Psychosocial Treatments

Key Readings in Addiction Psychiatry

Edited by
American Academy of Addiction Psychiatry

Sevarino	*Treatment of Substance Use Disorders*
Rosenthal	*Dual Diagnosis*
McCance-Katz & Clark	*Psychosocial Treatments*

PSYCHOSOCIAL TREATMENTS

Edited by

Elinore F. McCance-Katz, M.D., Ph.D.
H. Westley Clark, M.D., J.D., M.P.H.

BRUNNER-ROUTLEDGE
New York • London

Published in 2004 by
Brunner-Routledge
29 West 35th Street
New York, NY 10001
www.brunner-routledge.com

Published in Great Britain by
Brunner-Routledge
27 Church Road
Hove, East Sussex
BN3 2FA
www.brunner-routledge.com.uk

Brunner-Routledge is an imprint of the Taylor & Francis Group.
Printed in the United States of America on acid-free paper.

10 9 8 7 6 5 4 3 2 1

Library of Congress Cataloging-in-Publication Data
Psychosocial treatments / edited by Elinore F. McCance-Katz and H. Westley Clark.
    p. ; cm. — (Key readings in addiction psychiatry)
Includes bibliographical references and index.
    ISBN 0-415-94781-2 (pbk.)
1. Substance abuse—Relapse—Prevention. 2. Substance abuse—Treatment.
3. Psychiatric social work.
    [DNLM: 1. Substance-Related Disorders—therapy. 2. Psychotherapy—methods.
WM 270 P9737 2004] I. McCance-Katz, Elinore F. II. Clark, H. Westley. III. Series.

RC564.P855 2004
616.86'0651—dc21
                                                                    2003012668

Contents

Introduction to the Key Readings in Addiction Psychiatry Series

The American Academy of Addiction Psychiatry is pleased to announce a new book series, entitled Key Readings in Addiction Psychiatry. Substance abuse adversely affects a very large portion of the world's population, causing more deaths, illnesses, and disabilities than any other preventable health condition. According to Dr. Alan I. Leshner, director of the National Institute on Drug Abuse, "addiction has so many dimensions and disrupts so many aspects of an individual's life, treatment for this illness is never simple."[1] Scientific advances are occurring at an increasingly rapid rate, leading to an array of effective pharmacologic and behavioral treatment approaches. These new advances are stimulating a new level of scientific curiosity and research and accelerating the application of scientific findings in the clinical setting.

Through the compilations of up-to-date articles on various aspects of substance use disorders, the American Academy of Addiction Psychiatry, through the Key Readings series, seeks to:

- advance the knowledge of those committed to the treatment of substance abuse;
- introduce those new to the field of addictions to recent advances in substance use disorders;
- inspire those without knowledge of substance use disorders and reinvigorate those with a nihilistic view of their treatment to work to advance the field of addiction medicine beyond its current knowledge base.

Each book will serve as a quick guide to research studies and treatment approaches in the addiction field. They will serve as reference tools, edited by an expert in the field, keeping today's busy professional informed of timely, critical, and interesting research and clinical treatment issues. Each book within the series will present outstanding articles from leading clinical journals of relevance to the addiction psychiatrist, whether in clinical, research, administrative, or academic roles. The Key Readings in Addiction Psychiatry series will be presented in several volumes focused on treatment, dual diagnosis, and psychosocial therapies.

A new book in the series will be published annually, providing a continuous flow of new information in a handy, easily accessible form. This compilation of key readings in one source will be an excellent supplement to textbooks and can be used not only to keep up with rapid change in our field but also in preparation for the certification or recertification examinations in addiction psychiatry.

> Stephen L. Dilts, M.D., Ph.D.
> Immediate Past President
> American Academy of Addiction Psychiatry

NOTE

1. *Principles of Drug Addiction Treatment,* National Institute on Drug Abuse, 1999.

Introduction

Elinore F. McCance-Katz, M.D., Ph.D.
H. Westley Clark, M.D., J.D., M.P.H.

This book is the third in the series of Key Readings in Addiction Psychiatry and follows texts that summarize pharmacotherapies for addiction and the treatment of dual disorders. The focus of this book is on current psychosocial therapies utilized in the treatment of substance use disorders.

The field of addiction psychiatry has made substantial strides through the last decade with the development of several psychosocial interventions that have been shown in controlled research studies to have efficacy in the treatment of addiction. This book contains key articles that provide a discussion of the elements of each of several commonly used psychosocial interventions in the treatment of substance use disorders. The goal of inclusion of these articles was to provide a concise but comprehensive text that would give the practitioner information necessary to understand the theory underpinning psychotherapeutic interventions and the necessary tools and references needed for the practitioner to implement these therapies in practice. In addition, articles summarizing research data showing efficacy of psychosocial interventions have been included so that the reader can evaluate the available therapies and make informed decisions regarding whether a particular therapy might be utilized in his or her practice.

The major areas of psychosocial intervention for the treatment of addictive disorders supported by research data collected in controlled trials include relapse prevention therapy, community reinforcement, voucher-based programs, self-help therapies, and motivational enhancement therapy. These interventions vary in approach to the substance-using patient and range from techniques designed to assist individuals in understanding the components of substance use unique to them and developing interventions designed to curtail drug and alcohol use, to programs based on discouraging drug/alcohol-using behaviors and rewarding drug-free behaviors, to self-help strategies that are effective in substance abuse treatment, to techniques designed to resolve ambivalence about substance use and assist individuals in making positive behavior changes. Other articles in this text discuss current psychosocial interventions efficacious in a variety of patient-care settings, including outpatient, office-based practice, and specialized settings with a high prevalence of drug- and alcohol-abusing individuals, including adolescents, people in the criminal justice system, and homeless veterans.

The selections in this book on psychosocial treatments for substance use disorders will provide the reader with a broad overview of the field as well as the specific information needed to use these therapies in patient care. The review articles will also give the reader resources useful to expanding one's understanding of the theoretical basis of these interventions. This text has been compiled with the goal of placing the major, efficacious psychosocial therapies for the treatment of addiction in one incisive text that will encourage the use of these therapies by clinicians working with many types of patients in a variety of clinical settings.

Chapter 1

Relapse Prevention

An Overview of Marlatt's Cognitive-Behavioral Model

Mary E. Larimer, Ph.D.
Rebekka S. Palmer
G. Alan Marlatt, Ph.D.

Relapse prevention (RP) is an important component of alcoholism treatment. The RP model proposed by Marlatt and Gordon suggests that both immediate determinants (e.g., high-risk situations, coping skills, outcome expectancies, and the abstinence violation effect) and covert antecedents (e.g., lifestyle factors and urges and cravings) can contribute to relapse. The RP model also incorporates numerous specific and global intervention strategies that allow therapist and client to address each step of the relapse process. Specific interventions include identifying specific high-risk situations for each client and enhancing the client's skills for coping with those situations, increasing the client's self-efficacy, eliminating myths regarding alcohol's effects, managing lapses, and restructuring the client's perceptions of the relapse process. Global strategies comprise balancing the client's lifestyle and helping him or her develop positive addictions, employing stimulus control techniques and urge-management techniques, and developing relapse road maps. Several studies have provided theoretical and practical support for the RP model.

Keywords: AODD (alcohol and other drug dependence) relapse; relapse prevention; treatment model; cognitive therapy; behavior therapy; risk factors;

Mary E. Larimer, Ph.D., is a research assistant professor of psychology, Rebekka S. Palmer is a graduate student in clinical psychology, and G. Alan Marlatt, Ph.D., is a professor of psychology at the Addictive Behaviors Research Center, Department of Psychology, University of Washington, Seattle, Washington.

coping skills; self-efficacy; expectancy; AOD (alcohol and other drug) absti-
nence; lifestyle; AOD craving; intervention; alcohol cue; reliability (research
methods); validity (research methods); literature review

Relapse, or the return to heavy alcohol use following a period of abstinence or moderate use, occurs in many drinkers who have undergone alcoholism treatment. Traditional alcoholism treatment approaches often conceptualize relapse as an end-state, a negative outcome equivalent to treatment failure. Thus, this perspective considers only a dichotomous treatment outcome—that is, a person is either abstinent or relapsed. In contrast, several models of relapse that are based on social-cognitive or behavioral theories emphasize relapse as a transitional process, a series of events that unfold over time (Annis, 1986; Litman et al., 1979; Marlatt & Gordon, 1985). According to these models, the relapse process begins prior to the first post-treatment alcohol use and continues after the initial use. This conceptualization provides a broader conceptual framework for intervening in the relapse process to prevent or reduce relapse episodes and thereby improve treatment outcome.

This article presents one influential model of the antecedents of relapse and the treatment measures that can be taken to prevent or limit relapse after treatment completion. This relapse prevention (RP) model, which was developed by Marlatt and Gordon (1985) and which has been widely used in recent years, has been the focus of considerable research. This article reviews various immediate and covert triggers of relapse proposed by the RP model, as well as numerous specific and general intervention strategies that may help patients avoid and cope with relapse-inducing situations. The article also presents studies that have provided support for the validity of the RP model.

OVERVIEW OF THE RP MODEL

Marlatt and Gordon's (1985) RP model is based on social-cognitive psychology and incorporates both a conceptual model of relapse and a set of cognitive and behavioral strategies to prevent or limit relapse episodes (for a detailed description of the development, theoretical underpinnings, and treatment components of the RP model, see Dimeff & Marlatt, 1998; Marlatt, 1996; Marlatt & Gordon, 1985). A central aspect of the model is the detailed classification (i.e., taxonomy) of factors or situations that can precipitate or contribute to relapse episodes. In general, the RP model posits that those factors fall into two categories: immediate determinants (e.g., high-risk situations, a person's coping skills, outcome expectancies, and the abstinence violation effect) and covert antecedents (e.g., lifestyle imbalances and urges and cravings).

Treatment approaches based on the RP model begin with an assessment of the environmental and emotional characteristics of situations that are potentially associated with relapse (i.e., high-risk situations). After identifying those characteristics, the therapist works forward by analyzing the individual drinker's response to these situations, as well as backward to examine the lifestyle factors that increase the drinker's exposure to high-risk situations. Based on this careful examination of the relapse process, the therapist then devises strategies to target weaknesses in the client's cognitive and behavioral repertoire and thereby reduce the risk of relapse.

Immediate Determinants of Relapse

High-Risk Situations. A central concept of the RP model postulates that high-risk situations frequently serve as the immediate precipitators of initial alcohol use after abstinence (see Figure 1.1). According to the model, a person who has initiated a behavior change, such as alcohol abstinence, should begin experiencing increased self-efficacy or mastery over his or her behavior, which should grow as he or she continues to maintain the change. Certain situations or events, however, can pose a threat to the person's sense of control and, consequently, precipitate a relapse crisis. Based on research on precipitants of relapse in alcoholics who had received inpatient treatment, Marlatt (1996) categorized the emotional, environmental, and interpersonal characteristics of relapse-inducing situations described by study participants. According to this taxonomy, several types of situations can play a role in relapse episodes, as follows:

- Negative emotional states, such as anger, anxiety, depression, frustration, and boredom, which are also referred to as intrapersonal high-risk situations, are associated with the highest rate of relapse (Marlatt & Gordon, 1985). These emotional states may be caused by primarily intrapersonal perceptions of certain situations (e.g., feeling bored or lonely after coming home from work to an empty house) or by reactions to environmental events (e.g., feeling angry about an impending layoff at work).
- Situations that involve another person or a group of people (i.e., interpersonal high-risk situations), particularly interpersonal conflict (e.g., an argument with a family member), also result in negative emotions and can precipitate relapse. In fact, intrapersonal negative emotional states and interpersonal conflict situations served as triggers for more than one-half of all relapse episodes in Marlatt's (1996) analysis.
- Social pressure, including both direct verbal or nonverbal persuasion and indirect pressure (e.g., being around other people who are drinking), contributed to more than 20 percent of relapse episodes in Marlatt's (1996) study.
- Positive emotional states (e.g., celebrations), exposure to alcohol-related stimuli or cues (e.g., seeing an advertisement for an alcoholic beverage or passing by one's favorite bar), testing one's personal control (i.e., using "willpower" to limit consumption), and nonspecific cravings also were identified as high-risk situations that could precipitate relapse.

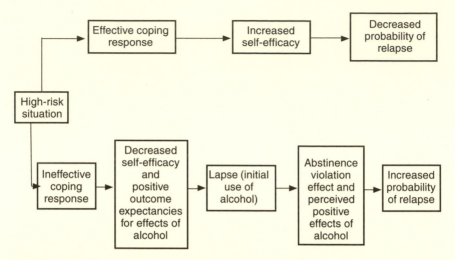

FIGURE 1.1. The cognitive-behavioral model of the relapse process posits a central role for high-risk situations and for the drinker's response to those situations. People with effective coping responses have confidence that they can cope with the situation (i.e., increased self-efficacy), thereby reducing the probability of a relapse. Conversely, people with ineffective coping responses will experience decreased self-efficacy, which, together with the expectation that alcohol use will have a positive effect (i.e., positive outcome expectancies), can result in an initial lapse. This lapse, in turn, can result in feelings of guilt and failure (i.e., an abstinence violation effect). The abstinence violation effect, along with positive outcome expectancies, can increase the probability of a relapse. NOTE: This model also applies to users of drugs other than alcohol.

Coping. Although the RP model considers the high-risk situation the immediate relapse trigger, it is actually the person's *response* to the situation that determines whether he or she will experience a lapse (i.e., begin using alcohol). A person's coping behavior in a high-risk situation is a particularly critical determinant of the likely outcome. Thus, a person who can execute effective coping strategies (e.g., a behavioral strategy, such as leaving the situation, or a cognitive strategy, such as positive self-talk) is less likely to relapse compared with a person lacking those skills. Moreover, people who have coped successfully with high-risk situations are assumed to experience a heightened sense of self-efficacy (i.e., a personal perception of mastery over the specific risky situation) (Bandura, 1977; Marlatt et al., 1995, 1999; Marlatt & Gordon, 1985). Conversely, people with low self-efficacy perceive themselves as lacking the motivation or ability to resist drinking in high-risk situations.

Outcome Expectancies. Research among college students has shown that those who drink the most tend to have higher expectations regarding the positive effects of alcohol (i.e., outcome expectancies) and may anticipate only the immediate positive effects while ignoring or discounting the potential negative consequences of excessive drinking (Carey, 1995). Such positive outcome expectancies may become particularly salient in high-risk situations, when the person expects alcohol use to help him or her cope with negative emotions or conflict (i.e., when drinking serves as "self-medication"). In these situations, the drinker focuses primarily on the anticipation of immediate gratification, such as stress reduction, neglecting possible delayed negative consequences.

The Abstinence Violation Effect. A critical difference exists between the first violation of the abstinence goal (i.e., an initial lapse) and a return to uncontrolled drinking or abandonment of the abstinence goal (i.e., a full-blown relapse). Although research with various addictive behaviors has indicated that a lapse greatly increases the risk of eventual relapse, the progression from lapse to relapse is not inevitable.

Marlatt and Gordon (1980, 1985) have described a type of reaction by the drinker to a lapse called the abstinence violation effect, which may influence whether a lapse leads to relapse. This reaction focuses on the drinker's emotional response to an initial lapse and on the causes to which he or she attributes the lapse. People who attribute the lapse to their own personal failure are likely to experience guilt and negative emotions that can, in turn, lead to increased drinking as a further attempt to avoid or escape the feelings of guilt or failure. Furthermore, people who attribute the lapse to stable, global, internal factors beyond their control (e.g., "I have no willpower and will never be able to stop drinking") are more likely to abandon the abstinence attempt (and experience a full-blown relapse) than are people who attribute the lapse to their inability to cope effectively with a specific high-risk situation. In contrast to the former group of people, the latter group realizes that one needs to "learn from one's mistakes" and, thus, they may develop more effective ways to cope with similar trigger situations in the future.

Covert Antecedents of High-Risk Situations

Although high-risk situations can be conceptualized as the immediate determinants of relapse episodes, a number of less obvious factors also influence the relapse process. These covert antecedents include lifestyle factors, such as overall stress level, as well as cognitive factors that may serve to "set up" a relapse, such as rationalization, denial, and a desire for immediate gratification (i.e., urges and cravings) (see Figure 1.2). These factors can increase a person's vulnerability to relapse both by increasing his or her exposure to high-risk situations and by decreasing motivation to resist drinking in high-risk situations.

In many cases, initial lapses occur in high-risk situations that are completely unexpected and for which the drinker is often unprepared. In relapse "setups," however, it may be possible to identify a series of covert decisions or choices, each of them seemingly inconsequential, which in combination set the person up for situations with overwhelmingly high risk. These choices have been termed "apparently irrelevant decisions" (AIDs), because they may not be overtly recog-

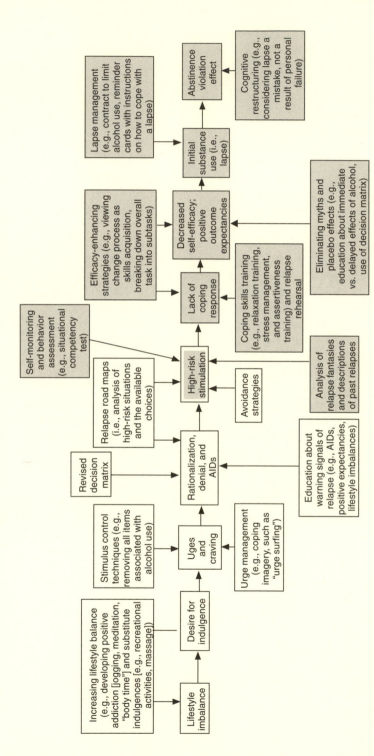

FIGURE 1.2. Covert antecedents and immediate determinants of relapse and intervention strategies for identifying and preventing or avoiding those determinants. Lifestyle balance is an important aspect of preventing relapse. If stressors are not balanced by sufficient stress management strategies, the client is more likely to use alcohol in an attempt to gain some relief or escape from stress. This reaction typically leads to a desire for indulgence that often develops into cravings and urges. Two cognitive mechanisms that contribute to the covert planning of a relapse episode—rationalization and denial—as well as apparently irrelevant decisions (AIDs) can help precipitate high-risk situations, which are the central determinants of a relapse. People who lack adequate coping skills for handling these situations experience reduced confidence in their ability to cope (i.e., decreased self-efficacy). Moreover, these people often have positive expectations regarding the effects of alcohol (i.e., outcome expectancies). These factors can lead to initial alcohol use (i.e., a lapse), which can induce an abstinence violation effect that, in turn, influences

nized as related to relapse but nevertheless help move the person closer to the brink of relapse. One example of such an AID is the decision by an abstinent drinker to purchase a bottle of liquor "just in case guests stop by." Marlatt and Gordon (1985) have hypothesized that such decisions may enable a person to experience the immediate positive effects of drinking while disavowing personal responsibility for the lapse episode ("How could anyone expect me not to drink when there's a bottle of liquor in the house?").

Lifestyle Factors. Marlatt and Gordon (1985) have proposed that the covert ante-cedent most strongly related to relapse risk involves the degree of balance in the person's life between perceived external demands (i.e., "shoulds") and internally fulfilling or enjoyable activities (i.e., "wants"). A person whose life is full of demands may experience a constant sense of stress, which not only can generate negative emotional states, thereby creating high-risk situations, but also enhances the person's desire for pleasure and his or her rationalization that indulgence is justified ("I owe myself a drink"). In the absence of other non-drinking pleasur-able activities, the person may view drinking as the only means of obtaining plea-sure or escaping pain.

Urges and Cravings. The desire for immediate gratification can take many forms, and some people may experience it as a craving or urge to use alcohol. Although many researchers and clinicians consider urges and cravings primarily physiologi-cal states, the RP model proposes that both urges and cravings are precipitated by psychological or environmental stimuli. Ongoing cravings, in turn, may erode the client's commitment to maintaining abstinence as his or her desire for immediate gratification increases. This process may lead to a relapse setup or increase the client's vulnerability to unanticipated high-risk situations.

Although they are often used interchangeably, the terms "urges" and "cravings" can be associated with distinct meanings. Thus, Marlatt and Gordon (1985) have defined an urge as a relatively sudden impulse to engage in an act such as alcohol consumption, whereas craving is defined as the subjective desire to experience the effects or consequences of such an act. Nevertheless, the same processes may mediate both urges and cravings. Two such processes have been

---

FIGURE 1.2. *Caption continued*
the risk of progressing to a full relapse. Self-monitoring, behavior assessment, analyses of relapse fantasies, and descriptions of past relapses can help identify a person's high-risk situations. Specific intervention strategies (e.g., skills training, relapse rehearsal, education, and cognitive restructuring) and general strategies (e.g., relaxation training, stress management, efficacy-enhancing imagery, contracts to limit the extent of alcohol use, and reminder cards) can help reduce the impact of relapse determinants. Shaded boxes indicate steps in the relapse process and intervention measures that are specific to each client and his or her ability to cope with alcohol-related situations. White boxes indicate steps in the relapse process and intervention strategies that are related to the client's general lifestyle and coping skills. High-risk situations are related to both the client's general and specific coping abilities.

proposed: (1) conditioning[1] elicited by stimuli associated with past gratification and (2) cognitive processes associated with anticipated gratification (i.e., the expectancies for the immediate pleasurable effects of alcohol).

RP INTERVENTION STRATEGIES

The RP model includes a variety of cognitive and behavioral approaches designed to target each step in the relapse process (see Figure 1.2). These approaches include specific intervention strategies that focus on the immediate determinants of relapse as well as global self-management strategies that focus on the covert antecedents of relapse. Both the specific and global strategies fall into three main categories: skills training, cognitive restructuring, and lifestyle balancing.

Specific Intervention Strategies

The goal of the specific intervention strategies—identifying and coping with high-risk situations, enhancing self-efficacy, eliminating myths and placebo effects, lapse management, and cognitive restructuring—is to teach clients to anticipate the possibility of relapse and to recognize and cope with high-risk situations. These strategies also focus on enhancing the client's awareness of cognitive, emotional, and behavioral reactions in order to prevent a lapse from escalating into a relapse. The first step in this process is to teach clients the RP model and to give them a "big picture" view of the relapse process. For example, the therapist can use the metaphor of behavior change as a journey that includes both easy and difficult stretches of highway and for which various "road signs" (e.g., "warning signals") are available to provide guidance. According to this metaphor, learning to anticipate and plan for high-risk situations during recovery from alcoholism is equivalent to having a good road map, a well-equipped toolbox, a full tank of gas, and a spare tire in good condition for the journey.

Identifying and Coping with High-Risk Situations. To anticipate and plan accordingly for high-risk situations, the person first must identify the situations in which he or she may experience difficulty coping and/or an increased desire to drink. These situations can be identified using a variety of assessment strategies. For example, the therapist can interview the client about past lapses or relapse episodes and relapse dreams or fantasies in order to identify situations in which the client has or might have difficulty coping. Several self-report questionnaires also can help assess the situations in which clients have been prone to drinking heavily in the past as well as the clients' self-efficacy for resisting future drinking in these situations (Annis & Davis, 1988; Annis, 1982a). Furthermore, clients who have not yet initiated abstinence are encouraged to self-monitor their drinking behavior—for example, by maintaining an ongoing record of the situations, emotions, and interpersonal factors associated with drinking or urges to drink. Such a record allows clients to become more aware of the immediate precipitants of drinking. Even in clients who have already become abstinent, self-monitoring can still be used to assess situations in which urges are more prevalent.

Once a person's high-risk situations have been identified, two types of intervention strategies can be used to lessen the risks posed by those situations. The first strategy involves teaching the client to recognize the warning signals associated with imminent danger—that is, the cues indicating that the client is about to enter a high-risk situation. Such warning signals to be recognized may include, for example, AIDs, stress and lack of lifestyle balance, and strong positive expectancies about drinking. As a result of identifying those warning signals, the client may be able to take some evasive action (e.g., escape from the situation) or possibly avoid the high-risk situation entirely.

The second strategy, which is possibly the most important aspect of RP, involves evaluating the client's existing motivation and ability to cope with specific high-risk situations and then helping the client learn more effective coping skills. Relevant coping skills can be behavioral or cognitive in nature and can include both strategies to cope with specific high-risk situations (e.g., refusing drinks in social situations and assertive communication skills) and general strategies that can improve coping with various situations (e.g., meditation, anger management, and positive self-talk).

Assessing a client's existing coping skills can be a challenging task. Questionnaires such as the situational confidence test (Annis, 1982b) can assess the amount of self-efficacy a person has in coping with drinking-risk situations. Those measures do not necessarily indicate, however, whether a client is actually able or willing to use his or her coping skills in a high-risk situation. To increase the likelihood that a client can and will utilize his or her skills when the need arises, the therapist can use approaches such as role plays and the development and modeling of specific coping plans for managing potential high-risk situations.

Enhancing Self-Efficacy. Another approach to preventing relapse and promoting behavioral change is the use of efficacy-enhancement procedures—that is, strategies designed to increase a client's sense of mastery and of being able to handle difficult situations without lapsing. One of the most important efficacy-enhancing strategies employed in RP is the emphasis on collaboration between the client and therapist instead of a more typical "top down" doctor-patient relationship. In the RP model, the client is encouraged to adopt the role of colleague and to become an objective observer of his or her own behavior. In developing a sense of objectivity, the client is better able to view his or her alcohol use as an addictive behavior and may be more able to accept greater responsibility both for the drinking behavior and for the effort to change that behavior. Clients are taught that changing a habit is a process of skill acquisition rather than a test of one's willpower. As the client gains new skills and feels successful in implementing them, he or she can view the process of change as similar to other situations that require the acquisition of a new skill.

Another efficacy-enhancing strategy involves breaking down the overall task of behavior change into smaller, more manageable subtasks that can be addressed one at a time (Bandura, 1977). Thus, instead of focusing on a distant end goal (e.g., maintaining lifelong abstinence), the client is encouraged to set smaller, more manageable goals, such as coping with an upcoming high-risk situation or making it through the day without a lapse. Because an increase in self-efficacy is closely tied to achieving preset goals, successful mastery of these individual smaller tasks is the best strategy to enhance feelings of self-mastery.

Therapists also can enhance self-efficacy by providing clients with feedback concerning their performance on other new tasks, even those that appear unrelated to alcohol use. In general, success in accomplishing even simple tasks (e.g., showing up for appointments on time) can greatly enhance a client's feelings of self-efficacy. This success can then motivate the client's effort to change his or her pattern of alcohol use and increase the client's confidence that he or she will be able to successfully master the skills needed to change.

Eliminating Myths and Placebo Effects. Counteracting the drinker's misperceptions about alcohol's effects is an important part of relapse prevention. To accomplish this goal, the therapist first elicits the client's positive expectations about alcohol's effects using either standardized questionnaires or clinical interviews. Positive expectancies regarding alcohol's effects often are based on myths or placebo effects of alcohol (i.e., effects that occur because the drinker expects them to, not because alcohol causes the appropriate physiological changes). In particular, considerable research has demonstrated that alcohol's perceived positive effects on social behavior are often mediated by placebo effects, resulting from both expectations (i.e., "set") and the environment (i.e., "setting") in which drinking takes place (Marlatt & Rohsenow, 1981). Subsequently, the therapist can address each expectancy, using cognitive restructuring (which is discussed later in this section) and education about research findings. The therapist also can use examples from the client's own experience to dispel myths and encourage the client to consider both the immediate and the delayed consequences of drinking.

Even when alcohol's perceived positive effects are based on actual drug effects, often only the immediate effects are positive (e.g., euphoria), whereas the delayed effects are negative (e.g., sleepiness), particularly at higher alcohol doses. Asking clients questions designed to assess expectancies for both immediate and delayed consequences of drinking versus not drinking (i.e., using a decision matrix) (see Table 1.1) often can be useful in both eliciting and modifying expectancies. With such a matrix, the client can juxtapose his or her own list of the delayed negative consequences with the expected positive effects.

Lapse Management. Despite precautions and preparations, many clients committed to abstinence will experience a lapse after initiating abstinence. Lapse-management strategies focus on halting the lapse and combating the abstinence violation effect to prevent an uncontrolled relapse episode. Lapse management includes

TABLE 1.1. An Example of a Decision Matrix for Alcohol Abstinence
or Alcohol Use*

	Immediate Consequences		Delayed Consequences	
	Positive	Negative	Positive	Negative
Remain Abstinent	Improved self-efficacy and self-esteem, family approval, better health, more energy, save money and time, greater success at work	Frustration and anxiety, denied pleasures of drinking, unable to go to bars, anger at not being able to do what one wants without "paying the price"	Greater control over one's life, better health and longevity, learn about one's self and others without being intoxicated, more respect from others	Not able to enjoy drinking while watching sports, bored and depressed, not able to remain friends with heavy-drinking buddies
Resume Alcohol Use	Automatic pleasure, reduced stress and anxiety, not feel pain, not worry about one's problems, able to enjoy sports and drink with buddies	Feel weak from drinking, risk of accidents and embarrassment, anger of wife and family, arrive late to or miss work, hangovers, waste money	Maintain friendships with drinking buddies, able to drink while watching sports, not have to cope with wife and family by staying out drinking	Possible loss of family and job, deterioration of health and early death, loss of nondrinking or light-drinking friends, ridicule by others, low self-esteem

*In such a matrix, the client lists both the positive and negative immediate and delayed consequences of remaining abstinent versus resuming drinking. This list can facilitate the client's decision making process regarding his or her future alcohol consumption.

contracting with the client to limit the extent of use, to contact the therapist as soon as possible after the lapse, and to evaluate the situation for clues to the factors that triggered the lapse. Often, the therapist provides the client with simple written instructions to refer to in the event of a lapse. These instructions reiterate the importance of stopping alcohol consumption and (safely) leaving the lapse-inducing situation. Lapse management is presented to clients as an "emergency preparedness" kit for their "journey" to abstinence. Many clients may never need to use their lapse-management plan, but adequate preparation can greatly lessen the harm if a lapse does occur.

Cognitive Restructuring. Cognitive restructuring, or reframing, is used throughout the RP treatment process to assist clients in modifying their attributions for and perceptions of the relapse process. In particular, cognitive restructuring is a critical component of interventions to lessen the abstinence violation effect. Thus, clients are taught to reframe their perception of lapses—to view them not as failures or indicators of a lack of willpower but as mistakes or errors in learning that signal the need for increased planning to cope more effectively in similar situations in the future. This perspective considers lapses key learning opportunities resulting from an interaction between coping and situational determinants, both of which can be modified in the future. This reframing of lapse episodes can help decrease the clients' tendency to view lapses as the result of a personal failing or moral weakness and remove the self-fulfilling prophecy that a lapse will inevitably lead to relapse.

Global Lifestyle Self-Control Strategies

Although specific intervention strategies can address the immediate determinants of relapse, it is also important to modify individual lifestyle factors and covert antecedents that can increase exposure or reduce resistance to high-risk situations. Global self-control strategies are designed to modify the client's lifestyle to increase balance as well as to identify and cope with covert antecedents of relapse (i.e., early warning signals, cognitive distortions, and relapse setups).

Balanced Lifestyle and Positive Addiction. Assessing lifestyle factors associated with increased stress and decreased lifestyle balance is an important first step in teaching global self-management strategies. This assessment can be accomplished through approaches in which clients self-monitor their daily activities, identifying each activity as a "want," "should," or combination of both. Clients also can complete standardized assessment measures, such as the Daily Hassles and Uplifts Scale (Delongis et al., 1982), to evaluate the degree to which they perceive their life stressors to be balanced by pleasurable life events.

Many clients report that activities they once found pleasurable (e.g., hobbies and social interactions with family and friends) have gradually been replaced by drinking as a source of entertainment and gratification. Therefore, one global self-management strategy involves encouraging clients to pursue again those previously satisfying, non-drinking recreational activities. In addition, specific cognitive-behavioral skills training approaches, such as relaxation training, stress management, and time management, can be used to help clients achieve greater lifestyle balance.

Helping the client to develop "positive addictions" (Glaser, 1976)—that is, activities (e.g., meditation, exercise, or yoga) that have long-term positive effects on mood, health, and coping—is another way to enhance lifestyle balance. Self-efficacy often increases as a result of developing positive addictions, largely caused by the experience of successfully acquiring new skills by performing the activity.

Stimulus-Control Techniques. Although achieving a more balanced lifestyle may reduce the risk of cravings and urges to use alcohol, urges and cravings might still result from exposure to conditioned stimuli previously associated with drinking. Stimulus-control techniques are relatively simple but effective strategies that can be used to decrease urges and cravings in response to such stimuli, particularly during the early abstinence period. Simply stated, these techniques encourage the client to remove all items directly associated with alcohol use from his or her home, office, and car. This includes eliminating, at least temporarily, all alcohol supplies, including those typically kept for "guests," as well as packing away wine or shot glasses, corkscrews, and similar items. Clients who used to hide or stash alcoholic beverages should make a concerted effort to remember and remove alcohol from all possible hiding places, because these hidden or forgotten bottles can serve as a powerful temptation when found "accidentally" after a period of sobriety.

Other, more subtle items that may serve as conditioned cues for drinking may include the favorite living room easy chair or the music the client typically listened to while unwinding in the evening with several of his or her favorite drinks. In these cases, a temporary change in seating or listening habits may be helpful while the client develops alternative coping strategies. Similarly, certain social events or other high-risk situations may have become associated with excessive drinking to such an extent that they may induce classically conditioned urges or cravings, particularly in the early stages of abstinence. Accordingly, approaches that provide the client with a range of avoidance strategies for turning down invitations, leaving risky situations, or otherwise avoiding problematic places or events also can serve as stimulus-control measures that may help prevent a lapse.

Urge-Management Techniques. Even with effective stimulus-control procedures in place and an improved lifestyle balance, most clients cannot completely avoid experiencing cravings or urges to drink. Therefore, an important aspect of the RP model is to teach clients to anticipate and accept these reactions as a "normal" conditioned response to an external stimulus. According to this approach, the client should not identify with the urge or view it as an indication of his or her "desire" to drink. Instead, the client is taught to label the urge as an emotional or physiological response to an external stimulus in his or her environment that was previously associated with heavy drinking, similar to Pavlov's dog, which continued to salivate at the sound of a bell that had previously signaled food.

In one clinical intervention based on this approach, the client is taught to visualize the urge or craving as a wave, watching it rise and fall as an observer and not to be "wiped out" by it. This imagery technique is known as "urge surfing" and refers to conceptualizing the urge or craving as a wave that crests and then washes onto a beach. In so doing, the client learns that rather than building interminably until they become overwhelming, urges and cravings peak and subside rather quickly if they are not acted on. The client is taught not to struggle against the wave or give in to it, thereby being "swept away" or "drowned" by the sensation, but to imagine "riding the wave" on a surfboard. Like the conceptualization of urges and cravings as the result of an external stimulus, this imagery fosters detachment from the urges and cravings and reinforces the temporary and external nature of these phenomena.

Relapse Road Maps. Finally, therapists can assist clients with developing relapse road maps—that is, cognitive-behavioral analyses of high-risk situations that emphasize the different choices available to clients for avoiding or coping with these situations as well as their consequences. Such a "mapping out" of the likely outcomes associated with different choices along the way can be helpful in identifying AIDs. For example, if arguments with a former spouse are a high-risk situation, the therapist can help the client map out several possible scenarios for interacting with the ex-spouse, including the likelihood of precipitating an argument in each scenario. The therapist can then help identify coping responses that can be used to avoid a lapse at each point in the interaction.

THEORETICAL AND PRACTICAL SUPPORT FOR THE RP MODEL

Several studies over the past two decades have evaluated the reliability and predictive validity[2] of the RP model as well as the efficacy of treatment techniques based on this model. One recent large-scale research effort assessing the RP model was the Relapse Replication and Extension Project (RREP), which was funded by the National Institute on Alcohol Abuse and Alcoholism (Lowman et al., 1996). This collaborative research project evaluated the reliability of raters' categorizations of high-risk situations using Marlatt's taxonomy and assessed whether a prior situation could predict future lapse episodes.

As described earlier in this article, the original relapse taxonomy sought to categorize the environmental or emotional stimuli associated with an initial return to drinking in order to enhance the long-term effectiveness of aversion therapy. The resulting taxonomy contained three levels of categorization of high-risk situations with increasing specificity to help clinicians obtain detailed information about the causes underlying each relapse episode. In the RREP study, researchers from three study sites were trained in coding relapse episodes. The researchers then coded key, or baseline, relapse episodes[3] described by study participants entering treatment at the study sites. The study addressed three major issues, as follows:

- It determined the inter-rater reliability of the relapse episode coding—that is, whether different researchers coded a given relapse episode in an identical or similar manner.
- It evaluated whether the key relapse episodes predicted the types of relapse episodes that study participants reported after undergoing treatment (Maisto et al., 1996; Stout et al., 1996).
- It extended research on the RP model beyond the taxonomy by evaluating alternative methods for assessing high-risk situations as well as evaluating the relative contribution of negative affect, abstinence violation effect, coping, and expectancies on the likelihood of relapse.

The results reported in the RREP study indicate that the original relapse taxonomy of the RP model has only moderate inter-rater reliability at the highest level of specificity, although reliability of the more general categories (e.g., negative affect and social pressure) was better. The model's predictive validity also was modest; however, the definition of the key relapse episodes utilized in these studies failed to clarify whether these were voluntary change episodes or simply a return to drinking following a short period of abstinence that did not represent a serious attempt to quit drinking. Therefore, the RREP studies do not represent a good test of the predictive validity of the taxonomy.

Nevertheless, the study provides relatively good support for other aspects of the RP model. For example, Miller and colleagues (1996) found that although mere exposure to specific high-risk situations did not predict relapse, the manner in which people coped with those situations strongly predicted subsequent relapse or continued abstinence. Furthermore, in that study the majority of relapse episodes after treatment occurred during situations involving negative emotional states, a finding that has been replicated in other studies (Cooney et al., 1997; McKay, 1999; Shiffman, 1992). Finally, the results of Miller and colleagues (1996) support the role of the abstinence violation effect in predicting which participants would experience a full-blown relapse following an initial lapse. Specifically, those participants who had a greater belief in the disease model of alcoholism and a higher commitment to absolute abstinence (who were most likely to experience feelings of guilt over their lapse) were most likely to experience relapse in that study. In a recent review of the literature on relapse precipitants, Dimeff and Marlatt (1998) also concluded that considerable support exists for the notion that an abstinence violation effect can precipitate a relapse.

Several recent review articles and meta-analyses have examined the effectiveness of treatments based on the RP model in preventing relapse (Dimeff & Marlatt, 1998; Rawson et al., 1993; Carroll, 1996; Irvin et al., 1999). The RP-based treatments included in those analyses were delivered both as stand-alone treatments for initiating abstinence and as adjuncts to other treatment programs. Although the reviews differ in their methodology and in their criteria for including or excluding certain treatments, the conclusions regarding overall effectiveness of the RP approach are similar. The findings can be summarized as follows:

- The studies conducted to date tend to support the effectiveness of cognitive-behavioral RP-based approaches in reducing the frequency of relapse episodes as well as the intensity of lapse and/or relapse episodes among people who resumed alcohol use after treatment (Irvin et al., 1999). The effectiveness of RP was particularly great in studies that compared relapse rates in patients before and after treatment or that compared patients receiving RP-based treatment with controls receiving no treatment.
- Despite its benefits, RP-based treatment is not associated with higher abstinence rates compared with other valid treatment approaches (Carroll, 1996; Irvin et al., 1999). RP-based treatment is, however, often associated with lower

drinking rates and fewer drinking problems among patients who have experienced a relapse (e.g., Chaney et al., 1978).

- RP is associated with "delayed emergence effects"—that is, significant effects favoring RP as compared with other treatment approaches are often found only at later follow-up points (i.e., 1 year or more after treatment) (Carroll, 1996). This delayed effectiveness may result from the fact that it takes time to learn new skills and that consequently RP effects become more obvious as patients acquire additional practice.
- Although RP has been applied with some success to various addictive behaviors, the effects of RP-based approaches are greatest in the treatment of alcoholism or multiple drug use (Irvin et al., 1999).
- Combining RP with medications (e.g., disulfiram or naltrexone) to treat alcoholism leads to improved outcomes as compared with either RP or medication alone (Irvin et al., 1999).

SUMMARY

The RP model of relapse is centered around a detailed taxonomy of emotions, events, and situations that can precipitate both lapses and relapses to drinking. This taxonomy includes both immediate relapse determinants and covert antecedents, which indirectly increase a person's vulnerability to relapse. Based on the classification of relapse determinants and high-risk situations proposed in the RP model, numerous treatment components have been developed that are aimed at helping the recovering alcoholic cope with high-risk situations. The results of recent research, particularly the RREP study, likely will lead to modifications of the original RP model, particularly with regard to the assessment of high-risk situations as well as the conceptualization of covert and immediate antecedents of relapse. Overall, however, research findings support both the overall model of the relapse process and the effectiveness of treatment strategies based on the model.

ACKNOWLEDGMENTS

Preparation of this manuscript was supported by National Institute on Alcohol Abuse and Alcoholism grants R3A–AA–05591 to G. Alan Marlatt and 5RO1–AA–10772–03 to Mary E. Larimer.

NOTES

1. Classical or Pavlovian conditioning occurs when an originally neutral stimulus (e.g., the sight of a beer bottle) is repeatedly paired with a stimulus (e.g., alcohol consumption) that induces a certain physiological response. After the two stimuli have been paired repeatedly, the neutral stimulus becomes a conditioned stimulus that elicits the same physiological response.

2. The term "reliability" refers to the ability of a test or method to provide stable results (e.g., when different patients are compared or different investigators rate the same patient). The term "predictive validity" refers to the ability of a test or method to predict a certain outcome (e.g., relapse risk) accurately.
3. The key relapse episode was defined as the most recent use of alcohol following at least 4 days of abstinence (Longabaugh et al., 1996).

REFERENCES

Annis, H. M. (1982a). *Inventory of Drinking Situations.* Toronto, Canada: Addiction Research Foundation.

Annis, H. M. (1982b). *Situational Confidence Questionnaire.* Toronto, Canada: Addiction Research Foundation.

Annis, H. M. (1986). A relapse prevention model for treatment of alcoholics. In W. R. Miller & N. Heather (Eds.), *Treating addictive behaviors: Processes of change* (pp. 407–433). New York: Plenum Press.

Annis, H. M., & Davis, C. S. (1988). Assessment of expectancies. In D. M. Donovan & G. A. Marlatt (Eds.), *Assessment of addictive behaviors: Behavioral, cognitive, and physiological procedures* (pp. 198–213). New York: Guilford Press.

Bandura, A. (1977). Self-efficacy: Toward a unifying theory of behavioral change. *Psychological Review, 84*(2), 191–215.

Carey, K. B. (1995). Alcohol-related expectancies predict quantity and frequency of heavy drinking among college students. *Psychology of Addictive Behaviors, 9*(4), 236–241.

Carroll, K. M. (1996). Relapse prevention as a psychosocial treatment: A review of controlled clinical trials. *Experimental and Clinical Psychopharmacology, 4*, 46–54.

Chaney, E. R., O'Leary, M. R., & Marlatt, G. A. (1978). Skill training with alcoholics. *Journal of Consulting and Clinical Psychology, 46*, 1092–1104.

Cooney, N. L., Litt, M. D., Morse, P. A., Bauer, L. O., & Guapp, L. (1997). Alcohol cue reactivity, negative-mood reactivity, and relapse in treated alcoholic men. *Journal of Abnormal Psychology, 106*, 243–250.

Delongis, A., Coyne, J. C., Dakof, G., Folkman, S., & Lazarus, R. S. (1982). Relationship of daily hassles, uplifts, and major life events to health status. *Health Psychology, 1*(2), 119–136.

Dimeff, L. A., & Marlatt, G. A. (1998). Preventing relapse and maintaining change in addictive behaviors. *Clinical Psychology: Science & Practice, 5*(4), 513– 525.

Glaser, W. (1976). *Positive addiction.* New York: Harper & Row.

Irvin, J. E., Bowers, C. A., Dunn, M. E., & Wang, M. C. (1999). Efficacy of relapse prevention: A metaanalytic review. *Journal of Consulting and Clinical Psychology, 67*, 563–570.

Litman, G. K., Eiser, J. R., Rawson, N. S. B., & Oppenheim, A. N. (1979). Differences in relapse precipitants and coping behaviours between alcohol relapsers and survivors. *Behaviour Research and Therapy, 17*, 89–94.

Longabaugh, R., Rubin, A., Stout, R. L., Zywiak, W. H., & Lowman, C. (1996). The reliablity of Marlatt's taxonomy for classifying relapses. *Addiction, 91*(suppl.), 73–88.

Lowman, C., Allen, J., Stout, R. L., & The Relapse Research Group. (1996). Replication and extension of Marlatt's taxonomy of relapse precipitants: Overview of procedures and results. *Addiction, 91*(suppl.), 51–72.

Maisto, S. A., Connors, G. J., & Zywiak, W. H. (1996). Construct validation analyses on the Marlatt typology of relapse precipitants. *Addiction, 91*(suppl.), 89–98.

Marlatt, G. A. (1996). Taxonomy of high-risk situations for alcohol relapse: Evolution and development of a cognitive-behavioral model. *Addiction, 91*(suppl.), 37–49.

Marlatt, G. A., & Gordon, J. R. (1980). Determinants of relapse: Implications for the maintenance of behavior change. In P. O. Davidson & S. M. Davidson (Eds.), *Behavioral medicine: Changing health lifestyles* (pp. 410–452). New York: Brunner/Mazel.

Marlatt, G. A., & Gordon, J. R. (Eds.). (1985). *Relapse prevention: Maintenance strategies in the treatment of addictive behaviors*. New York: Guilford Press.

Marlatt, G. A., & Rohsenow, D. J. (1981). The think-drink effect. *Psychology Today, 15*, 60–93.

Marlatt, G. A., Baer, J. S., & Quigley, L. A. (1995). Self-efficacy and addictive behavior. In A. Bandura (Ed.), *Self-efficacy in changing societies* (pp. 289–315). New York: University Press.

Marlatt, G. A., Barrett, K., & Daley, D. C. (1999). Relapse prevention. *The American Psychiatric Press textbook of substance abuse treatment* (2d ed.), pp. 393–407.

McKay, J. R. (1999). Studies of factors in relapse to alcohol, drug and nicotine use: A critical review of methodologies and findings. *Journal of Studies on Alcohol, 60*, 566–576.

Miller, W. R., Westerberg, V. S., Harris, R. J., & Tonigan, J. S. (1996). What predicts relapse? Prospective testing of antecedent models. *Addiction, 91*(suppl), 155–172.

Rawson, R. A., Obert, J. L., McCann, M. J., & Marinelli-Casey, P. (1993). Relapse prevention models for substance abuse treatment. *Psychotherapy, 30*(2), 284–298.

Shiffman, S. (1992). Relapse process and relapse prevention in addictive behaviors. *Behavior Therapist*, 9–11.

Stout, R. L., Longabaugh, R., & Rubin, A. (1996). Predictive validity of Marlatt's relapse taxonomy versus a more general relapse code. *Addiction, 91*(suppl.), 99–110.

Chapter 2

Motivational Interviewing

William C. Noonan, M.S.W.
Theresa B. Moyers, Ph.D.

Motivational interviewing (MI) is a directive client-centered counseling style that is designed to assist clients in exploring and resolving ambivalence to increase motivation for change. It proposes a model of motivation as a dynamic client characteristic that is particularly subject to the influence of therapist behaviors. From a transtheoretical perspective, MI assists client movement through the stages of change to the "action" stage where engaging in change behaviors begins. MI is distinguished from other approaches by its empathic non-confrontive style and the stage-specific strategies it utilizes.

Eleven clinical trials have evaluated MI with several populations (nine with problem drinkers and two with drug abusers) in a variety of settings. Two studies have evaluated MI as a stand-alone intervention, three as an enhancement to existing treatment, five utilized MI in hospital settings, and one study compared it to an alternative group treatment. Most of these studies support MI as a useful clinical intervention. MI appears to be an effective, efficient, and adaptive therapeutic style worthy of further development, application, and research.

INTRODUCTION

Client motivation has been consistently recognized as a critical factor in the treatment of alcohol problems. It has often been seen as a stable client attribute and is

William C. Noonan, M.S.W., NRSA Predoctoral Fellow, Department of Psychology, University of New Mexico, Albuquerque, NM, USA.

Theresa B. Moyers, Ph.D., Associate Director, Substance Abuse Treatment Program, Albuquerque Veterans Administration Medical Center, Albuquerque, NM, USA.

typically inferred from client behavior (Miller, 1985). Treatment personnel often expect alcoholics to be poorly motivated as a result of powerful constitutional defense mechanisms that operate to protect the alcoholic's drinking (Moyers & Miller, 1993). From this perspective, confrontive treatment strategies can be viewed as imperative, since they are seen as the only methods powerful enough to break through these character defense mechanisms.

An alternative model of motivation was proposed by Miller in the early 1980s (Miller, 1983, 1985). It construes motivation as a dynamic characteristic rather than a static client trait, and one that can be influenced by external factors including specific therapist behaviors. Based upon this early model and a recently published review of the brief intervention literature that identified the effective ingredients in these interventions (Miller & Sanchez, 1994), a therapeutic method was developed for enhancing motivation for change called motivational interviewing (MI) (Miller & Rollnick, 1991). The efficacy of MI has subsequently been evaluated in a series of clinical trials and has been adapted to a broader array of clinical concerns and settings. This paper will review and evaluate the empirical findings on the efficacy of MI and describe potential future applications.

WHAT IS MI?

Rollnick and Miller (1995) offer their current definition of MI as a "directive, client-centered counseling style for eliciting behavior change by helping clients to explore and resolve ambivalence." They emphasize that the spirit of MI is better understood as an interpersonal style rather than a set of therapeutic techniques. It emphasizes the value-driven and health-seeking component of client behavior and asserts that clients will be more likely to make choices consistent with their core values when they are helped to recognize them.

MI is directive in that it facilitates the expression, clarification, and resolution of the ambivalence that may block a client from making a commitment to change. While confrontation is the implicit goal of MI, immediate, direct confrontation and persuasion are explicitly proscribed because they generally increase resistance and reduce the probability of change (Miller et al., 1993; Miller & Rollnick, 1991). Finally, the therapeutic relationship is seen as a partnership where the client's autonomy, freedom of choice, and efficacy are actively supported rather than being directed by a therapist in the "expert" role.

Utilizing the transtheoretical perspective proposed by Prochaska and DiClemente (1982), MI seeks to assist clients in moving from the early stages of change (precontemplation or contemplation) to the determination or action stage. It uses stage-specific strategies to foster a commitment to take action for change. The active ingredients of MI which help facilitate this movement are in the following prescription:

- Express empathy with reflective listening.
- Develop discrepancy between client goals or values and current problem behavior.
- Avoid argumentation and direct confrontation.
- Roll with resistance rather than opposing it directly.
- Support self-efficacy and optimism for change (Miller & Rollnick, 1991).

The empathic, client-centered therapeutic approach developed by Rogers (1957, 1959) provides the foundation of MI (Miller & Rollnick, 1991). In contrast to confrontive techniques, MI attempts to elicit the reasons for change from the client rather than attempting to persuade that change is necessary. In essence, MI assists clients to convince *themselves* that change is necessary. For problem drinkers who are not considering change (Precontemplators) MI attempts to elicit concerns regarding the extent, impact, and risk of the current level of drinking in order to create ambivalence about change. These concerns may arise out of personal values and goals or may be stimulated by objective assessment results that provide normative and risk level information. For Contemplators, who are ambivalent about change, MI attempts to reflect or even amplify the discrepancy between the client's values or goals and the problem behavior. Juxtaposition of the conflicting values and goals with the impact of the problem behavior may be used to reduce the desirability of the behavior. MI also emphasizes the client's freedom and responsibility to decide about, and implement, change and supports their self-efficacy for doing so. If ambivalence is resolved and a desire to change is elicited, MI attempts to clarify the change desired and to solidify the commitment to do so. Finally, the client is assisted in determining the next step, which may or may not involve further therapeutic assistance. Frequently, a menu of effective change options may be provided so that a client may choose the option(s) with greatest appeal.

Rollnick and Miller (1995) emphasize the importance of distinguishing the interpersonal style of MI from a number of different specific interventions that have been derived from or confused with it. The Drinker's Check-up (DCU; Miller & Sovereign, 1989) is a brief assessment-based intervention. It provides meaningful, personal feedback that can be compared with some normative reference utilizing the MI style. MI may also be provided without formal assessment (Miller, 1983) and, alternatively, assessment feedback may also be provided in a nonconfrontive style without any interpersonal interaction (Agostinelli et al., 1995).

Motivational Enhancement Therapy (MET; Miller et al., 1992) is a four-session adaptation of the DCU and is one of three therapies being evaluated in Project MATCH (1993). MATCH is a clinical trial in the USA of 1726 treatment-seeking problem drinkers randomized to MET, Cognitive-Behavioral Skills training, or Twelve-Step Facilitation Therapy.

Brief motivational interviewing utilizes a menu of quick, concrete strategies designed for use in brief medical consultations (Rollnick et al., 1992a). A 5–15 minutes strategy that matches the degree of readiness to change in the patient is selected from a menu of strategies. The strategies are designed to manifest the spirit of MI and allow for an approximately 40-minute consultation.

Finally, brief interventions have often been confused with MI because they share many of the same effective ingredients identified by Miller and Sanchez (1994). These active ingredients are summarized by the acronym FRAMES, which stands for *Feedback* of personal risk or impairment, emphasizing the personal *Responsibility* for change, *Advice* to change, a *Menu* of alternative change strategies, an *Empathic* therapeutic style, and an enhancement of client *Self-efficacy* and optimism. Many of these ingredients are consistent with MI, while others (e.g., advice-giving) may require alteration for a motivational interviewing style. To avoid confusion, Rollnick and Miller (1995) recommend that only those interventions aimed at increasing readiness to change and embodying the "spirit" described above should be termed motivational interviewing.

Eleven clinical trials evaluating MI have been completed with a variety of populations and a number of other trials are currently under way. Two of the studies have provided MI to self-identified concerned drinkers with no additional treatment (Miller et al., 1988, 1993), three have offered MI at treatment entry as an enhancement to regular treatment (Bien et al., 1993; Brown & Miller, 1993; Saunders et al., 1995), five have utilized MI in medical settings with patients seeking help for other medical issues (Handmaker, 1993; Kuchipudi et al., 1990; Heather et al., 1995; Richmond et al., 1995; Senft et al., 1995), and a final controlled study has compared a brief motivational interview to an extended alternative treatment (Stephens et al., 1993). Most of these studies have used some variation of the DCU (Miller & Sovereign, 1989) while others have used a brief motivational intervention. All but two studies have evaluated changes in alcohol use. Table 2.1 provides a summary of sample characteristics and other important information for each of the studies. Nine of the studies that provide support for the efficacy of MI will be reviewed first; they are divided according to settings. The last section will review the two studies that did not support MI as an effective clinical intervention.

EVIDENCE SUPPORTING THE EFFICACY OF MI

MI as the Sole Intervention with Self-Selected Help Seekers

The DCU was first evaluated by Miller et al. (1988). They advertised a free and confidential DCU that was not connected with a treatment program, was not for alcoholics but for drinkers in general, did not result in a diagnosis or label, and provided objective feedback about their alcohol use. Subjects were encouraged to use this information in whatever way they found most useful.

The DCU consisted of a 2-hour assessment followed by a 1-hour feedback session 1 week later. The assessment included quantity and frequency of alcohol intake, blood tests to assess possible liver damage from alcohol, and neuropsychological tests sensitive to cognitive impairment that might be caused by alcohol. Feedback was presented in the empathic MI style described above. In the immediate DCU group, both weekly alcohol consumption and weekly peak blood alcohol level were significantly reduced at both six weeks and 18 months. The waiting-list control group initially showed no change in consumption, but had similar outcomes after receiving the DCU intervention.

A similar study compared the DCU in one of two conditions: presented in either an MI style or a confrontive style (Miller et al., 1993). The confrontive DCU included therapist behaviors such as arguing, disagreeing, and labeling. Audiotapes of all sessions were coded by two raters to provide a frequency measure of both therapist and client behaviors. Both groups demonstrated significantly less weekly consumption, lower peak BAC levels, and fewer drinking days relative to waiting-list controls at the 6-week and 12-month follow-up.

In this study, assigned therapist style failed to produce any significant difference in drinking behavior; however, the confrontive condition did evoke significantly more client resistance behaviors (arguing, ignoring, and interrupting). Actual therapist behavior was also examined in delivery of their assigned styles. A correlational analysis revealed that therapist confrontation significantly predicted client drinking behavior at 1 year. Four client resistance behaviors (interrupting, arguing, off-task responses, and negative responses) also predicted client drinking during the same time interval. The more the therapist confronted, the more the client resisted and the more he or she was drinking 1 year later. The authors emphasized that the relative absence of client resistance behaviors, which only comprised 3% of total client responses, was more strongly related to successful outcomes than the presence of the positive behaviors (agreeing with the therapist, expressing concern, determination, or optimism) usually associated with motivation to change. They suggested that the most successful therapeutic styles may be those that elicit positive motivational responses from clients without evoking resistance.

MI as an Enhancement to Treatment

Three trials have attempted to use MI to enhance existing interventions in both alcohol and methadone maintenance treatment settings. The first study to provide MI enhancement to a severely alcohol-impaired population was conducted at a veterans' hospital outpatient program (Bien et al., 1993). Participants were randomly assigned to receive a DCU or brief confrontive feedback prior to their regular treatment. The mean MAST score for the sample was 33 and they reported drinking an average of 92 drinks per week. The 3-month follow-up analysis using a composite variable of drinking measures (e.g., total consumption, peak BAC level, and days abstinent) for the past 30 days demonstrated a significantly lower value on the composite variable for the MI group. No significant differences among the groups were evident at 6 months which may reflect the difficulty of sustaining treatment gains in a severely disabled population.

Brown and Miller (1993) provided an MI-style DCU prior to regular treatment in an inpatient alcohol unit at a private psychiatric hospital. Consecutive admissions with a primary diagnosis of alcohol dependence were randomly assigned to receive the two-session DCU procedure or not prior to inpatient treatment. The sample was comparable to those in the above study (Bien et al., 1993) with a slightly lower MAST score of 25.8 and slightly lower drink consumption of 85.9 drinks per week. In addition to the usual drinking outcome measures, this study evaluated treatment involvement and the extent to which clients received what they wanted from treatment.

Both the MI and control groups showed significant reductions in weekly consumption and BAC levels; however, the MI group showed a significantly greater reduction in weekly consumption over the control condition. In addition, blind ratings of client involvement by three different therapists indicated superior treatment involvement by the MI group and this rating also predicted drinking outcomes. These data suggest that the improved outcomes produced by MI may be mediated, in part, by greater engagement in treatment and more positive therapist perceptions.

The first trial with a population of opiate abusers was conducted in an Australian methadone maintenance program (Saunders et al., 1995). They compared MI with an educational control condition prior to regular treatment. The MI provided by these authors was a more structured intervention and did not involve assessment feedback. The therapist elicited the "good" and then the "less good" consequences of heroin use and juxtaposed these with considerations of the client's life satisfaction and areas of greatest concern. This process was aided by the use of a self-completed decision matrix allowing the comparison of the positive and negative consequences of opiate use, and the costs and benefits of stopping. The hour-long interview was followed 1 week later by a 10–15 minute review session.

Over the 6-month follow-up period, participants in the MI group initially moved further along the stages of change, made greater initial commitments to abstinence, saw more positive outcomes from abstaining, and remained engaged in treatment longer. They relapsed less quickly to opiate use and reported a greater reduction in opiate-related problems.

MI in Medical Settings

The use of MI in primary medical settings is generating considerable interest because it offers the possibility of a brief and effective intervention for a population with an elevated rate of substance abuse. Some of these patients may be at risk from medical complications secondary to their drinking or they may lack the problem recognition that could motivate behavior change and/or the seeking of alcohol treatment. Patients with specific high-risk primary medical conditions, such as high blood pressure or diabetes, may also be targeted for intervention with potentially similar benefits. Below are five studies that have specifically targeted alcohol problems in medical settings.

Handmaker (1993) targeted pregnant women who were screened as at-risk drinkers (at least one drink in the last 30 days) at a university hospital prenatal clinic and were randomized to an MI-style DCU or no intervention. At the 2-month follow-up, the overall sample showed significant reductions in peak BAC level and total abstinent days but no differences in drinking measures were apparent between the experimental groups. The author speculated that the assessment procedure alone may have contributed to increased awareness of drinking behavior in the control group which resulted in enough behavior change to eliminate any difference between the two groups. However, among the heavier drinkers (BACs > 222 mg%) the DCU did produce a significantly greater reduction in peak BACs indicating positive changes in the amount of alcohol consumed per occasion.

A large-scale study employing "naturalistic" or "opportunistic" recruitment procedures in a primary medical setting also found a brief MI intervention to be effective (Senft et al., 1995). These authors recruited patients from those appearing for their regular appointments who were then randomized to a "usual care" condition or an immediate 15-minute MI after seeing their general practitioner (GP). Seventy-nine percent of the MI patients actually completed the intervention interview; follow-up was completed by phone at 6 and 12 months. Patients in the MI group reported significantly less total consumption at 6 months and significantly fewer drinking days per week at both the 6- and 12-month follow-up relative to controls. The number of drinks per drinking day did not differ at any comparison.

Finally, Heather et al. (1996) tested a matching hypothesis that heavy drinking medical inpatients who were not ready to change their drinking behavior would see greater drinking reductions following an MI intervention, while those who were ready to change would benefit more from a brief skills-based approach. Patients were screened from a variety of inpatient wards using an instrument that had questions regarding alcohol consumption embedded in it. To be selected, patients needed to report drinking more than 28 standard drinks per week or more than 11 standard drinks in a single session during the prior month. Patients with severe alcohol dependence or organic conditions requiring total abstinence, major psychiatric problems, or treatment for alcohol problems were excluded.

Using block randomization, the subjects were assigned to three conditions:

• MI
• Skills-based counseling (SBC)
• Usual care.

All subjects received a baseline assessment which included a weekly quantity–frequency measure of alcohol consumption and the Readiness to Change Questionnaire (RCQ; Rollnick et al., 1992b) which is designed to measure a patient's readiness to reduce heavy alcohol consumption. The MI session explored the "good things" and "not so good things" about heavy drinking, provided information, and explored concerns raised by patients in a style that allowed them to make their own decisions. The SBC provided normative feedback, information on the dangers of heavy drinking, and recommended safe drinking limits. It also provided instruction on self-monitoring, drink reduction, identification of high-risk situations, and alternative activities associated with a changed lifestyle. The usual care condition may or may not have included advice about drinking from medical staff.

At the 8-month follow-up both the MI and the SBC groups showed reduced drinking. While there was no overall difference between the MI and SBC interventions, the MI proved superior to the SBC intervention for the problem drinkers who were less ready to change. The SBC did not produce better results with the "ready-to-change" patients, indicating that only half of the authors' matching hypothesis was confirmed.

MI COMPARED TO OTHER TREATMENTS

One final study by Stephens et al. (1994) has compared an adaptation of the DCU with an extended treatment and delayed treatment control condition. Participants

TABLE 2.1. Sample and Study Characteristics for Controlled Trials of Motivational Interviewing

					Effect sizes[a]	
Study	n[b]	FU[c]	% Male[d]	Outcome[e]	Within	Between
Bien et al. (1993)	28	3	94	MI > TC		0.72
Brown & Miller (1993)	30	3	75	MI > TC		1.06
Handmaker (1993)	42	2	0	MI = NT	1.80	0.39[f]
Heather et al. (1995)	174	8	100	MI > BT, NI		0.45[h]
Kuchipudi et al. (1990)	114	4	100	MI = NT		0.00[g]
Miller et al. (1988)	42	18	71	MI > WL	0.33	
Miller et al. (1993)	42	12	57	MI > WL	0.64	
Richmond et al. (1995)	378	12	57	MI = BT, NT	0.27	
Saunders et al. (1995)	122	6	64	MI > TC	i	
Senft et al. (1995)	516	12	71	MI > NT		0.20
Stephens et al. (1993)	291	16	77	MI > ET, WL	0.87	

[a] Effect sizes computed on largest significant difference between group drinking behavior effect where applicable and largest within-group effect when not; computation of largest within-group effect size = (intake mean – follow-up mean)/weighted pooled standard deviation; computation of largest between-group effect size = (comparison follow-up mean – follow-up mean)/weighted pooled standard deviation.
[b] n: total number randomized in study sample.
[c] FU: longest follow-up period in study.
[d] % males in study sample.
[e] TC = treatment control; T = no treatment; WL = waiting list.
[f] Effect size computed for subjects with peak blood alcohol levels > 0.222 mg % ($n = 4$).
[g] Effect size statistic, w, computed from χ^2 contingency table data.
[h] Effect size computed for subjects identified as "not ready to change."
[i] Data not available for computation.

were media-recruited marijuana abusers who wanted help stopping their use and were required to have used marijuana on at least 50 days out of the last 90 to participate in the study.

The DCU was modified to assess for marijuana use and utilized the typical two-session assessment and feedback format separated by 1 month. Problem-solving training was included in the marijuana DCU intervention and the attendance at the second session by a supportive other was encouraged, and 31% of the participants complied.

The extended treatment was a 14-session Relapse Prevention Support Group (RPSG) modeled on Marlatt and Gordon's (1985) cognitive-behavioral treatment. Participants were randomized to one of the three conditions and evaluated five times in the following 16 months. All groups showed significant reductions in days of marijuana use and rates of abstinence at 4 months, but differences for both the MI and relapse prevention groups were more significant than those of the delayed treatment group. In addition, both the MI and RPSG groups showed significant reductions in use-related problems and dependence symptoms when compared to the delayed treatment condition.

EVIDENCE NOT SUPPORTING THE EFFICACY OF MI

The two studies that have found no support for the efficacy of MI have both been conducted in medical settings. One study compared an MI-style intervention to brief advice from a GP, an assessment only condition, and a control group (Richmond et al., 1995). These authors were interested in evaluating more naturalistic recruitment procedures with non-treatment seekers, because previous studies had found positive effects for both brief GP advice and assessment conditions but used self-selected treatment seeking subjects.

The MI intervention was a structured behavioral change program with a goal of moderate drinking that was delivered with an MI-style. The program consisted of five brief GP consultations conducted over a 5-month period for approximately 80 minutes. It included a self-help manual and utilized intervention strategies appropriate for different stages of change. Patients not suited to a moderation goal (severe alcohol dependence and problems or medical conditions where drinking was contraindicated) and those with psychiatric problems or previous or current alcohol treatment were eliminated from the study. Results failed to demonstrate any differences in consumption among the groups at the 6- and 12-month follow-up although the MI group did show a reduction in alcohol-related problems at 6 months.

This study is notable for a loss of 49% in the MI-designated subject pool, occurring before the MI component of the behavioral change program began on session two. When these subjects were left out of the analysis, the MI group did demonstrate a greater reduction in drinking than the other two groups. Initial poor compliance is precisely one of the behaviors meant to be influenced by motivational interviewing and previous studies have demonstrated its positive impact upon the client engagement process. Brown and Miller (1993) and Saunders et al. (1995) have suggested that this may be one of the ways that MI mediates positive outcomes. Therefore, using motivational interviewing in initial client contacts may increase both compliance and available data in a study design of this type.

The markedly different outcomes of the Richmond et al. (1995) and the Senft et al. (1995) studies are especially difficult to reconcile given their design and population similarities. A likely explanation may be the immediacy and brevity of the Senft et al. MI intervention which may have encouraged greater patient participation than the more infrequent schedule in the Richmond et al. study. Another explanation may be that patients in Australia often choose their GP on a convenience and availability basis due to a fee-for-service system and have less of a sense that the GP is their doctor (Richmond et al., 1995). This may produce a relationship that is less conducive to lifestyle interventions than in other systems where the patient–GP bond may be more personal.

Kuchipudi et al. (1990) described a motivational intervention using a drinkers check-up format that was provided to inpatient gastroenterology patients. The subjects had recurrent gastrointestinal diseases and had been advised by their physicians to discontinue alcohol consumption. Eligible patients had also been drinking up to the time of admission and had not been involved in alcohol treatment for the previous 2 months. Subjects were randomly assigned to the motivational intervention or a no-treatment control.

The motivational intervention consisted of interviews with three different individuals over a period of several days. In addition, a social worker contacted each subject in the motivational intervention group to discuss available alcohol treatment programs and how they might specifically benefit the patient. Motivational intervention subjects were also mandated to attend a weekly 45-minute group discussion of alcoholism programs at the hospital.

No significant differences were found between the two groups on measures of treatment initiation, compliance with clinic appointments, or self-reports of drinking at 3 months. The authors attributed the failure of their motivational intervention to produce the more positive outcomes seen in other studies to the unselected status of their subjects. They reported that a significant number of subjects ($n = 38$) refused to cooperate with some component of the study and that this was prognostic of negative outcomes. They point out that consent procedures used in other studies select only these willing subjects and may thus produce more positive outcomes.

As with the Richmond et al. (1995) study, there is a question as to whether Kuchipudi et al. (1990) provided a true test of MI. The procedures they describe do not seem to reflect the "spirit" of MI (i.e., overreliance on "medical authority") or even the more structured formal feedback procedures of the DCU. In addition, the motivational interviews were apparently conducted by at least 18 and possibly 24 or more different individuals. It is unclear what training or quality control procedures were employed to minimize variability with such a large group of therapists.

SUMMARY

The reviewed studies generally support the efficacy of MI with a variety of problematic behaviors (alcohol, marijuana, and opiate use) in a variety of settings (inpatient, outpatient, and primary care). The variable effect sizes for MI in the different studies require further examination. As some authors suggest, it is likely that the effectiveness of MI is linked to specific client variables which have not yet been measured in outcome studies. In particular, severity of impairment, co-existing personality disorganization, and degree of ambivalence toward substance use appear to be variables that would indicate differential response to MI. As with other interventions for substance abuse, it is unlikely that MI would be uniformly effective for all recipients. Investigation of client (or other) factors which predict favorable response to MI may eliminate the variability in effect sizes seen in outcome studies to date.

CURRENT AND FUTURE DIRECTIONS FOR MI

One of the important questions to be explored is the efficacy of MI with new problem areas, populations, settings, and formats. Motivation for change and compliance with treatment are common concerns for professionals treating a wide variety of health-related problems. Compliance with medical advice is the common denominator in most of these attempts (Rollnick et al., 1992a) and specific applications have or are being explored in the areas of diabetes (Stott et al., 1995), pain management (Jensen, in press), HIV risk reduction (Baker & Dixon, 1991), coronary heart disease rehabilitation, and eating disorders. Other applications are occurring in the treatment of sex offenders (Garland & Dougher, 1991; Mann & Rollnick, 1996), couples (Zweben, 1991), other concerned family members, smokers, and violent families.

Another area of interest has been the application of MI to teenagers. One trial evaluating a DCU as an enhancement to treatment in an adolescent substance abuse program is under way (Aubrey, 1995). The DCU is a one-session assessment and feedback procedure following the usual intake protocol. The 3-month follow-up will evaluate substance abuse related behaviors and treatment involvement and compliance.

New applications must be balanced by the ongoing exploration of many unanswered questions about MI. One important area of exploration concerns the effectiveness of MI relative to other established treatments. This is especially important for cost-conscious managed care environments. How do interventions using MI compare to the generally more extensive and costly treatments now in use? A recent meta-analysis (Miller et al., 1995) suggests that many of the more established treatments are more expensive and less effective than briefer interventions of which MI is only one.

Another area of inquiry concerns the mechanism, action, and duration of MI. How brief can an MI intervention be to still trigger behavior change? Senft et al. (1995) have demonstrated positive effects on drinking behavior at 6 months following a 15-minute motivational interview in a primary health clinic. While this finding needs replication, it encourages speculation about the wider application of such brief contacts. How long-lasting are behavior changes catalyzed by MI? Few studies have conducted follow-ups beyond 6 months. While some of the studies reviewed here do demonstrate longer-lasting effects, their findings need to be replicated and extended for even longer time periods.

A third question focuses on the active ingredients of MI. What are the necessary and/or sufficient conditions for successful MI? Are some components more useful than others? Can MI be accomplished with reflective listening alone? How important is structured feedback? Agostinelli et al. (1995) have demonstrated reductions in drinking behavior in a college population with personalized non-labeling feedback by mail. Further, how much of a role does subject-reactivity to the assessment process play in instigating change?

A fourth essential question to be explored is who benefits from MI and, importantly, who does not? What client characteristics predict responsiveness to MI? Since MI utilizes the assumption that clients respond according to their core values, it is possible that MI, like many other therapeutic interventions, may be less useful for clients with a diagnosis of antisocial personality disorder. A related issue is the effectiveness of MI in different cultures where values and expectations of help-seeking and the role of care providers may differ. Healers in some cultural contexts are expected to take directive, persuasive, and confrontive roles which may be inconsistent with the spirit of MI.

Other potential factors impacting the efficacy of MI are the expectations of both therapist and client. For example, Brown and Miller (1993) found the fulfillment of patient treatment expectations to be predictive of successful outcomes. Similarly, therapist expectations formed early in treatment are predictive of client outcome in substance abuse settings (Leake & King, 1977; Moyers & Love, 1995). Can such therapist and patient expectations influence the effectiveness of MI and might positive expectations be one of the active ingredients of MI?

A final question concerns the diffusion of MI into the treatment community. Much interest has certainly been generated in the research oriented clinical community and MI has been enthusiastically embraced in some countries such as the UK. However, MI has not made many inroads with the clinicians who provide the majority of alcohol and other drug treatments in the USA. What are the variables responsible for these differences and how can this knowledge be utilized to encourage the dissemination of MI into appropriate clinical communities? A related question is how to best train clinicians in the MI style. One study (Rubel et al.,

1995) has recently evaluated the effectiveness of an MI workshop. They found significant improvements in clinician knowledge and MI techniques assessed with paper and pencil questionnaires but no significant change in therapist behavior from audiotaped therapy sessions. More research in this area is essential if MI is to be effectively implemented in the treatment community. A final question that has been asked previously (Miller et al., 1988, p. 265) is "will any of this research, present and future, have a noticeable impact on how society addresses the prevention and resolution of the alcohol problem?" The authors certainly hope so!

ACKNOWLEDGMENT

This research was supported, in part, by a National Research Services Award (NRSA) grant (T32-AA07460) from the National Institute of Alcohol Abuse and Alcoholism awarded to the University of New Mexico. The authors also wish to acknowledge the editorial assistance of William R. Miller in the preparation of this review.

REFERENCES

Agostinelli, G., Brown, J. M., & Miller, W. R. (1995). Effects of normative feedback on consumption among heavy drinking college students. *Journal of Drug Education, 25*(1), 31–40.

Aubrey, L. (1994). *Motivational induction for adolescents seeking treatment.* National Institute on Alcohol Abuse and Alcoholism (Grant no. 1 R03 AA10648–01).

Baker, A., & Dixon, J. (1991). Motivational interviewing for HIV risk reduction. In W. R. Miller & S. Rollnick (Eds.), *Motivational interviewing: Preparing people to change addictive behavior.* New York: Guilford Press.

Bien, T., Miller, W. R., & Burroughs, J. M. (1993). Motivational interviewing with alcohol outpatients. *Behavioral and Cognitive Psychotherapy, 21*(4), 347–356.

Brown, J., & Miller, W. R. (1993). Impact of motivational interviewing on participation and outcome in residential alcoholism treatment. *Psychology of Addictive Behaviors, 7*(4), 211–218.

Garland, R. J., & Dougher, M. J. (1991). Motivational intervention in the treatment of sex offenders. In W. R. Miller & S. Rollnick (Eds.), *Motivational interviewing: Preparing people to change addictive behavior.* New York: Guilford Press.

Handmaker, N. S. (1993). *Motivating pregnant drinkers to abstain: Prevention in prenatal care clinics.* Doctoral dissertation, University of New Mexico.

Heather, N., Rollnick, S., Bell, A., & Richmond, R. (1996). Effects of brief counseling among male heavy drinkers identified on general hospital wards. *Drug and Alcohol Review, 15,* 29–38.

Jensen, M. P. (in press). Enhancing motivation to change in pain treatment. In D. C. Turk & R. J. Gatchel (Eds.), *Psychological treatment for pain: A practitioner's handbook.* New York: Guilford Press.

Kuchipudi, V., Hobein, K., Flickinger, A., & Iber, F. L. (1990). Failure of a 2-hour motivational intervention to alter recurrent drinking behavior in alcoholics with gastrointestinal disease. *Journal of Studies on Alcohol, 51*(4), 356–360.

Leake, G. J., & King, A. S. (1977). Effect of counselor expectations on alcoholic recovery. *Alcohol Health and Research World, 11*(3), 16–22.

Marlatt, G. A., & Gordon, J. R. (1985). *Relapse prevention: Maintenance strategies in the treatment of addictive behaviors.* New York: Guilford Press.

Mann, R. E., & Rollnick, S. (1996). Motivational interviewing with a sex offender who believed he was innocent. *Behavioural and Cognitive Psychotherapy, 24,* 127–134.

Miller, W. R. (1983). Motivational interviewing with problem drinkers. *Behavioural Psychotherapy, 11,* 147–172.

Miller, W. R. (1985). Motivation for treatment: A review with special emphasis on alcoholism. *Psychological Bulletin, 98*(1), 84–107.

Miller, W. R., & Rollnick, S. (1991). *Motivational interviewing: Preparing people to change addictive behavior.* New York: Guilford Press.

Miller, W. R., & Sanchez, V. C. (1994) Motivating young adults for treatment and lifestyle change. In G. Howard (Ed.), *Issues in alcohol use and misuse by young adults* (pp. 55–82). Notre Dame, IN: University of Notre Dame Press.

Miller, W. R., & Sovereign, R. G. (1989). The check-up: A model for early intervention in addictive behaviors. In T. Loberg, W. R. Miller, P. E. Nathan, & G. A. Marlatt (Eds.), *Addictive behaviors: Prevention and early intervention* (pp. 219–231). Amsterdam: Swets & Zeitlinger.

Miller, W. R., Sovereign, R. G., & Krege, B. (1988). Motivational interviewing with problem drinkers: II. The Drinker's Check-up as a preventive intervention. *Behavioural Psychotherapy, 16*(4), 251–268.

Miller, W. R., Zweben, A., DiClemente, C. C., & Rychtarik, R. G. (1992). *Motivational enhancement therapy manual: A clinical research guide for therapists treating individuals with alcohol abuse and dependence.* National Institute on Alcohol Abuse and Alcoholism, Rockville, MD.

Miller, W. R., Benefield, R. G., & Tonigan, J. S. (1993). Enhancing motivation for change in problem drinking: A controlled comparison of two therapist styles. *Journal of Consulting and Clinical Psychology, 61*(3), 455–461.

Miller, W. R., Brown, J. M., Simpson, T. L., et al. (1995). What works? A methodological analysis of the alcohol treatment outcome literature. In R. K. Hester & W. R. Miller (Eds.), *Handbook of alcoholism treatment approaches: Effective alternatives* (pp. 12–44). Boston: Allyn & Bacon.

Moyers, T. M., & Love, J. (1995). Alcohol therapists' conceptualizations of clients: Do they affect treatment? Paper presented at the 28th Annual Convention of the Association for Advancement of Behavior Therapy, November 1994, San Diego, CA.

Moyers, T. B., & Miller, W. R. (1993). Therapists' conceptualizations of alcoholism: Measurement and implications for treatment. *Psychology of Addictive Behaviors, 7*(4), 238–245.

Prochaska, J. O., & DiClemente, C. C. (1982). Transtheoretical therapy: Toward a more integrative model of change. *Psychotherapy: Theory, Research, and Practice, 19,* 276–288.

Project MATCH Research Group. (1993). Project MATCH: Rationale and methods for a multisite clinical trial matching patients to alcoholism treatment. *Alcoholism: Clinical and Experimental Research, 17,* 1130–1145.

Richmond, R., Heather, N., Wodak, A., Kehoe, L., & Webster, I. (1995). Controlled evaluation of a general practice-based brief intervention for excessive drinking. *Addiction, 90,* 119–132.

Rogers, C. R. (1957). The necessary and sufficient conditions for therapeutic personality change. *Journal of Consulting Psychology, 21,* 95–103.

Rogers, C. R. (1959). A theory of therapy, personality, and interpersonal relationships as developed in the client-centered framework. In S. Koch (Ed.), *Psychology: The study of a science. Vol. 3. Formulations of the person and the social context.* New York: McGraw-Hill.

Rollnick, S., & Miller, W. R. (1995). What is motivational interviewing? *Behavioural and Cognitive Psychology, 23,* 325–334.

Rollnick, S., Heather, N., & Bell, A. (1992a). Negotiating behaviour change in medical settings: The development of brief motivational interviewing. *Journal of Mental Health, 1,* 25–37.

Rollnick, S., Heather, N., Gold, R., & Hall, W. (1992b). Development of a short "readiness to change" questionnaire for use in brief, opportunistic interventions among excessive drinkers. *British Journal of Addiction, 87,* 743–754.

Rubel, E. C., Sobell, L. C., & Miller, W. R. (1995). Effectiveness of a workshop on motivational interviewing with alcohol abusers. Manuscript submitted for publication.

Saunders, B., Wilkinson, C., & Phillips, M. (1995). The impact of a brief motivational intervention with opiate users attending a methadone programme. *Addiction, 90,* 415–424.

Senft, R. A., Polen, M. R., Freeborn, D. K., & Hollis, J. F. (1995). Drinking patterns and health: A randomized trial of screening and brief intervention in a primary care setting. *Final report to the National Institute on Alcohol Abuse and Alcoholism* (Grant No. AA08976).

Stephens, R. S., Roffman, R. A., Cleaveland, B. L., Curtin, L., & Wertz, J. (1994). Extended versus minimal intervention with marijuana dependent adults. Paper presented at the 28th Annual Convention of the Association for Advancement of Behavior Therapy, San Diego, CA.

Stott, N. C. H., Rollnick, S., Pill, P., & Rees, M. (1995). Innovation in clinical method: Diabetes care and negotiating skills. *Family Practice.*

Zweben, A. (1991). Motivational counseling with alcoholic couples. In W. R. Miller & S. Rollnick (Eds.), *Motivational interviewing: Preparing people to change addictive behavior.* New York: Guilford Press.

Chapter 3

Motivational Interviewing to Enhance Treatment Initiation in Substance Abusers

An Effectiveness Study

Kathleen M. Carroll, Ph.D.
Bryce Libby, M.S.W.
Joseph Sheehan, M.S.
Nancy Hyland, C.A.C.

Sixty individuals referred for a substance abuse evaluation by a child welfare worker were randomly assigned to either a standard evaluation or an evaluation enhanced by Motivational Interviewing techniques, each delivered in a single session. Participants who received the enhanced evaluation were significantly more likely to attend at least one additional treatment session after the initial evaluation (59% versus 29%). This finding suggests that comparatively inexpensive modifications of "standard" initial evaluations with substance-using parents may increase engagement of substance-abusing parents in treatment. Moreover, this study adds to an overwhelmingly positive literature supporting Motivational Interviewing with alcohol-using populations and extends prior findings to non-research community settings. (American Journal of Addictions 2001;10:335–339)

From the Department of Psychiatry, Division of Substance Abuse, Yale University School of Medicine, New Haven, Conn. (Dr. Carroll); Advanced Behavioral Health, Middletown, Conn., (Mr. Libby); the Department of Children and Families, State of Connecticut, Hartford (Mr. Sheehan); and the Genesis Center, Manchester, Conn. (Ms. Hyland).

A comparatively strong relationship between parental substance abuse and child abuse and neglect has been established.[1,2] Providing effective treatment for substance-abusing parents is thus a promising strategy for preventing further neglect.[2-4] Unfortunately, however, efforts to provide treatment to this population have been hampered by major gaps between the child welfare and the substance abuse treatment systems, including limited access to treatment.[3,4]

In response to increasing incidence of child abuse associated with parental substance abuse in Connecticut,[5] the Department of Children and Families (DCF) initiated Project SAFE (Substance Abuse Family Evaluation). Through a contract with Advanced Behavioral Health Incorporated, a network of 43 substance abuse treatment providers, Project SAFE provides DCF child welfare workers with immediate access to substance abuse treatment for parents suspected of substance abuse. Rather than relying on the parents to make the initial contact with treatment providers, DCF caseworkers call a centralized intake system to make the initial evaluation appointment, which is scheduled within 24 hours of the call. After the evaluation, outpatient treatment is offered free of charge through the provider network.

Project SAFE's success has been notable in several respects:[6] since its inception in 1995, 23,447 individuals have been referred to Project SAFE, and approximately 68% of those completed an evaluation. However, engaging this population in treatment has proven more difficult, as only 36% of those referred have attended one or more subsequent treatment sessions.

Brief motivational approaches that focus on mobilizing the individual's own resources to change[7] have high levels of empirical support in the substance abuse treatment literature, particularly for cigarette and alcohol users,[8-10] but they have not been widely evaluated in community treatment programs nor as a strategy to foster treatment engagement in non-treatment-seeking populations. Motivational approaches typically focus on reviewing objective information about the individual's substance use as well as on eliciting any concerns that the individual or their significant others may have about the individual's substance use.[7] By increasing the individual's awareness regarding the consequences of substance use as well as their own ambivalence toward use within an empathic and non-confrontational context, motivational approaches seek to increase motivation for changing substance use and related behaviors.[7] This trial evaluated whether integrating these motivational strategies into standard substance abuse evaluations would increase rates of initiation of substance abuse treatment among individuals referred through Project SAFE.

METHODS

An important aim of this trial was to evaluate interventions intended to enhance treatment engagement in "real world" community settings.[11] Thus, several design features were included to emphasize external validity. For example, the study was conducted within a community treatment clinic with no prior involvement in research, clinicians were drawn from the existing program staff, assessments were limited to those already in place for Project SAFE, training was comparatively brief, and inclusion/exclusion criteria were nonrestrictive to enhance the generalizability of the sample.

Participants were 60 individuals referred for evaluation by their DCF caseworkers for a substance abuse evaluation between March and June of 1999 at the Genesis Center in Manchester, Conn. At the time the individual presented for the evaluation, he or she was approached by a study clinician who explained the purpose of the study and obtained written informed consent. The participant was then randomly assigned to either the standard or enhanced evaluation.

To minimize attrition that may have resulted from delaying the time between randomization and the evaluation (e.g., by requiring participants to return to the clinic for the evaluation at another time), the entire study process (informed consent, random assignment, delivery of standard or enhanced evaluation) was completed within a single 2-hour sequence.

Clinicians and Training

Four clinicians (2 master's-, 2 bachelor's-level) conducted the experimental evaluations, and four conducted the standard evaluations (1 master's-, 3 bachelor's-level). The clinicians who provided the enhanced evaluation completed one day of training in Motivational Interviewing,[7] utilizing a therapist training protocol demonstrated to facilitate competent implementation of motivational techniques in a previous major multisite trial[12,13] and provided by one of the original supervisors from that project.

Interventions

Standard Evaluation. The standard evaluation was conducted according to the practice standards established for Project SAFE. This involved collecting information on the participant's reason for referral, substance use history, history, and current status of psychosocial problems, and collection of a urine specimen. The clinician then provided a treatment recommendation and referral. The evaluation process required approximately 1 hour.

Motivational Evaluation. In this condition, clinicians elicited the same information as in the standard evaluation; however, the clinicians integrated Motivational Interviewing techniques throughout the interview.[7] These included (1) heightening participants' awareness of the personal consequences of substance use (e.g., "What bothers you about your cocaine use?"), (2) expressing empathy (e.g., "It must have been difficult for you to come here today"), and (3) avoiding resistance (e.g., "What you decide to do about your substance use is up to you"). The motivational evaluation was the same length as the standard evaluation (1 hour).

Assessments

Because the major focus of the trial was treatment initiation, the primary outcome measures were the rates of participants who attended one or three subsequent drug abuse treatment sessions after the evaluation. For both conditions, a standard clinical summary was used to obtain basic demographic data and substance abuse history. Data on treatment utilization was drawn from the Project SAFE database.

RESULTS

Of 75 individuals who were approached and invited to participate, 60 elected to participate and were randomized. Reasons for refusal were: reluctance to cooperate with DCF (n = 8), not interested (n = 4), concerns about confidentiality (n = 2), or insufficient proficiency in English (n = 1). Baseline demographic data are provided in Table 3.1. Regarding substance use in the previous month, 92% reported some alcohol use, 77% reported marijuana use, and 53% reported some cocaine use, although the reported frequency of marijuana or cocaine use was low (less than two days per month).

The rate of participants attending at least one treatment session at the Genesis Center ("treatment initiation") following the evaluation was 59.3% in the motivational group compared with 29.2% of the standard group (chi square = 4.6, $p = .03$). The percentage attending three or more treatments continued to favor the motivational condition but was lower for both conditions; differences between the groups were not statistically significant (29.6% versus 16.7%, chi square = 1.2, NS).

DISCUSSION

Results of this study suggest that modifying clinicians' interviewing style to include motivational strategies can substantially increase the likelihood of treatment initiation in this resistant and challenging population. Although the rate of treatment inception for the group assigned to the motivational condition was twice that of the group assigned to the standard evaluation, further treatment participation dropped off sharply in both groups. There are several possible reasons for the weakening effect. First, the clinician who conducted the evaluation was rarely the same one who provided subsequent treatment. Thus, prior to the first session, participants did not know that they would be seeing a different clinician from the one who conducted the initial evaluation. Second, the clinicians who provided subsequent treatment were likely to use more traditional, confrontational approaches, which may have led to poorer engagement.

Limitations of the current study include the somewhat specialized study population and the lack of substance abuse outcome data. Nevertheless, as one of very

TABLE 3.1. Baseline Demographic and Substance Use Data
by Group, N = 60

Characteristic	Standard Evaluation N = 29	Motivational Interviewing Enhanced Evaluation N = 31	F or X2, df., *p*
Number (%) female	18 (62.1%)	25 (80.6%)	ns
Number (%) African American	1 (3.4%)	2 (6.5%)	ns
Hispanic	3 (10.3%)	3 (9.7%)	
Caucasian	25 (86.2%)	25 (80.6%)	
Other		1 (3.2%)	
Number (%) single/divorced	15 (51.7%)	15 (48.4%)	ns
Number (%) unemployed	8 (27.6%)	5 (16.1%)	ns
Mean (SD) age	34.0 (10.0)	34.7 (9.3)	ns
Mean (SD) years of education	11.4 (1.0)	12.1 (0.9)	7.83, (1,58), .007
Mean (SD) of days alcohol use in past month	5.0 (6.7)	2.3 (2.8)	ns
Mean (SD) days of marijuana use in past month	1.8 (6.2)	1.7 (4.3)	ns
Mean (SD) days of cocaine use in past month	0.1 (0.3)	0.3 (0.8)	ns
Number (%) has SO who is substance user	16 (55.2%)	14 (45.2%)	ns
Number (%) family history of substance use	25 (86.2%)	26 (83.9%)	ns
Mean (SD) number of children	2.17 (1.34)	2.42 (1.39)	ns
Mean (SD) number of minor children residing w/participant	1.55 (1.33)	1.90 (1.64)	ns
Number (%) with history of psychiatric treatment	14 (48.3%)	11 (35.5%)	ns
Number (%) on probation or parole	3 (10.3%)	3 (9.7%)	ns

few clinical trials evaluating Motivational Interviewing with drug abusers, this study adds to an overwhelmingly positive literature supporting this approach with alcohol-using populations[8–10] and extends prior findings to nonresearch community settings. It should be noted that these dramatic initial effects were achieved through minor variations in clinician style, delivered in a single session by community substance abuse counselors who had completed very abbreviated training in Motivational Interviewing.

These findings suggest, first, that Motivational Interviewing techniques can be taught to and used by "real world" clinicians. Second, Motivational Interviewing techniques, provided in one session, are powerful and practical in the short term, in this case doubling the return rate of this client population. Finally, a single session of Motivational Interviewing may not produce enduring engagement effects, at least when followed by traditional counseling techniques. Additional motivationally focused sessions or greater integration of these techniques into ongoing counseling might be associated with improved long-term engagement.

ACKNOWLEDGMENTS

Support was provided by NIDA grants P50-DA09241 (Bruce Rounsaville, M.D.) and K05-DA00457 (Dr. Carroll.) Project SAFE is a contract supported by the Department of Children and Families (DCF) of the State of Connecticut. The contributions of Theresa Babuscio, Tami Frankforter, Deborah Beckwith, Mike Socha, Roz Liss, Cindy Morgan, and the staff of the Genesis Center are gratefully acknowledged.

REFERENCES

1. Child Welfare League of America. (1992). *Children at the front: A different view of the war on alcohol and drugs.* Washington, DC: Author.
2. Kelleher, K., Chaffin, M., Hollenberg, J., & Fischer, E. (1994). Alcohol and drug disorders among physically abusive and neglectful parents in a community-based sample. *American Journal of Public Health, 84,* 1586–1590.
3. Institute of Medicine. (1996). *Fetal alcohol syndrome: Diagnosis, epidemiology, prevention, and treatment.* Washington, DC: National Academy Press.
4. Juliana, P., & Goodman, C. (1997). Children of substance abusing parents. In J. H. Lowinsohn, P. Ruiz, & R. B. Millman (Eds.), *Comprehensive textbook of substance abuse* 3rd ed. (pp. 665–671). New York: Williams & Wilkins.
5. Connecticut Department of Children and Families. (1997). *A report to the general assembly: Child protective services and adult substance abuse treatment.* Hartford, CT: Connecticut Department of Children and Families.
6. Center on Addiction and Substance Abuse at Columbia University. (1998). *No safe haven: Children of substance-abusing parents.* New York: CASA.
7. Miller, W. R., & Rollnick, S. (1991). *Motivational interviewing: Preparing people to change addictive behavior.* New York: Guilford.
8. Babor, T. F. (1994). Avoiding the horrid and beastly sin of drunkenness: Does dissuasion make a difference? *Journal of Consulting and Clinical Psychology, 62,* 1127–1140.
9. Bien, T. H., Miller, W. R., & Tonigan, J. S. (1993). Brief interventions for alcohol problems: A review. *Addiction, 88,* 315–335.
10. WHO Brief Intervention Study Group. (1996). A randomized cross-national clinical trial of brief interventions with heavy drinkers. *American Journal of Public Health, 86,* 948–955.
11. Institute of Medicine. (1998). *Bridging the gap between practice and research: Forging partnerships with community-based drug and alcohol treatment.* Washington, DC: National Academy Press.
12. Project MATCH Research Group. (1997). Matching alcohol treatments to client heterogeneity: Project MATCH posttreatment drinking outcomes. *Journal of Studies on Alcohol, 58,* 7–29.
13. Carroll, K. M., Connors, G. J., Cooney, N. L., et al. (1998). Internal validity of Project MATCH treatments: Discriminability and integrity. *Journal of Consulting and Clinical Psychology, 66,* 290–303.

Chapter 4

Network Therapy for Cocaine Abuse

Use of Family and Peer Support

Marc Galanter, M.D.
Helen Dermatis, Ph.D.
Daniel Keller, Ph.D.[†]
Manuel Trujillo, M.D.

Cocaine-dependent subjects were treated by psychiatric residents in a 24-week sequence of Network Therapy. This approach, developed for practitioners in solo practice, employs a cognitive-behavioral orientation in sessions with family and peers as well as in individual sessions. Of 47 subjects, 73% of all observed weekly urines were negative for cocaine, and 20 (45%) of the subjects had negative toxicologies in the last three scheduled samples. A positive outcome was associated with the number of network (but not individual) sessions attended and completion of the full treatment sequence. Results suggest the utility of Network Therapy, even in the hands of relatively naive therapists. (American Journal on Addictions 2002;11:161–166)

From the Division of Alcoholism and Drug Abuse, Department of Psychiatry, NYU School of Medicine, New York, NY (Drs. Galanter, Dermatis, and Trujillo); and the Department of Psychiatry, Mount Sinai Medical Center, New York, NY (Dr. Keller).

†Deceased.

Network Therapy is an approach to the management of the substance-abusing patient in which individual sessions are augmented by ones where the patient's social support network (i.e., peers, and family members) engaged to help secure the patient's abstinence.[1,2] Three key elements are introduced in Network Therapy (NT): (1) a cognitive behavioral approach to relapse prevention, already found to be valuable in addiction treatment;[3] (2) support of the patient's natural social network, as involvement of spouse[4] and peer support,[1] to be effective in enhancing the outcome of professional therapy; (3) community reinforcement techniques, which have been employed to provide support for rehabilitation by focusing on activities outside the session context.[5] The study on network therapy outcome reported here was carried out under a Phase I Behavioral Therapies Development initiative of the National Institute on Drug Abuse to implement innovative therapies that have a theoretical basis.

METHOD

The Treatment Procedure

Therapists employed in this study were 28 PGY-III and PGY-IV psychiatry residents who received a 13-week video-assisted didactic seminar on network therapy. They received weekly supervision of a member of the faculty of the NYU Division of Alcoholism and Drug Abuse. None had prior training in substance abuse treatment other than periodic exposure to substance abuse patients on their inpatient and emergency room rotations.

Subjects were drawn from a pool of applicants solicited from the NYU and Bellevue Hospital substance abuse referral sources and from advertisements in local newspapers. To be included, they had to experience appreciable ongoing compromise from cocaine or dependence by *DSM-IV* criteria and be able to bring to intake a collateral, family member, or friend who agreed to support them in their recovery. Applicants with pre-existing major Axis I disorders were excluded.

Members of the network, who were not substance abusers themselves, were chosen by mutual agreement of the therapist and patient. The network is used by the therapist to aid in instituting a pragmatic treatment plan to undercut denial and initiate and stabilize abstinence. A cognitive-behavioral framework was provided by beginning each network session with the patient recounting events related to cue exposure or to substance use since the last meeting. Network members are invited to comment on this report to assure that all are engaged in a mutual task with correct, shared information.

As applied here, this clinical approach involved two therapy sessions a week for 24 weeks. Generally, one network session is scheduled each week for an initial month, with subsequent sessions held less frequently, typically on a monthly basis by the end of the treatment period. The remaining sessions are dedicated to individual therapy. Patients received no external incentives from the therapist for complying with the treatment, such as contingency reinforcers, and paid a $20 fee for each session.

Training

In order to ensure standardized application of the approach, a 122-page treatment manual was prepared based on our previously published volume on the NT technique.[2] The manual focuses on the three basic components of NT as described above: cognitive-behavioral assessment of the patient with implementation of appropriate behavioral strategies, teaching the network to provide a supportive environment for the patient's abstinence, and training the network to assist the patient to follow through in adherence to behavioral strategies (e.g., avoiding triggers). The manualized format of Network Therapy has been shown to be discriminable from other addiction treatment using family members.

Therapist adherence to the network therapy protocol was assessed by supervisors on videotape of sessions made monthly with the Network Therapy Rating Scale (NTRS),[6] a 14-item scale comprised of two components that rate therapists' use of network and non-network techniques, respectively, in a given session. Results of these assessments based on evaluation of videotaping of sessions will be reported elsewhere.

Outcome Measures

Subjects were screened prior to entry into treatment for the quantity of admission cocaine use and for the ability to present at evaluation with a collateral who could participate in a network. The success of the treatment was determined for each subject by means of two outcome variables based on weekly urine toxicologies collected under observation. One was the portion of that subject's urine toxicologies that was found to be negative for cocaine during the course of treatment. This reflected the subject's compliance with abstinence expectations while in treatment. The second outcome variable was whether or not all of the last three urine toxicologies scheduled for the subject were found to be negative for cocaine. This reflected the likelihood that the subject achieved a cocaine-free state at the end of treatment.

Three groups of variables were studied to determine whether they were associated with a relatively better response to treatment. One group reflected antecedent pathology and treatment: a self-reported history of general psychiatric or substance abuse treatment, previous attendance at Twelve-Step meetings, number of years of cocaine use, and the number of days of cocaine or crack cocaine use during the 30 days prior to entry into the study. A second group of variables reflected the status of the subject's psychopathology or substance use at the time of intake into the study. These were determined by scores on the Global Severity Index[7] and urine toxicology at the time of admission. A third set of variables involved the degree a subject participated in therapy sessions during the study, as reflected in the number of network and individual sessions attended.

RESULTS

Subjects

The study population consisted of 47 subjects whose mean age was 35.5 (SD = 7.0) years, of whom most (40, 85%) were male. Twenty-nine (62%) were White, 10 (21%) were Black, and 8 (17%) were Hispanic. They had an average of 14.6 (SD = 2.37) years of education. Twenty-six (55%) worked full-time or were students, while 5 (11%) worked part-time and 16 (34%) were unemployed. Thirty-one (66%) were living with a significant other or with family. The subjects had spent an average of $709 (SD = 1046) on cocaine the previous month, and 27 (57%) had received treatment for substance abuse at some previous time. Mean score for the subjects on the Global Severity Index was .934 (SD = .471).

Treatment Outcome

Overall, the 47 subjects who agreed to enter treatment continued for an average of 12.9 (SD = 12.45) weeks. Twelve (26%) dropped out within the first week, and of those who continued beyond that point, almost half (17, 36% of the entire sample) completed a full 24-week course. Thirty-six (77%) of the 47 subjects established a network. Among those who established a network, the mean number of collaterals across all network sessions was 1.47 (SD = .677), with attendees about evenly divided among family members (45.5%, SD = 45.4) and friends (54.5%, SD = 45.5). The mean portion of all urine toxicology samples negative for cocaine across all the subjects was 73.1%, and 20 subjects (43% of the entire sample) had negative toxicologies for each of the last three scheduled urines.

Correlates of Outcome

Patients' status at admission was predictive of urine toxicology results during treatment, as follows: a lower (less pathologic) mean score on the Global Severity Index was correlated with a greater portion of urines negative for cocaine during subsequent treatment ($r = .37$, $p < .05$). Similarly, subjects whose urine toxicology on admission was negative for cocaine also had a higher portion of cocaine negative urines during treatment (0 = 84.1%, SD = 16.0) than those who did not (0 = 59.6%, SD = 29.1; $t = 3.1$ $p < .01$). There was, however, no significant relationship between the former admission variables (the GSI and the admission cocaine toxicology) and results on the last 3 urine toxicologies. A self-reported history of psychiatric or addiction treatment was not predictive of either of the two outcome variables (percent negative or last 3 urines). Neither were prior Twelve-Step participation, the number of years of cocaine use, or the number of days cocaine was used in the 30 days prior to entry into the study.

Completion of the full 24-week sequence was associated with a better outcome as measured by urine toxicologies. Among those who continued beyond one week, those who completed the 24-week program (N = 17) were compared to those who did not (N = 18). The preponderance of completers (15 of 17) had their last three urine tests prove negative for cocaine, a portion much greater than that among the non-completers (4 of 18; Fisher's Exact Test, $p < .01$). The completers also had a higher portion of negative urines over the course of the entire treatment (0 = 82.88, SD = 16.23) than did the non-completers (0 = 58.17, SD = 29.45; t = 2.73, $p < .05$).

Individual and Network Sessions

Across all subjects, there was a significant correlation between the number of network sessions attended and the portion of a subject's urine toxicologies that were negative (r = .39, $p < .05$). Similarly, in the entire sample of 47, those subjects who had negative toxicologies in their last 3 urines had attended almost twice the number of network sessions as those who did not (0 = 11.7, SD = 5.14 vs. 0 = 5.82, SD = 3.66; t = 3.35, $p < .01$). There was, however, no significant relationship between the number of individual sessions and the portion of negative urines over the entire course of treatment.

DISCUSSION

Network Therapy was developed to enhance the ability of the office-based practitioner to secure abstinence in substance-abusing patients. In the private office, modalities available in multi-modal clinics, such as social work support, milieu treatments, and ongoing group therapy, are generally unavailable. In the format employed here, subjects selected for this study had to meet one criterion of ancillary support necessary to initiate implementation of the network approach: they had to have access to a friend or family member who could serve as a nidus for Network support. Once treatment was initiated, more than three quarters (77%) of the subjects did establish a network, i.e., bring in at least one member for a Network session. In fact, 1.47 collaterals on average attended any given Network session, across all the subjects and sessions. This is notable, since compliance after initial screening was not necessarily assured. No incentives, monetary or otherwise, were provided, and subjects paid a $20 fee for treatment out of pocket.

Notably, it was the number of network sessions and not individual sessions that was significantly associated with a good outcome, as measured by urine toxicologies. This suggests the central role of the meetings with collaterals in shaping outcome. Also important in terms of outcome is whether subjects completed the 24-week sequence. Almost all of those who completed the sequence (15 of 17) produced urines negative for cocaine in their last three toxicologies. On the other hand, only the minority of those who attended the first week but did not complete the sequence (4 of the 18) met this outcome criterion. A similar differential between completers and non-completers was observed for the mean portion of urines that were negative in all samples produced over the course of treatment, reflecting the association between ongoing compliance with non-use of cocaine and a positive outcome. The treatment variables of network attendance and completion of the sequence were associated with urinalysis results both during treatment and in final outcome. Stated otherwise, patients with a good outcome had been more compliant with the format of treatment throughout.

Only two variables measured at the outset of treatment were associated with the portion of urinalyses negative for cocaine *during* treatment: admission urines taken at the outset of treatment negative for cocaine and a lower score on the Global Severity index. The GSI is noted here because subjects' T scores (72 for males and 63 for females) reflected elevated distress, as it exceeded that of same gender non-patient reference groups, as reported by Derogatis,[7] by more than two standard deviations.

Network Therapy combines a number of psychosocial approaches: social and family support, relapse prevention techniques, and individual therapy. Is it beneficial to employ such psychosocial treatments in combination? Observations on psychotherapeutic options suggest that combining modalities in treating substance abusers can enhance the clinician's effectiveness. The outcome of a behaviorally oriented marital approach to alcoholism, for example, was enhanced by adding post-treatment sessions directed at relapse prevention.[8] Additionally, when outcome of a treatment program for cocaine dependence was compared to the same option enhanced with cocaine-specific coping skills, a significant improvement was achieved; enhanced outcome was also found when behavioral couples therapy was used to augment a package for drug-abusing outpatients, most of whom were referred by the criminal justice system.[9] Our therapists also employed individual therapy in addition to the network sessions. Although the effectiveness of individual therapy for substance abuse, either alone or in combination with other modalities, has not been fully explored, it should be noted that in one study on psychotherapy for alcoholism, this modality was found comparable in effect to that of a multi-modal behavioral therapy.[10]

In this study, relatively naive therapists embarked on treating substance-dependent patients. We undertook the training of psychiatric residents in an approach somewhat different from the training they would be undergoing in individual psychotherapy in their third postgraduate year by orienting the residents' individual therapy toward a cognitive behavioral, symptom-focused approach found useful in treating substance abuse. This was combined with the use of a substance abuse-oriented approach of a support group of family members and/or peers, since either type of collateral might be suitable for a given patient.

Education for the treatment of addiction has emerged in recent years as an issue of increasing importance, and addiction psychiatry residencies have been important in establishing models for clinical competency. There is a need for training in psychosocial approaches applicable in the practitioner's office, necessary as both a stand-alone option and in combination with pharmacotherapy. Network Therapy and the associated training program were employed in this study to address this need. Altogether, both the treatment embodied here, grounded in a theoretical model, and related training were found to be workable on a practical level and warrant further controlled evaluation.

ACKNOWLEDGMENT

This study was funded by grant R01DA10728 from the National Institute on Drug Abuse, Bethesda, Md. (Dr. Galanter).

REFERENCES

1. Galanter, M. (1993). Network therapy for addiction: A model for office practice. *American Journal of Psychiatry, 150,* 28–36.
2. Galanter, M. (1999). *Network therapy for alcohol and drug abuse: A new approach in practice.* Expanded edition. New York: Guilford.
3. Carroll, K. M., & Schottenfeld, R. (1997). Nonpharmacologic approaches to substance abuse treatment. *Medical Clinics of North America, 81,* 927–944.
4. McCrady, B. (1986). The family in the change process. In W. N. Miller & N. Heather (Eds.), *Treating addictive behaviors: Processes of change* (pp. 305–318). New York: Plenum.
5. Hunt, G. M., & Azrin, N. H. (1973). A community-reinforcement approach to alcoholism. *Behavior Research and Therapy, 11*: 91–104.
6. Keller, D., Galanter, M., & Weinberg, S. (1997). Validation of a scale for Network therapy: A technique for systematic use of peer and family support in addiction treatment. *Journal of Drug and Alcohol Abuse, 23,* 115–127.
7. Derogatis, L. R. (1993). *Brief symptom inventory (BSI): Administration, scoring and procedures manual.* 3rd ed. Baltimore: National Computer Systems, Inc.
8. O'Farrell, T. J., & Cutter, H. S. G. (1984). Behavioral marital therapy couples groups for male alcoholics and their wives. *Journal of Substance Abuse Treatment, 1,* 191–204.
9. Monti, P. M., Rohsenow, D. J., Michalec, E., Martin, R. A., & Abrams, D. B. (1997). Brief coping skills treatment for cocaine abuse: Substance use outcomes at three months. A*ddiction, 92,* 1717–1728.
10. Ojehagen, A., Berglund, M., & Appel, C. P. (1992). A randomized study of long-term out-patient treatment in alcoholics. Psychiatric treatment versus multimodal behavioural therapy, during 1 versus 2 years of treatment. *Alcohol and Alcoholism, 27,* 649–658.

Chapter 5

The Community-Reinforcement Approach

William R. Miller, Ph.D.
Robert J. Meyers, M.S.
with Susanne Hiller-Sturmhöfel, Ph.D.

The community-reinforcement approach (CRA) is an alcoholism treatment approach that aims to achieve abstinence by eliminating positive reinforcement for drinking and enhancing positive reinforcement for sobriety. CRA integrates several treatment components, including building the client's motivation to quit drinking, helping the client initiate sobriety, analyzing the client's drinking pattern, increasing positive reinforcement, learning new coping behaviors, and involving significant others in the recovery process. These components can be adjusted to the individual client's needs to achieve optimal treatment outcome. In addition, treatment outcome can be influenced by factors such as therapist style and initial treatment intensity. Several studies have provided evidence for CRA's effectiveness in achieving abstinence. Furthermore, CRA has been successfully integrated with a variety of other treatment approaches, such as family therapy and motivational interviewing, and has been tested in the treatment of other drug abuse.

KEY WORDS: AODU (alcohol and other drug use) treatment method; reinforcement; AOD (alcohol and other drug) abstinence; motivation; AOD use pattern; AODD (alcohol and other drug dependence) recovery; treatment outcome; cessation of AODU; professional client relations; family therapy; motivational interviewing; spouse or significant other; literature review

William R. Miller, Ph.D., is director of research and Robert J. Meyers, M.S., is a senior research scientist at the Center on Alcoholism, Substance Abuse, and Addiction, University of New Mexico, Albuquerque, New Mexico.

Susanne Hiller-Sturmhöfel, Ph.D., is a science editor of *Alcohol Research and Health*.

In nearly every review of alcohol treatment outcome research, the community-reinforcement approach (CRA) is listed among approaches with the strongest scientific evidence of efficacy. Yet many clinicians who treat alcohol problems have never heard of it, despite the fact that the first clinical trial of CRA was published over a quarter of a century ago—an example of the continuing gap between research and practice.

The underlying philosophy of CRA is disarmingly simple: In order to overcome alcohol problems, it is important to rearrange the person's life so that abstinence is more rewarding than drinking. The use of alcohol as well as other drugs can be highly reinforcing: The user experiences effects that motivate him or her to continue drinking, which can lead to alcohol dependence.

What then would make a dependent drinker want to give up drinking? One common approach is to "turn up the pain"—that is, to confront the person with unpleasant and costly consequences of drinking. This approach attempts to render drinking less attractive, and can include aversion therapies, pharmacotherapy with the medication disulfiram, confrontational counseling, and infliction of negative consequences (i.e., punishment). Such negative approaches, however, frequently have been found to be ineffective in decreasing drinking and alcohol problems (Miller et al., 1998).

Even seasoned clinicians are often amazed at how much adversity an alcoholic will endure in order to continue drinking. In fact, it has been said that if punishment worked, there would be no alcoholics.

CRA takes a different approach to overcoming alcohol problems, one that is based on providing incentives to stop drinking rather than punishment for continued drinking. To that end, client, therapist, and significant others work together to change the drinker's lifestyle (e.g., his or her social support system and activities) so that abstinence becomes more rewarding than drinking. Since its introduction by Hunt and Azrin in 1973, CRA treatment has evolved considerably, and the clientele has expanded to include spouses of alcoholics and users of drugs other than alcohol. This article summarizes the components of CRA as well as factors influencing its effectiveness. In addition, the article briefly reviews clinical studies demonstrating CRA's efficacy in treating clients with alcohol and other drug (AOD) problems.

WHAT IS CRA?

To provide an alcoholic with the incentive to quit drinking, CRA has the following two major goals:

- Elimination of positive reinforcement for drinking
- Enhancement of positive reinforcement for sobriety.

To achieve those goals, CRA therapists combine a variety of treatment strategies, such as increasing the client's motivation to stop drinking, initiating a trial period of sobriety, performing a functional analysis of the client's drinking behavior, increasing positive reinforcement through various measures, rehearsing new coping behaviors, and involving the client's significant others. Other factors, such as therapist style and initial treatment intensity, also may influence the client's outcome. These treatment components and treatment-related factors are described in the following sections.

Building Motivation

The initial step in CRA generally is an exploration of the client's motivations for change. Particularly in early versions of CRA, this process involved the identification of positive reinforcers (e.g., praise and shared pleasant events) that could serve as effective incentives for the client to change his or her behavior. The CRA therapist also reviews with the client the current and future negative consequences of the client's drinking patterns. For example, the therapist may offer an "inconvenience review checklist"—a list of frequent negative consequences of drinking, such as medical problems, marital problems, or difficulties at work. The client then checks all those negative consequences that apply to his or her current situation or are likely to occur in the future. This assessment can be conducted in an empathic motivational interviewing style rather than a confrontational style (Miller & Rollnick, 1991), thereby encouraging the client, rather than the therapist, to voice the advantages of change and the disadvantages of his or her current drinking.

Initiating Sobriety

Once the client has identified factors that provide the motivation to change his or her drinking behavior, the therapist moves on to setting goals for achieving abstinence. Because many clients are reluctant to commit themselves to immediate total and permanent abstinence, a procedure called sobriety sampling can be helpful. This procedure uses various counseling strategies to negotiate intermediate goals, such as a trial period of sobriety (see Miller & Page, 1991). For example, the therapist may encourage the client to try not drinking for 1 month, to see how it feels and to learn more about the ways in which he or she has been depending on alcohol. Sanchez-Craig and colleagues (1984) found that clients who explicitly were given a choice about a trial period of abstinence were more likely to abstain than were clients who were given a firm prescription for abstinence.

Analyzing Drinking Patterns

CRA involves a thorough functional analysis of the client's drinking patterns. This analysis helps identify situations in which drinking is most likely to occur (i.e., high-risk situations) as well as positive consequences of alcohol consumption that may have reinforced drinking in the past. This step, which is often underemphasized in cognitive-behavioral therapy, is useful in individualizing treatment and in determining specific treatment components, or modules, that are most likely to be successful for a particular client.

Increasing Positive Reinforcement

Once the analysis of the client's drinking patterns is completed, both the client and therapist select appropriate modules from a menu of treatment procedures to address the client's individual needs. Many of these treatment modules focus on increasing the client's sources of positive reinforcement that are unrelated to drinking. For example, as people become increasingly dependent on alcohol, their range of non-drinking activities (e.g., hobbies, sports, and social involvement) narrows substantially, resulting in increasing isolation. Consequently, an important component of recovery for the drinker is to reverse this isolation process by becoming involved with other non-drinking people and by increasing the range of enjoyable activities that do not involve drinking.

Several treatment modules can help in this process. For example, social and recreational counseling is used to help the client choose positive activities to fill time that was previously consumed by drinking and recuperating from its effects. If the client cannot easily decide on such activities, an approach called activity sampling can encourage him or her to try out or renew various activities that might be, or once were, fun and rewarding. For this strategy, the therapist and client schedule activities that the client will try between counseling sessions and plan where, when, how, and with whom the client will participate in those activities. Those plans emphasize activities that bring the client into contact with other people in non-drinking contexts. Such activities might include involvement in a church, attendance of 12-Step meetings or classes, participation in common-interest clubs (e.g., sports clubs), visits to alcohol-free establishments, or participation in volunteer programs. The choice of programs is tailored to the client's personal interests to ensure that the client experiences the activities as positive reinforcers.

Other components of CRA are designed to help clients organize not only their leisure activities but also, if necessary, their regular daily lives. For example, a component called access counseling addresses practical barriers, such as the lack of information sources and means of communication, that stand between the client and those activities that provide positive reinforcement. Thus, access counseling assists the client in obtaining everyday necessities, such as a telephone, a newspaper, a place to live, or a job. Another approach to helping clients find rewarding work involves job club procedures (e.g., interview skills training and résumé development), which have been shown to be successful even for difficult-to-employ people (Azrin & Besalel, 1980). The common goal of all these CRA treatment modules is to make the client's alcohol-free life more rewarding and affirming and to re-engage the client in his or her community.

Behavior Rehearsal

CRA therapists do not just talk about new behavior; instead, they have clients actually practice new coping skills, particularly those involving interpersonal communication, during the counseling sessions. For example, a therapist may first demonstrate the new behavior (e.g., drink refusal or assertive communication), then reverse roles and guide the client in practicing the new skill. Again, the therapist gives praise for any and all steps in the right direction.

Involving Significant Others

Because CRA emphasizes change not only in the client's behavior but also in his or her social environment, this treatment approach emphasizes and encourages, whenever possible, the cooperation of other people who are close and significant to the drinker. Significant others, particularly those who live with a drinker, can be helpful in identifying the social context of the client's drinking behavior and in supporting change in that behavior. Consequently, even early versions of CRA included brief relationship counseling (Hunt & Azrin, 1973). Rather than providing protracted marital therapy, this counseling offers practical skills training to improve positive communication and reinforcement between the client and his or her significant other, reduce aversive communication (e.g., arguments), and facilitate the negotiation of specific changes in the drinker's behavior (Meyers & Smith, 1995). In addition, CRA therapists may coach significant others on how to avoid inadvertent reinforcement of drinking (sometimes called "enabling") and increase positive reinforcement for sobriety—for example, by spending time with the drinker when he or she is sober and withdrawing attention when he or she is drinking.

Factors Influencing CRA Effectiveness

In addition to the treatment components previously described, several factors related to treatment delivery may influence treatment effectiveness and, consequently, the patient's outcome. Two of those factors are therapist style and initial treatment intensity.

Therapist Style. An important aspect of CRA that is sometimes underemphasized is the therapeutic style with which this treatment approach is delivered. An optimal CRA therapist is consistently positive, energetic, optimistic, supportive, and enthusiastic. Any and all signs of progress, no matter how small—even the client just showing up for a counseling session—are recognized and praised. CRA counseling is provided in a personal, engaging style, not in the form of a businesslike negotiation or impersonal education. With a therapist who successfully executes this counseling approach, clients look forward to coming back for future sessions and leave those sessions feeling hopeful and good about themselves.

Although many therapists can deliver CRA, some clinicians might find this approach easier to adopt than will other clinicians. For example, therapists with generally optimistic or enthusiastic personalities might be best suited for CRA. In contrast, therapists who have been trained to use a relatively confrontational approach in order to break down denial may find the CRA approach more difficult to practice.

Initial Treatment Intensity. Another characteristic of CRA that may contribute to the success of this approach is its "jump-start" quality. Ideally, a client who is ready for change can schedule an appointment for the same or following day, rather than being placed on a waiting list for 1 or more months. In addition, during the initial treatment phase, counseling sessions may be scheduled more frequently than once per week. The intervals between sessions can then be extended as the client's abstinence becomes more stable.

Finally, CRA can involve procedures to initiate abstinence immediately. For example, in some cases the client can be evaluated right away as to whether he or she is a candidate for taking disulfiram, an agent that induces unpleasant effects (e.g., nausea and vomiting) after alcohol consumption and is used to discourage drinking. In those cases, a medical staff member of the treatment facility can promptly issue and fill a disulfiram prescription, and the client can take the first dose in the therapist's presence. If a concerned significant other is willing to help the client, he or she can be trained along with the client in procedures to ensure that the client takes the medication regularly. This process also can be used to promote patient compliance with other medication regimens.

EVIDENCE FOR CRA'S EFFICACY

During the past 25 years, numerous studies have demonstrated the efficacy of CRA in the treatment of alcoholism. In the first evaluation, Hunt and Azrin (1973) compared CRA with traditional disease-model treatment[1] for alcohol-dependent people receiving inpatient treatment. In that study, the patients who received CRA fared much better than did the patients who received traditional treatment—in fact, almost no overlap existed in the distribution of the two groups on several outcome measures at follow-up. The CRA clients drank substantially less and less often, had fewer institutionalized days and more days of employment, and exhibited greater social stability compared with patients who were treated with the traditional approach.

Additional improvements to CRA, such as monitored disulfiram administration, mood monitoring, and spousal involvement, further increased the difference in outcome between patients who received CRA and those who received traditional treatment (Azrin, 1976). For example, with these improvements, drinking days in the CRA group dropped to 2% of all days during a 6-month follow-up period compared with 55% of all days in the standard treatment group.

Whereas those initial studies were conducted in an inpatient setting, CRA subsequently was shortened and adapted for use in outpatient settings (e.g., by instituting immediate disulfiram administration). The modified CRA approach also was considerably more effective than traditional outpatient treatment mirroring the Minnesota model (Azrin et al., 1982). As in previous studies, CRA clients showed substantially increased rates of abstinence and employment and less institutionalization and incarceration.

In another study, researchers assessed the effectiveness of a social intervention consistent with CRA. They provided an alcohol-free club where clients could socialize and have fun without drinking. Clients given access to this club evidenced better outcomes than did clients without such access (Mallams et al., 1982). Because these studies employed scientifically sound methodology, they provided strong evidence for the effectiveness of CRA.

Other evaluations of CRA's effectiveness have been conducted at the University of New Mexico's Center on Alcoholism, Substance Abuse, and Addictions (CASAA). In one outpatient treatment study (Meyers & Miller, in press), CRA was found to be more successful in suppressing drinking than was a traditional disease-model counseling treatment approach.

After Meyers and Smith (1995) published the first manual delineating the components of CRA for therapists treating patients with alcohol problems, CASAA researchers conducted a study on CRA's efficacy among homeless alcohol-dependent men and women at a large day shelter. The study found that compared with the standard 12-Step-oriented group therapy provided at the shelter, CRA, when implemented as described in the manual, resulted in significantly improved outcomes during the 1-year follow-up period (Smith et al., 1998). As in previous studies, alcohol consumption in the CRA group was almost completely suppressed during 1 year of follow-up. In contrast, patients in the standard care group reported drinking on about 40% of the days as well as high levels of intoxication.

CRA as Family Therapy

In recent years, CRA also has been integrated into a unilateral family therapy (FT) approach in which the person seeking help is not the drinker (who refuses to get treatment) but a concerned spouse or other family member—resulting in the community reinforcement and family training (CRAFT) approach (Meyers & Smith, 1997). The CRAFT treatment approach is based on studies demonstrating that the involvement of family members can help initiate and promote the treatment of people with alcohol problems (Sisson & Azrin, 1986).

Without the drinker present, the CRAFT therapist works with the family member to change the drinker's social environment in a way that removes inadvertent reinforcement for drinking and instead reinforces abstinence. The therapist also helps the family member prepare for the next opportunity when the drinker may respond favorably to an offer of help and support and may be willing to enter treatment.

A recently completed clinical trial funded by the National Institute on Alcohol Abuse and Alcoholism evaluated the efficacy of CRAFT (Miller et al., in press). In that study, 64% of the clients who received CRAFT counseling succeeded in recruiting their loved one into treatment following an average of four to five counseling sessions. In contrast, two traditional methods for engaging unmotivated problem drinkers into treatment—the Johnson Institute intervention[2] and counseling to engage in Al-Anon—resulted in significantly lower proportions of significant others (30% and 13%, respectively) motivating their loved ones to enter treatment. In a parallel study sponsored by the National Institute on Drug Abuse that focused on abusers of other drugs, family members receiving CRAFT successfully engaged 74% of initially unmotivated drug users in treatment (Meyers et al., 1999).

CRA in the Treatment of Other Drug Abuse

CRA also has been used in the treatment of other drug abuse and dependence. For example, researchers at CASAA conducted a trial in which heroin addicts receiving methadone maintenance therapy were randomly assigned to CRA or standard treatment approaches. Although both CRA and the traditional approaches resulted in good treatment outcomes in this study, CRA was associated with a modest but statistically significant advantage over the standard care approaches (Abbott et al., 1998). Furthermore, researchers studying the treatment of cocaine addicts found substantially better outcomes for clients who received CRA combined with positive reinforcement in the form of monetary vouchers issued when the clients tested drug free compared with clients who participated in an outpatient 12-Step counseling program (Higgins et al., 1991).

Can CRA Be Used in Ordinary Treatment Settings?

CRA has sometimes been delivered in relatively expensive ways (e.g., in inpatient programs, through home visits, and in combination with vouchers). However, CRA is also amenable to and effective in the typical outpatient treatment context, in which the client is seen weekly at a clinic. Furthermore, in outpatient studies that demonstrated good treatment outcomes with CRA, alcohol-dependent patients received an average of five to eight CRA sessions (e.g., Azrin et al., 1982). Similarly, the study by Miller and colleagues (in press) demonstrated that approximately five CRAFT sessions with a concerned significant other frequently resulted in the drinker's entry into treatment. This treatment duration is well within the guidelines of most managed care systems.

Although CRA is based on a comprehensive treatment philosophy, its procedures generally are familiar to clinicians who have been trained in cognitive-behavioral treatment approaches. For example, CRA involves a functional analysis and the individualized application of specific components chosen from a menu of problem-solving procedures. Furthermore, CRA can be combined with other treatment methods. For example, at CASAA, CRA has recently been combined with motivational interviewing to form an integrated treatment. Similarly, CRA is consistent with involvement in 12-Step programs. Finally, combinations of CRA and other treatment approaches can be tailored to address the needs of particular client populations (for an example of such an approach targeted to a specific population, see sidebar).

Sidebar: CRA and Special Populations

The community-reinforcement approach (CRA) is a highly flexible treatment approach that allows therapists and clients to choose from an extensive menu of treatment options to meet the specific needs of the client. This flexibility also enables CRA to be adapted easily to client populations with special needs, such as ethnic or cultural minorities. For example, CRA has been adapted creatively at the Na'nizhoozhi Center, Inc. (NCI) in Gallup, New Mexico, a treatment facility that primarily serves the *Dine'* (Navajo) Native Americans. The NCI staff has developed an intensive, 16-day residential program for alcohol-dependent Native Americans who have not responded to treatment programs based on the Minnesota model, which emphasizes a loss-of-control disease methodology and a 12-Step approach to recovery.

Among the *Dine'*, clan ties remain strong even when the trust between the drinker and his or her family has been broken repeatedly. Accordingly, when treating clients from this cultural group, alcoholism treatment professionals should work with both the family and community networks using traditional Native American ceremonies and extended clan ties. The NCI program connects or reconnects the clients with Native American spirituality through the *Hiina'ah Bits'os* (Eagle Plume) Society. For example, traditional practices, such as the talking circle (i.e., the passing of an object that designates who is speaking while all others listen) and the sacred use of tobacco, are integrated into the treatment program, replacing alcohol with the *Dine'* way of seeking harmony with all of creation (i.e., "walking in beauty"). A special compound built adjacent to the Na'nizhoozhi Center includes ceremonial grounds, tepees, and sweat lodges.

For many NCI clients, the path into this program has been long and painful. Most clients are unemployed, destitute, hopeless, physically ill, and depressed after multiple treatment failures. Researchers have begun to evaluate the effectiveness of the modified CRA approach practiced at the NCI in this challenging patient population. Preliminary results indicate that at the 6-month follow-up, a substantial portion of clients have achieved continuous abstinence and many other clients are free of alcohol-related problems, despite occasional drinking, or have improved considerably even if they have experienced some ongoing problems. These initial indications of effectiveness bear witness to the *Hiina'ah Bits'os* Society's motto, "Against all odds, we walk in beauty."

—William R. Miller and Robert J. Meyers with Susanne Hiller-Sturmhöfel

SUMMARY

CRA is a comprehensive, individualized treatment approach designed to initiate changes in both lifestyle and social environment that will support a client's long-term sobriety. CRA focuses on finding and using the client's own intrinsic reinforcers in the community and is based on a flexible treatment approach with an underlying philosophy of positive reinforcement. Those characteristics make CRA (with certain modifications) applicable to a wide range of client populations.

Numerous clinical trials have found CRA to be effective in treating AOD abuse and dependence and in helping relatives recruit their loved ones into AOD-abuse treatment. The trials were conducted in a variety of geographic regions, treatment settings (e.g., inpatient and outpatient), and individual and family therapy approaches. Furthermore, the clients in those studies suffered from various AOD-related problems and included homeless people as well as people of different ethnic or cultural backgrounds. Consistently, CRA was more effective than the traditional approaches with which it was compared or to which it had been added. Because the scope and duration of CRA are compatible with the guidelines of most managed care services, this approach may play an increasingly important role in the treatment of people with alcoholism.

ACKNOWLEDGMENTS

The authors gratefully acknowledge the support of the National Institute on Alcohol Abuse and Alcoholism and the National Institute on Drug Abuse for several of the clinical studies summarized in this report.

NOTES

1. Traditional disease-model treatment is similar to the Minnesota model, which posits that alcoholism is a disease characterized by loss of control over drinking and which emphasizes a 12-Step approach to recovery.
2. The Johnson Institute intervention entails five therapy sessions that prepare the client and his or her family members for a family confrontation meeting.

REFERENCES

Abbott, P. J., Weller, S. R., Delaney, H. D., & Moore, B. A. (1998). Community reinforcement approach in the treatment of opiate addicts. *American Journal of Drug and Alcohol Abuse, 24,* 17–30.

Azrin, N. H. (1976). Improvements in the community-reinforcement approach to alcoholism. *Behavior Research and Therapy, 14,* 339–348.

Azrin, N. H., & Besalel, V. A. (1980). *Job Club Counselor's Manual.* Baltimore: University Park Press.

Azrin, N. H., Sisson, R. W., Meyers, R., & Godley, M. (1982). Alcoholism treatment by disulfiram and community reinforcement therapy. *Journal of Behavior Therapy and Experimental Psychiatry, 13*, 105–112.

Higgins, S. T., Delaney, D. D., Budney, A. J., Bickel, W. K., Hughes, J. R., & Foerg, F. (1991). A behavioral approach to achieving initial cocaine abstinence. *American Journal of Psychiatry, 148*, 1218–1224.

Hunt, G. M., & Azrin, N. H. (1973). A community-reinforcement approach to alcoholism. *Behavior Research and Therapy, 11*, 91–104.

Mallams, J. H., Godley, M. D., Hall, G. M., & Meyers, R. A. (1982). A social-systems approach to resocializing alcoholics in the community. *Journal of Studies on Alcohol, 43*, 1115–1123.

Meyers, R. J., & Miller, W. R. (Eds.). (in press). *A community reinforcement approach to addiction treatment*. Cambridge, UK: Cambridge University Press.

Meyers, R. J., & Smith, J. E. (1995). *Clinical guide to alcohol treatment: The community reinforcement approach*. New York: Guilford Press.

Meyers, R. J., & Smith, J. E. (1997). Getting off the fence: Procedures to engage treatment-resistant drinkers. *Journal of Substance Abuse Treatment, 14*, 467–472.

Meyers, R. J., Miller, W. R., Hill, D. E., & Tonigan, J. S. (1999). Community reinforcement and family training (CRAFT): Engaging unmotivated drug users in treatment. *Journal of Substance Abuse, 10*(3), 1–18.

Miller, W. R., & Page, A. (1991). Warm turkey: Other routes to abstinence. *Journal of Substance Abuse Treatment, 8*, 227–232.

Miller, W. R., & Rollnick, S. (1991). *Motivational interviewing: Preparing people to change addictive behavior*. New York: Guilford Press.

Miller, W. R., Andrews, N. R., Wilbourne, P., & Bennett, M. E. (1998). A wealth of alternatives: Effective treatments for alcohol problems. In W. R. Miller & N. Heather, (Eds.), *Treating addictive behaviors: Processes of change* 2d ed. (pp. 203–216). New York: Plenum Press.

Miller, W. R., Meyers, R. J., & Tonigan, J. S. (in press). Engaging the unmotivated in treatment for alcohol problems: A comparison of three strategies for intervention through family members. *Journal of Consulting and Clinical Psychology*.

Sanchez-Craig, M., Annis, H. M., Bornet, A. R., & MacDonald, K. R. (1984). Random assignment to abstinence and controlled drinking: Evaluation of a cognitive-behavioral program for problem drinkers. *Journal of Consulting and Clinical Psychology, 52*, 390–403.

Sisson, R. W., & Azrin, N. H. (1986). Family-member involvement to initiate and promote treatment of problem drinkers. *Journal of Behavior Therapy and Experimental Psychiatry, 17*, 15–21.

Smith, J. E., Meyers, R. J., & Delaney, H. D. (1998). Community reinforcement approach with homeless alcohol-dependent individuals. *Journal of Consulting and Clinical Psychology, 66*, 541–548.

Chapter 6

Voucher-Based Incentives

A Substance Abuse Treatment Innovation

Stephen T. Higgins
Sheila M. Alessi
Robert L. Dantona

In this report we provide an overview of research on the voucher-based incentives approach to substance abuse treatment. This approach was originally developed as a novel method for improving retention and increasing cocaine abstinence among cocaine-dependent outpatients. The efficacy of vouchers for those purposes is now well established, and plans are underway to move the intervention into effectiveness testing in community clinics. The use of vouchers also has been extended to the treatment of alcohol, marijuana, nicotine, and opioid dependence. Particularly noteworthy is that vouchers hold promise as an efficacious intervention with special populations of substance abusers, including pregnant and recently postpartum women, adolescents, and those with serious mental illness. Overall, voucher-based incentives hold promise as an innovative treatment intervention that has efficacy across a wide range of substance abuse problems and populations.

Keywords: Contingency management; Substance abuse treatment; Incentives

Stephen T. Higgins, Department of Psychiatry, Department of Psychology, University of Vermont.
Sheila M. Alessi, Department of Psychiatry, University of Vermont.
Robert L. Dantona, Department of Psychiatry, University of Vermont.

INTRODUCTION

This report provides an overview of research on the use of voucher-based incentives to treat cocaine and other substance abuse. This treatment approach was initially developed as a novel method to manage cocaine dependence in outpatient settings (Higgins et al., 1991). At that time, no psychosocial treatments for cocaine dependence had been shown to be efficacious, and the few promising pharmacotherapies were not panning out in randomized clinical trials (Higgins & Wong, 1998; Mendelson & Mello, 1996). Details of the voucher-based incentives approach are described below, but at its essence it involves the delivery of vouchers exchangeable for retail items contingent on patients meeting a predetermined therapeutic target. The target that has been most thoroughly researched is biochemically verified abstinence from recent drug use. Because patients must remain in treatment in order to collect vouchers for abstinence, the intervention often increases treatment retention as well. Retention in treatment is reliably associated with positive outcomes in substance abuse treatment and thus is an important feature of the efficacy of this approach (e.g., Simpson, 1984; Simpson, Joe, & Brown, 1997). This treatment approach is also efficacious with special populations of substance abusers and for increasing compliance with medication and other therapeutic regimens. Research supporting those applications is described below.

In much of our research, voucher-based incentives have been used in combination with an intensive behavioral therapy known as the Community Reinforcement Approach (CRA), a treatment originally developed for chronic alcoholism (Hunt & Azrin, 1973; Meyers & Smith, 1995). Indeed, a therapy manual has been published by the National Institute on Drug Abuse on the CRA + vouchers treatment for cocaine dependence (Budney & Higgins, 1998). CRA is not addressed in the present report. Readers with specific interests in CRA may want to consult the aforementioned manual or other sources focused on that component (e.g., Higgins, 1999; Meyers & Miller, 2001).

INCREASING ABSTINENCE FROM COCAINE USE

Drug-Free Clinics

The Voucher Intervention

The voucher program was first described in a report in which the efficacy of CRA + vouchers for treating cocaine-dependent outpatients was compared to drug abuse counseling among 25 consecutive clinic admissions (Higgins et al., 1991). In that report, the voucher program was 12 weeks in duration and implemented using a 4x/week (Monday, Wednesday, Friday, Saturday) schedule of urinalysis monitoring. Beginning with our next report comparing patients randomly assigned to these same two treatments (Higgins et al., 1993) the weekly Saturday test was omitted. A 3x/week (Monday, Wednesday, Friday) monitoring schedule has been used in each of our subsequent trials (Higgins et al., 1994; Higgins, Wong, Badger, Ogden, & Dantona, 2000).

Specimens are collected under the observation of a same-sex staff member and tested for the presence of benzoylecgonine, a cocaine metabolite, using an onsite enzyme multiplied immunoassay technique (EMIT, Syva, San Jose, CA). Cocaine-negative specimens earn points that are recorded on vouchers and provided to patients. Points are worth the equivalent of $.25 each, and the first negative specimen earns 10 points or $2.50 in purchasing power. The number of points earned increases by five with each consecutive negative test result, so that the second consecutive negative test result earns 15 points, the third earns 20 points, and so on. Further, each three consecutive cocaine-negative tests earn the equivalent of a $10 bonus. A cocaine-positive test result or failure to provide a scheduled specimen resets the voucher value back to the initial $.25/point or $2.50 value from which it can escalate again according to the same schedule. Five consecutive test results following a reset restores voucher value to where it was prior to the reset. Points cannot be lost once earned. No money is ever given directly to patients. Instead, points are used to purchase retail items, with clinic staff making all purchases. If patients earn all of the vouchers and bonuses possible, they earn a total of $997.50 in purchasing power. Average earnings among cocaine-dependent outpatients in our clinic have been about half of the total possible.

Efficacy Testing

As noted above, treatment retention rates and cocaine-abstinence levels were strikingly better among patients treated with CRA + vouchers in our initial trials comparing this treatment with drug abuse counseling (Higgins et al., 1991, 1993). Among the 19 patients treated with CRA + vouchers in our initial randomized trial, for example, 58% completed a recommended course of 24 weeks of outpatient treatment versus 11% of those who received drug abuse counseling. We were able to verify with urinalysis testing 8 or more weeks of continuous cocaine abstinence among 68% of those treated with CRA + vouchers, but only among 11% of those treated with drug abuse counseling either because of early dropout or ongoing cocaine use. The relatively dismal outcomes observed among those treated with drug abuse counseling in this trial were congruent with what was being reported at that time for outpatient treatments for cocaine dependence (e.g., Kang et al., 1991). The results observed with the CRA + vouchers intervention were the exception. The research design used in these initial two trials precluded isolation of the contribution of vouchers to the outcomes observed, but we hypothesized that the incentives were an active contributor.

The efficacy of vouchers was first demonstrated in a randomized clinical trial in which 40 outpatients were assigned to treatment with CRA + vouchers or CRA only (Higgins et al., 1994). Seventy-five percent of those treated with CRA

+ vouchers completed the recommended 24 weeks of treatment versus 40% of those treated with CRA only, thereby demonstrating the contribution of vouchers to the high retention rates previously observed with the CRA + vouchers treatment. More than 50% of those treated with CRA + vouchers were verified by urinalysis testing to have achieved at least 12 weeks of continuous cocaine abstinence versus approximately 20% with CRA only (Figure 6.1). Also, there was no precipitous drop-off in abstinence levels when the vouchers were discontinued during the second half of this 24-week treatment intervention. These results demonstrated the active contribution of contingent vouchers to the high levels of during-treatment abstinence observed previously with the CRA + vouchers treatment, and suggested that the effects of the vouchers remained discernible for at least 12 weeks after they were discontinued. Subsequent follow-up assessments with patients from this trial and those from the randomized trial comparing CRA + vouchers to drug abuse counseling suggested that effects continued through 6 months of posttreatment follow-up (Higgins et al., 1995).

Our next trial was focused on dissociating the effects of vouchers on cocaine abstinence from those on retention, and also assessing outcomes through 15 months after the vouchers were discontinued (Higgins, Wong, et al., 2000). While increasing retention is an important therapeutic goal, it obscured scientific interpretation of how vouchers increased abstinence rates in our prior studies. For example, whether vouchers were indirectly increasing abstinence by increasing the amount of counseling patients received or were doing so by directly reinforcing abstinence could not be determined. In this trial, 70 cocaine-dependent outpatients were randomized to one of two treatment groups: CRA + contingent vouchers or CRA + noncontingent vouchers. Recommended treatment duration was 24 weeks in both conditions, with vouchers available during weeks 1–12. The only difference between the two treatment conditions was that in the contingent vouchers condition, incentives were dispensed only when urinalysis results verified recent cocaine abstinence, whereas in the noncontingent voucher condition they were dispensed independent of urinalysis results.

Making vouchers available to both groups in this trial achieved the goal of keeping retention rates in the contingent and noncontingent conditions comparable, with 56% and 53% of patients completing 24 weeks of treatment, respectively. Despite comparable retention rates, the conditions differed in the amount of cocaine abstinence achieved. A larger percentage of patients assigned to the contingent than the noncontingent condition achieved sustained periods of cocaine abstinence during the 24 weeks of treatment (Figure 6.2).

Moreover, cocaine-abstinence levels were consistently higher in the contingent than the noncontingent condition during a 1-year period of posttreatment follow-up (Figure 6.3). These results further demonstrated the efficacy of the contingent voucher intervention, dissociated their effects on abstinence from those on retention, and demonstrated effects through 15 months after the voucher program was discontinued and 12 months after the recommended 24-week course of CRA therapy.

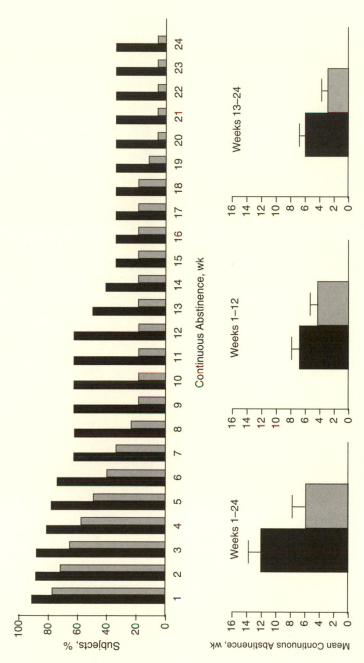

FIGURE 6.1. Top panel shows distributions of continuous cocaine abstinence verified by urinalysis testing in each treatment group. The height of each bar represents the percentage of patients achieving a duration of abstinence greater than or equal to the number of weeks indicated. Note that x-axis shows weeks of continuous abstinence and not consecutive treatment weeks. Bottom panel shows mean duration of continuous abstinence achieved in each treatment group during weeks 1–24, 1–12, and 13–24. Solid bars indicate the CRA + vouchers group; shaded bars represent the CRA-only group. Brackets in bottom panel represent ± S.E.M.

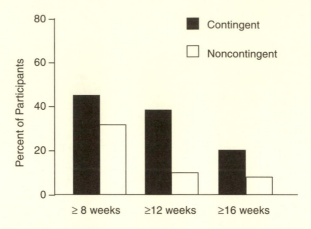

FIGURE 6.2. Percentage of patients in the contingent and noncontingent voucher conditions who were verified by urinalysis testing to have achieved durations of at least 8, 12, or 16 weeks of continuous cocaine abstinence during the 24-week treatment period.

Gaining Insights into Voucher Effects

From 1993 onward, our trials involved overlapping protocols in terms of always including a CRA + vouchers condition, a 24-week duration of treatment, and common follow-up assessments. That overlap permitted us to accumulate a database that can be used in retrospective studies. Below we describe results from one such study that we believe may provide important insights into how vouchers improve treatment outcomes.

One high priority issue is gaining insight into how vouchers may promote longer-term cocaine abstinence. In the Higgins, Badger, and Budney (2000) report where contingent voucher effects were discernible through 15 months after the intervention was discontinued, the duration of continuous cocaine abstinence achieved during treatment was a robust predictor of posttreatment abstinence in the contingent condition. Predictors of abstinence in the noncontingent condition were not examined. We used our cumulative database to more thoroughly examine this relationship between early and later abstinence using a larger number of subjects and both the CRA + vouchers and control treatment conditions (Higgins, Badger, et al., 2000). The relationship between abstinence achieved during treatment and the odds of posttreatment abstinence was examined among 190 patients treated with CRA + contingent vouchers (n = 125) or one of the several control treatments, including CRA + noncontingent vouchers, CRA alone, and drug abuse counseling (n = 65). The number of weeks of continuous abstinence achieved was the primary measure of during treatment abstinence. Two measures of posttreatment abstinence were used. Abstinence across each of the 6-, 9-, and 12-month follow-up assessments served as a measure of continuous abstinence and absti-

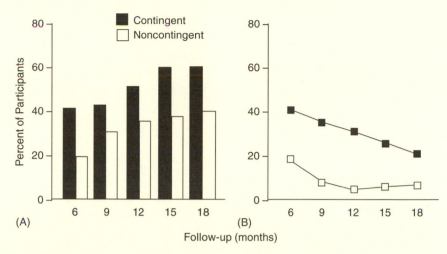

FIGURE 6.3. (A) Percentage of patients in the two treatment conditions who were verified by urinalysis testing to be cocaine abstinent and reported no cocaine use in the past 30 days at specific posttreatment assessments (i.e., point-prevalence abstinence). (B) Percentage of patients abstinent at the 6-month (end of treatment) assessment who sustained abstinence continuously between consecutive posttreatment assessments conducted at 9, 12, 15, and 18 months after treatment entry.

nence at the 12-month assessment only served as a measure of point-prevalence abstinence.

The estimated probability of continuous abstinence across all posttreatment assessments increased as an orderly function of the duration of continuous abstinence achieved during treatment (Figure 6.4). The probability of 12-month point-prevalence abstinence was similarly related to the amount of during-treatment abstinence achieved (not shown). Importantly, there were no significant differences noted between the CRA + vouchers and control treatments in that regard. The odds of achieving longer-term abstinence increased comparably independent of whether abstinence was achieved with the CRA + vouchers or control treatments. Where treatment type made a difference was in the proportion of patients who achieved a period of sustained abstinence during treatment. For example, significantly more patients treated with CRA + vouchers versus control treatments (37% vs. 14%) achieved 12 or more weeks of sustained abstinence during treatment. Thus, even though the predictive utility of during-treatment abstinence was comparable across the two treatment conditions, follow-up abstinence levels would still be predicted to differ between the treatment conditions given that a larger percentage of patients treated with CRA + vouchers achieved sustained levels of during-treatment abstinence. That prediction was generally supported by the data. Twenty-nine percent versus 14% of patients in the CRA + contingent vouchers and control treatments reported abstinence across all posttreatment

assessments (P = .02) and 21% versus 12% reported abstinence across all assessments that was verified by cocaine-negative urinalysis results (P = .15). More
research will be necessary, but results from this study suggested that the longer-
term efficacy of the CRA + vouchers treatment resides, at least in part, in its
ability to promote initial periods of sustained abstinence in a larger proportion of
patients than comparison treatments.

Generality to Other Drug-Free Clinics

The studies described above were all conducted in a university-based research
clinic located in a small metropolitan area. Demonstrating the generality of the
voucher-based intervention beyond this one clinic and to patients residing in large
metropolitan areas was an important step in the development of this treatment
approach. The studies by Silverman and colleagues with methadone maintenance
patients described below provided the seminal support for the generality of the
voucher-based approach to these other settings and populations, but establishing
generality to other drug-free clinics was important as well. At least two trials
provided that support (Kirby, Marlowe, Festinger, Lamb, & Platt, 1998; Rawson,
McCann, Huber, & Shoptaw, 1999). Kirby et al. (1998) demonstrated the efficacy

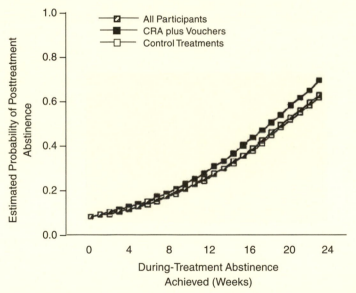

FIGURE 6.4. The estimated probability of continuous cocaine abstinence across 6 months
of posttreatment follow-up as a function of the longest duration of continuous cocaine
abstinence achieved during treatment. Estimated probabilities are shown from logistic
regression models based on all patients, those treated with CRA + vouchers, and those
treated with control treatments.

of a voucher intervention involving a slight schedule variation on the procedure described above in a population of cocaine-dependent adults treated in a drug-free clinic located in a large metropolitan area (Camden, NJ). Rawson et al. (1999) used essentially the same schedule as was used in our trials in a drug-free clinic located in a still larger metropolitan area (Los Angeles, CA). Both studies supported the efficacy of contingent vouchers for increasing cocaine abstinence in dependent outpatients. Results from the Rawson et al. trial are currently in preparation for publication, although the results have been reported at conferences. Those studies coupled with those reported below in methadone maintenance patients firmly established the generality of vouchers beyond our clinic and population.

Methadone Clinics

Efficacy Testing

Methadone maintenance is a highly effective treatment for reducing heroin abuse, but does not impact the serious problem of chronic cocaine abuse common among many patients enrolled in that therapy (Silverman, Chutuape, Bigelow, & Stitzer, 1999). The largest body of evidence on the use of vouchers with opiate-dependent cocaine abusers comes from a programmatic series of studies conducted by Silverman and colleagues (Silverman, Higgins, et al., 1996; Silverman, Svikis, Robles, Stitzer, & Bigelow, 2001; Silverman et al., 1998, 1999). Selected studies from that series are described below.

In the seminal report on vouchers in this population, 37 methadone maintenance patients who were regular cocaine abusers participated in a 12-week intervention (Silverman, Higgins, et al., 1996). Patients were randomly assigned to receive vouchers contingent on cocaine-negative urinalysis results or independent of urinalysis results and according to a schedule that was yoked to the contingent group. Voucher value and schedule were largely identical to those used in our trials. Results are shown in Figure 6.5. During baseline conditions, patients in both treatment conditions were positive for cocaine use throughout baseline monitoring. Following the introduction of the voucher intervention, abstinence levels increased substantially among those who received contingent vouchers but not those who received them noncontingently. Similarly, robust effects of vouchers were noted in a subsequent trial by this group (Silverman et al., 1998). Even though vouchers were contingent only on cocaine abstinence in this latter trial, opiate abstinence also increased. These trials firmly established the efficacy of the voucher intervention for increasing cocaine abstinence in methadone maintenance clinics.

What was also evident in these trials by Silverman and colleagues is that many patients resumed cocaine use when the vouchers were discontinued. That was not an unexpected finding considering that these patients were not cocaine abuse treatment seekers. Rather, these were individuals enrolled in methadone treatment for opiate dependence who happened to be observed to be using co-

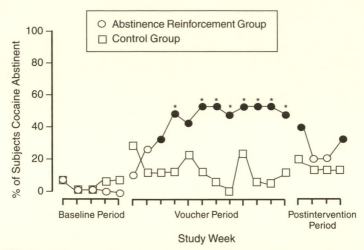

FIGURE 6.5. Percentage of patients in each condition verified by urinalysis testing to be cocaine abstinent during 25 successive weeks. Those in the abstinence reinforcement condition received contingent vouchers; those in the control group received them noncontingently during weeks 1–12. Solid circles and asterisks indicate the weeks on which the contingent vouchers group differed significantly from the control group.

caine during mandatory urinalysis monitoring and offered an opportunity to participate in a study where they could earn incentives by reducing their cocaine use. Nevertheless, the follow-up data underscored the need to consider additional strategies to achieve longer-term cocaine abstinence in this population. These patients very well may need a maintenance therapy to sustain abstinence from cocaine use much as they do to sustain abstinence from opiate use.

To begin examining this maintenance notion, Silverman and colleagues conducted a study designed to examine the feasibility of sustaining abstinence for 1 year in this population. Patients were randomly assigned to one of three conditions: a no-incentive control condition, a condition in which patients earned medication take-home privileges contingent on opiate and cocaine abstinence, or a condition in which patients earned vouchers and take-home privileges contingent on cocaine and opiate abstinence. In this third condition, patients could earn approximately $5000 in vouchers if they abstained from cocaine use continuously throughout the 1-year intervention. Medication take-home privileges permit patients to take home the next day's dose or several days' doses of medication to save the patient the inconvenience of having to attend the clinic daily. A full report on this trial is not yet published, but results were reported at a conference and published in abstract form (Silverman, Robles, Bigelow, & Stitzer, 2000). As hypothesized, abstinence levels in this trial were lowest in the control condition, intermediate in the take-home privileges only condition, and highest in the combined vouchers and take-home privileges condition. The results provided unequivocal evidence supporting the feasibility of maintaining high levels of cocaine and opiate abstinence through a 1-year period through the use of contingent incentives.

Silverman and colleagues have implemented this maintenance approach with pregnant and recently postpartum cocaine- and opiate-dependent women. Not surprisingly, many of these women have histories of chronic unemployment, poor educational attainment, and limited vocational skills. They are a very challenging group to treat. In the approach used by Silverman and colleagues, labeled the "therapeutic workplace" intervention, patients earn vouchers by simultaneously abstaining from cocaine use and participating in 3-h vocational training sessions on a Monday–Friday schedule. The first report on this intervention involved 40 women who were continuing to use cocaine despite being enrolled in a comprehensive substance abuse treatment program for pregnant women (Silverman et al., 2001). Results from the initial 6 months of the intervention were reported. Using random assignment, 20 women were enrolled in the therapeutic workplace while the remaining 20 continued in the comprehensive program only. The intervention significantly increased the percent of specimens negative for cocaine and opiate use during the 6-month period from an average of 33% in the control condition to 59% in the therapeutic workplace condition. These results provide further empirical support and a practical forum (vocational training) for a maintenance approach.

Another interesting feature of the therapeutic workplace project and the development of this maintenance approach is that the investigators are developing a data-entry business in which they can employ the patients. The strategy is to use the business to generate a revenue stream that can be used to support the cost of the maintenance voucher therapy. It is too early to determine the success of the business aspect of this project, but it appears promising. The therapeutic workplace approach is also being investigated with other populations, including HIV-infected substance abusers and homeless alcoholics (K. Silverman, personal communication, March 2002).

Efficacy testing on the use of vouchers to increase cocaine abstinence in the methadone maintenance population is that not limited to the work of Silverman and colleagues. Other investigators have conducted rigorous randomized clinical trials supporting the efficacy of vouchers in promoting cocaine abstinence in this population (e.g., Petry & Martin, 2002; Preston, Umbricht, Wong, & Epstein, 2001; Rawson, McMann, Huber, Thomas, & Ling, 2000). The report by Preston et al. (2001) included initial positive results on a potentially promising strategy of initially shaping successive approximations to complete cocaine abstinence rather than requiring complete abstinence from the outset as a strategy for increasing the proportion of patients who respond to the voucher intervention.

Moving the Approach to Community Clinics

The costs associated with the vouchers intervention are recognized as a barrier to its dissemination to community clinics. Petry and colleagues (Petry & Martin, 2002; Petry, Martin, Cooney, & Kranzler, 2000) have been researching a less expensive variation of the approach in community clinics. In this modified procedure, termed the "fish bowl" approach, patients earn opportunities to draw small pieces of paper from a bowl contingent on drug-negative urinalysis results. The bowl contains 250 slips of paper. To reduce costs, 50% of the slips are nonwinners and simply say "Sorry, try again"; others earn small prizes (109 slips at $1.00), large prizes (15 at maximum of $20.00), or a jumbo prize (1 at approximately $100.00). In a 12-week randomized clinical trial using this procedure, 42 cocaine-abusing methadone patients were assigned to drug abuse counseling with versus without the incentive procedure. Cocaine- or opiate-negative results earned a draw from the bowl. Specimens negative for both drugs earned four draws. An entire week of negative urinalysis results earned bonus draws, with the number of bonus draws increasing with each consecutive week of negative results. Positive results reset the bonus back to its original level from which it could again escalate. Across the 12-week trial, the percent of specimens negative for cocaine and opiates was significantly greater in the incentive compared to the no-incentive treatment condition supporting the efficacy of this innovation. For example, 47% of patients in the incentive condition achieved 4 or more weeks of continuous abstinence from cocaine and opiates compared to 16% in the no-incentives condition. Overall, patients in the incentive condition earned an average of $137 in prizes across the 12-week period. This represents a considerable reduction in incentive costs compared to the typical costs in the 12-week interventions by Higgins and colleagues and Silverman and colleagues where incentive earnings across 12 weeks were typically in the $500 range. We anticipate that abstinence levels are also likely to be less when lower value incentive values are used (Silverman et al., 1999), although the precise relation of incentive values to outcome in these interventions has not yet been thoroughly evaluated.

Such a possible tradeoff between incentive value/costs and outcomes achieved notwithstanding, Petry and colleagues' lower-cost strategy has already made headway in terms of moving the voucher-based incentives approach into community clinics. A variation of this intervention is now being investigated in a large multisite study involving drug-free and methadone maintenance clinics as part of the National Institute on Drug Abuse's Clinical Trials Network.

INCREASING ABSTINENCE FROM OTHER SUBSTANCES

The efficacy of vouchers at increasing cocaine abstinence has led investigators to also examine their use with other forms of drug abuse. Selected examples of those efforts are summarized below.

Opiate Abstinence

Initial efforts to extend voucher-based incentives to promoting abstinence from other drugs were focused on opiates, where there is a well-established literature demonstrating the efficacy of other contingent incentives for increasing abstinence from illicit drug use (Griffith, Rowan-Szal, Roark, & Simpson, 2000; Stitzer

& Higgins, 1995). Bickel, Amass, Higgins, Badger, and Esch (1997) demonstrated the efficacy of CRA + vouchers for increasing retention and opiate abstinence during a 24-week outpatient detoxification. The efficacy of vouchers in that trial could not be dissociated from CRA, but the combined CRA + vouchers intervention was more efficacious than drug abuse counseling.

Silverman, Wong, et al. (1996) isolated the efficacy of contingent vouchers for increasing opiate abstinence in a study completed with 13 opiate-dependent individuals enrolled in methadone maintenance therapy. Using the same voucher parameters as were used in their studies on cocaine use, patients were offered the opportunity to earn vouchers for 12 weeks contingent on opiate-negative urinalysis results. A within-subject research design was used wherein the voucher intervention was bracketed by two baseline periods. Percent opiate positive urinalysis results decreased significantly from an average of > 75% during an initial 5-week baseline to < 25% during the 12-week contingent vouchers intervention. During a subsequent 8-week return-to-baseline condition, percent opiate-positive specimens increased to approximately 45%.

Piotrowski et al. (1999) also reported positive outcomes using contingent vouchers to increase abstinence from opiates and other drug use in a randomized trial conducted with new admissions to methadone treatment. Downey, Helmus, and Schuster (2000), by contrast, failed to find a significant treatment effect in a trial comparing vouchers delivered contingent on abstinence from opiate and cocaine use to a noncontingent vouchers control condition in opiate-dependent patients maintained on buprenorphine. It is unclear why vouchers were not efficacious in the Downey et al. (2000) study. There was some suggestion in the results that perhaps requiring simultaneous abstinence from opiates and cocaine may have been too stringent for this sample in that it kept subjects from getting an opportunity to sample the reinforcement associated with vouchers. When the analyses were restricted to those individuals in the contingent voucher condition who earned at least one voucher, abstinence levels were higher in the contingent than the noncontingent condition. When considered across studies, there is compelling evidence that contingent vouchers can increase abstinence from illicit opiates.

Marijuana Abstinence

Results from several controlled studies demonstrate that marijuana use is sensitive to contingent incentives for abstinence (Budney, Higgins, Delaney, Kent, & Bickel, 1991; Budney, Higgins, Radonovich, & Novy, 2000; Sigmon, Steingard, Badger, Anthony, & Higgins, 2000). Budney et al. (2000), for example, randomly assigned 60 marijuana-dependent outpatients to one of three conditions: (1) motivational interviewing only, (2) motivational interviewing plus relapse prevention counseling, or (3) motivational interviewing and relapse prevention plus vouchers contingent on marijuana-negative urinalysis results. The study was 14 weeks in duration, involving twice-weekly urinalysis testing. The voucher intervention was in effect during weeks 3–14. Marijuana has a relatively long metabolic half-life. To permit adequate time for clearance of marijuana from the system prior to the start of the incentive program, patients in the voucher condition were instructed to begin abstaining from marijuana use at the beginning of week one if they desired negative urinalysis results when the vouchers became available at the start of week three.

As shown in Figure 6.6, significantly greater abstinence was observed in the voucher condition compared to the two other treatment conditions. The percentage of patients achieving 1–14 weeks of continuous marijuana abstinence and overall mean duration of continuous abstinence achieved during the 14-week intervention were greater in the group that received contingent vouchers than either comparison treatment. Longer-term effects in this population have yet to be reported. As is described in the special populations section, Sigmon et al. (2001) demonstrated the feasibility of this approach to increasing abstinence from marijuana use in schizophrenic outpatients.

Alcohol Abstinence

The seminal study on Petry et al.'s (2000) fish bowl method was conducted with 42 alcohol-dependent male veterans receiving intensive outpatient services. Patients were randomly assigned to receive standard treatment with or without the incentive program. Draws from the bowl were earned contingent on submitting negative breath alcohol samples and completing treatment goals (e.g., attending self-help meetings, increasing participation in family activities). Self-reported drinking did not affect incentive delivery. A number of significant differences in outcome were noted. Eighty-four percent of those assigned to the voucher condition were retained for the recommended 8 weeks of treatment compared to 22% in the no-incentive condition. By the end of treatment, 69% of patients in the

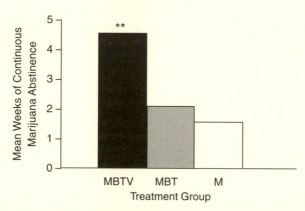

FIGURE 6.6. Mean weeks of continuous marijuana abstinence achieved in the three treatment groups. M = motivational interviewing; MBT = M plus coping skills therapy; MBTV = MBT plus contingent vouchers; * * between-group differences at P < .05.

incentive condition had not reported resumption of drinking compared to only 39% in the no-incentive condition. The percentage of patients who tested positive for illicit drug use in assessments completed at 4 and 8 weeks of treatment was lower in the incentive condition (10%) than the no-incentive condition (43%), even though incentives were not earned contingent on urinalysis results. Total incentive earnings during the 8-week intervention were approximately $200. These results are seminal findings in terms of the use of vouchers in this population that will need to be replicated. Certainly, they lend further support to the potential utility of this incentives approach to a wide range of substance abuse problems.

INCREASING ABSTINENCE FROM DRUG ABUSE IN SPECIAL POPULATIONS

The efficacy of vouchers in promoting abstinence in relatively treatment recalcitrant populations like cocaine-dependent and opiate-dependent outpatients spurred interest in the potential application of this approach with still other challenging populations. In this section, we describe studies focused on examining the efficacy of vouchers for increasing abstinence from (1) cigarette smoking and illicit drug abuse among individuals with serious mental illness, (2) cigarette smoking among pregnant women, and (3) cigarette smoking among adolescents. Preliminary results on the use of contingent vouchers to increase abstinence from cigarette smoking among methadone maintenance patients look promising (Shoptaw et al., 1999), but due to space constraints that work is not described further in this report.

Increasing Drug Abstinence Among Those with Severe Mental Illness

Substance abuse among individuals with serious mental illness is highly prevalent and associated with a broad array of untoward societal and individual consequences (Regier et al., 1990). To our knowledge, no consensus exists on how to effectively treat substance abuse among individuals with serious mental illness. Prompted by the positive outcomes using incentives with cocaine abusers without mental illness, Shaner et al. (1997) examined whether providing monetary incentives contingent on cocaine-negative urinalysis results might increase abstinence among two schizophrenic men whose cocaine abuse had proven recalcitrant to other interventions. During a 2-month intervention, these two individuals earned $25 per cocaine-negative urinalysis test. The percentage of cocaine-negative urinalysis results increased during the intervention phase compared to baseline levels in both subjects.

While encouraging, those results were obtained in only two subjects, and thus additional inquiry was necessary to evaluate the feasibility of using monetary incentives to promote abstinence from drug use among the mentally ill. We conducted several experiments to further examine this feasibility question. Our first experiment on this topic was conducted with 11 schizophrenic outpatients who were heavy cigarette smokers, but who were not currently trying to quit smoking (Roll, Higgins, Steingard, & McGinley, 1998). Our goal was to determine whether their substance use was sensitive to incentives for abstinence. Smoking was monitored daily across three consecutive 5-day periods (Monday–Friday). The first and third periods were treated as baseline conditions during which subjects smoked as usual. Breath carbon monoxide (CO) levels were collected once daily and subjects were paid cash independent of their CO levels. During the middle 5-day period, CO specimens were collected three times daily and payments were only made if the CO level was < 11 ppm. We recognized that this was a liberal abstinence criterion and that some undetected smoking might be possible. However, considering that the mean baseline CO level in this group was > 35 ppm, we were confident that meeting an < 11 ppm criterion would require substantial reductions in their usual smoking rate if not total cessation. Mean percentages of CO specimens meeting the abstinence criterion were 14%, 54%, and 12% during the baseline, intervention, and second baseline conditions, respectively, providing strong evidence in support of the sensitivity of cigarette smoking in these mentally ill subjects to monetary incentives for abstinence. We recently replicated this finding (Tidey, O'Neill, & Higgins, in press), although combining nicotine replacement therapy (21-mg transdermal patch) with the incentives did not improve abstinence rates above incentives only.

We have also demonstrated the feasibility of this approach with schizophrenic marijuana smokers (Sigmon et al., 2000). Ten adults with schizophrenia or other serious mental illness who were regular marijuana smokers completed a 25-week study involving five 5-week conditions (three incentive conditions bracketed by baseline conditions). Twice-weekly urinalysis testing was conducted throughout. During the two baseline conditions, participants received monetary incentives independent of urinalysis results. During the monetary incentive conditions, varying amounts of money were delivered contingent on marijuana-negative urinalysis results. Monetary values were $25, $50, and $100 per negative specimen. The mean number of negative specimens during the first and second baselines were 1.3 ± 0.62, and 1.8 ± 1.1 of a maximum of 10. The mean number of negative specimens during the $25, $50, and $100 contingent payment conditions were 4.2 ± 1.4, 4.1 ± 1.4, and 5.1 ± 1.4 of a maximum of 10. Those levels exceeded baseline levels, although there were no differences between the three incentive values. Worth explaining is that the two higher incentive values were examined in this study because the first three of the 10 subjects failed to respond at the $25 value. Surprisingly, those three subjects also failed to respond at the higher incentive values. By focusing on the recalcitrant subjects, however, we never examined whether abstinence was sustainable at lower incentive values in the responsive subjects. We are currently investigating that question in an ongoing study with mentally ill marijuana smokers using incentive values of $25.00, $12.50, and $6.25 per marijuana-negative test (Alessi, Sigmon, & Higgins, 2002). Three subjects have completed the study. Participants were paid $12.50 per specimen indepen-dent of urinalysis results during baseline conditions at the start and end of the study, with 96% and 88% of specimens being marijuana-positive, respectively. During the three 5-week periods when payment depended on marijuana-negative urinalysis results, 0%, 21%, and 46% of specimens were marijuana-positive at the $25.00, $12.50, and $6.25 values. These results suggest that abstinence can be maintained below baseline levels with lower-value vouchers, but that the frequency of marijuana use increases as incentive value decreases.

Increasing Abstinence from Cigarette Smoking Among Pregnant Women

Among the most exciting of the extensions of the vouchers approach is their use to promote smoking abstinence among pregnant women. Smoking during preg-nancy is a major preventable cause of fetal morbidity and mortality, and is par-ticularly prevalent among less educated women (Floyd, Rimer, Giovino, Mullen, & Sullivan, 1993; Mullen, 1999). Available interventions rarely achieve cessation rates in excess of 12–18%, and the majority of those who quit resume smoking following delivery. Several research groups are investigating the use of vouchers to promote abstinence during pregnancy and postpartum in this population. One group has reported results from a randomized trial supporting the efficacy of vouchers in this population (Donatelle, Prows, Champeau, & Hudson, 2000). In that trial, 220 pregnant smokers were randomly assigned to receive a smoking-cessation self-help kit only or the kit plus vouchers contingent on verified smok-ing abstinence. Those in the voucher condition were asked to designate a significant other (SO) to participate in the trial as a support person. The pregnant woman and her SO received vouchers monthly during the pregnancy and for 2 months post-partum contingent on verified smoking abstinence in the former. Vouchers were $50 per test for the smokers and $50 for the first test and $25 for each subsequent test for the SOs. Importantly, the costs of the vouchers in this study were covered through donations from local health care organizations, businesses, and founda-tions. Smoking cessation rates at end-of-pregnancy were 32% versus 9% in the voucher and control conditions, respectively, and 21% versus 6% at the 2-month postpartum assessment. The magnitude of this treatment effect may be the most impressive of any seen among pregnant women in several decades and has prompted considerable clinical and research interest.

Our research effort with this population is still in the pilot study phase, but already looks promising (Higgins et al., in press). In this ongoing study, all women receive encouragement from their provider to quit smoking and written materials that describe the benefits of doing so. Twenty-five consecutive admissions have been entered into the contingent voucher condition and 10 into a control condi-tion wherein vouchers are earned independent of smoking status. The voucher schedule is an adaptation of the one used in our studies with cocaine-dependent outpatients described above, and is in place throughout pregnancy and 3 months postpartum. A woman who entered this study at 12 weeks into her pregnancy, for example, and who sustained abstinence continuously through the pregnancy and postpartum period could earn $1147 in vouchers or approximately $127/month. Results are only available at this time from during pregnancy and may change as the study progresses. With those caveats noted, abstinence levels at the second and third antepartum assessments are 40% (10/25) and 40% (10/25) for women in the contingent voucher condition versus 10% (1/10) and 0% (0/3) for women in the noncontingent control condition. These preliminary results, considered in combination with the impressive trial results from Donatelle et al. (2000), bode well for the efficacy of vouchers for promoting smoking abstinence among pregnant and recently postpartum women.

Increasing Abstinence Among Adolescent Smokers

The vast majority of cigarette smokers begin smoking in adolescence (Centers for Disease Control, 1998). Approximately 18% of adolescents in the United States are current smokers. Relative to efforts to identify effective cessation interventions for adult smokers, there has been little research on treatments for adolescent smokers. Corby, Roll, Ledgerwood, and Schuster (2000) reported evidence supporting the feasibility of using monetary incentives to increase smoking abstinence in this population. The approach was based on the feasibility studies in schizophrenic smokers described above. Adolescent smokers who were not currently trying to quit were invited to participate in a study where they could earn monetary incentives by decreasing their smoking. Eight adolescents who reported smoking an average of 19 cigarettes per day (range = 15–25) and had a baseline breath CO >18 ppm participated. In a within-subject design, participants were monitored twice daily via breath CO testing for three consecutive 5-day periods (Monday–Friday). Smoking abstinence was defined as CO levels $\leq$ 8 ppm. During the first and third 5-day periods, subjects were encouraged to use their willpower to stop smoking, but incentives were dispensed independent of smoking status at a rate of $4 per test. During the second period, incentives were dispensed contingent on abstinence, with the overall payment amount equal to that available in the baseline conditions. Subjects were followed up 2 weeks after the end of the second baseline period. Of the 10 negative CO tests possible per 5-day period, subjects averaged 1.0 during the first baseline, 9.5 during the second period when incentives were contingent on abstinence, and 7.5 during the third baseline. By the 2-week follow-up assessment the carry-over effect evident in the second baseline period had dissipated, which is expected in this population who were not currently trying to quit smoking. The strikingly greater abstinence levels evident during the contingent compared to the baseline conditions, however, clearly support the sensitivity of smoking in this population to incentives for abstinence. The next step is to integrate this knowledge regarding the sensitivity of adolescent smoking to contingent incentives for abstinence into the development of effective smoking cessation interventions for this population.

INCREASING COMPLIANCE WITH MEDICATION REGIMENS

Results from several trials provide evidence supporting the efficacy of voucher-based incentives for increasing compliance with medication regimens among substance abusers (Carroll et al., 2001; Carroll, Sinha, Nich, Babuscio, & Rounsaville, 2002; Preston et al., 1999; Rigsby et al., 2000). All but the Rigsby et al. (2000) study have involved compliance with naltrexone, an opioid antagonist.

Naltrexone Compliance

Naltrexone is a long-acting opioid antagonist that blocks the effects of opioid agonists, is well tolerated, and does not produce physical dependence. While these characteristics suggest that naltrexone should be an effective pharmacotherapy for opiate dependence, difficulties with early attrition and poor medication compliance undermine its efficacy. The difficulty in maintaining naltrexone compliance appears to be largely due to the drug's lack of reinforcing effects. The rationale in these studies is to substitute the reinforcing effects of vouchers in order to engender regular medication compliance.

The seminal trial on this topic (Preston et al., 1999) was a 12-week study in which 58 recently detoxified opiate-dependent outpatients were randomized to one of three treatment conditions: vouchers delivered contingent on 3×/week naltrexone ingestion, vouchers delivered independent of naltrexone ingestion, and a no-voucher control. Voucher value and schedule of delivery were the same as in the studies on cocaine abstinence in methadone maintenance patients described above (Silverman, Higgins, et al., 1996). Contingent vouchers significantly increased retention in treatment and medication compliance. Of a total 36 possible, mean naltrexone ingestions in the contingent voucher, noncontingent voucher, and control conditions were 21.4 ± 3.5, 11.3 ± 3.0, and 4.4 ± 1.5, respectively. Generally, comparable results have been observed in subsequent trials (Carroll et al., 2001, 2002), thereby providing a fairly compelling case that naltrexone compliance can be increased with contingent vouchers. What value of vouchers is needed and whether outcomes are enhanced by also including vouchers contingent on drug-negative urinalysis results remain to be clarified.

Antiretroviral Therapy Compliance

The Rigsby et al. (2000) report described a 4-week pilot study examining the efficacy of monetary incentives for increasing compliance with antiretroviral therapy regimens in HIV infected patients, the vast majority of whom were cocaine and heroin abusers. Participants were randomized to three conditions: nondirective inquires about compliance, cue-dose training involving directive strategies for enhancing compliance, and cue-dose training plus cash payments for each dose of the primary medication taken within 2 h of the scheduled time. The value of the incentive began at $2 and escalated to $10 per day based on continuous compliance. Compliance with the primary and nonprimary medications was enhanced in the incentive condition from approximately 70% at baseline to 90% during the intervention, with little change in the other conditions. Compliance in the incentive condition returned to baseline levels when the incentive was removed. Other investigators are also examining this topic, but to our knowledge, results from those studies have not yet been reported.

CONCLUSIONS

The purpose of this report was to provide an overview of research on the vouchers approach to drug abuse treatment. Begun as a novel intervention for outpatient management of cocaine dependence, this approach has now gone in many unexpected and interesting directions. Indeed, the approach has gone in more directions than space permitted us to characterize in detail in this report. Perhaps what is most encouraging about the many new and varied directions being taken with this approach is that they appear to be driven by empirical evidence. Starting with the application to cocaine dependence, the positive results obtained with the intervention appear to drive further inquiry into whether the intervention will prove efficacious with still other clinically challenging populations or problems. The answers have often been positive, which continues the cycle.

Of course, how much this approach eventually influences everyday drug abuse treatment practices remains to be seen. The application of vouchers to treatment of cocaine dependence is the most thoroughly developed of the various applications, and the results obtained from the multisite trial mentioned above may be an important determinant of future directions in that area. Of course, the practice of moving efficacious treatments from specialized research clinics into community clinics for effectiveness testing is relatively new in drug abuse treatment development. Indeed, the trials planned with vouchers will be among the first ever conducted in the National Institute on Drug Abuse's Clinical Trials Network. One can imagine that the logistical and practical obstacles to be worked through are enormous. However, just the fact that there is a Clinical Trials Network and that a novel treatment approach such as vouchers can be moved into effectiveness testing bodes well for the growing influence of science in drug abuse treatment development, including behavioral as well as pharmacological interventions.

The therapeutic workplace intervention of Silverman et al. (2001) is a potentially important development within vouchers research specifically and drug abuse treatment generally. To our knowledge, the 6-month data they reported is the first evidence from a randomized clinical trial supporting an efficacious intervention to promote cocaine and opiate abstinence in pregnant and recently postpartum women (cf. Higgins, 2001). Achieving abstinence while simultaneously providing vocational training to these women is in many ways remarkable. The women in that trial resided in poverty-stricken communities where chronic unemployment and drug dependence were rampant. The epidemiologic evidence is clear on the strong positive association between those conditions (e.g., Substance Abuse and Mental Health Services Administration [SAMHSA], 2000). Silverman and colleagues offer a strategy for addressing chronic unemployment and drug dependence within a single therapeutic context. Of course, the need for addressing co-occurring chronic unemployment and drug dependence is not limited to women with children. There is a tremendous need in economically poorer communities to address these related problems among both genders and parents and nonparents alike. The work of Silverman and colleagues provides some initial and potentially important insights into how that might be done effectively. Epidemiologic trends suggest a growing need to tailor substance abuse interventions for use among the less educated and more economically disadvantaged (SAMHSA, 2000).

We are also enthusiastic about the promising results from the work being done on promoting cigarette smoking cessation among pregnant and newly postpartum women. Again, the relationship between low socioeconomic status and smoking is striking (e.g., Tseng, Yeatts, Millikan, & Newman, 2001). The abstinence levels achieved by Donatelle et al. (2000) far exceed those typically observed in pregnant smokers. Our pilot data further support the feasibility of achieving relatively high cessation rates in this population using contingent vouchers. The fact that Donatelle et al. were able to cover incentive costs through donations illustrates the willingness of communities to support this approach to decreasing smoking among pregnant women. These are new observations and we look forward to seeing how this promising area of inquiry develops.

The practical matter of how to cover the cost of incentive programs in substance abuse treatment is unresolved. To date, the vast majority of work in this area has been conducted through funds from research grants. We anticipate that should treatment outcome research continue to support the efficacy of incentives with special populations, there will be practical ways to support them. The work of Donatelle et al. (2000) indicates that, at least with pregnant women, communities are willing to financially support such programs. The same might be true for treatment programs for adolescents, for example, although that remains to be examined. Alternative strategies are being examined with other populations. As noted above, Petry and colleagues are conducting research towards developing less costly incentive programs that community clinics might be able to support with existing revenue streams, while Silverman and colleagues are examining the very promising approach of integrating incentives for drug abstinence with vocational training and paid employment. Also worth examining in community substance abuse treatment clinics is whether contingent access to already existing community services or facilities might be effective incentives (e.g., community recreational or cultural facilities). A single solution to the practical matter of covering the costs of using material incentives in substance abuse treatment seems unlikely. Instead, current directions in the field point towards variation across different target populations, clinics (e.g., private vs. publicly funded), geographical and cultural contexts, and other factors.

We close this report on a theoretical point. There is an extensive scientific literature demonstrating the fundamental role played by the positive reinforcing effects of drugs in the genesis and maintenance of repeated drug use and dependence (e.g., Griffiths, Bigelow, & Henningfield, 1980; Higgins, 1997). Indeed, one can reasonably argue that at its core, drug dependence is a reinforcement disorder, that is, a disorder wherein the behavioral repertoire of the user is monopolized by a single type of reinforcement, namely, drug-produced changes in the reinforcement centers of the central nervous system (Wise, 1998). The voucher-based research reviewed above illustrates how that same behavioral process of reinforcement can be systematically applied to foster recovery from drug dependence.

ACKNOWLEDGMENTS

Preparation of this report was supported by research grants RO1DA09378, RO1DA08076, RO1DA14028, and institutional training grant T32DA07242 from the National Institute on Drug Abuse.

REFERENCES

Alessi, S. M., Sigmon, S. C., & Higgins, S. T. (2002). [Urinalysis results from individuals with serious mental illness receiving monetary incentives contingent on marijuana abstinence]. Unpublished raw data.

Bickel, W. K., Amass, L., Higgins, S. T., Badger, G. J., & Esch, R. A. (1997). Effects of adding behavioral treatment to opioid detoxification with buprenorphine. *Journal of Consulting and Clinical Psychology, 65*, 803–810.

Budney, A. J., & Higgins, S. T. (1998). A community reinforcement plus vouchers approach: Treating cocaine addiction. Rockville, MD: U.S. Department of Health and Human Services.

Budney, A. J., Higgins, S. T., Delaney, D. D., Kent, L., & Bickel, W. K. (1991). Contingent reinforcement of abstinence with individuals abusing cocaine and marijuana. *Journal of Applied Behavior Analysis, 24*, 657–665.

Budney, A. J., Higgins, S. T., Radonovich, K. J., & Novy, P. L. (2000). Adding voucher-based incentives to coping skills and motivational enhancement improves outcomes during treatment for marijuana dependence. *Journal of Consulting and Clinical Psychology, 68*(6), 1051–1061.

Carroll, K. M., Ball, S. A., Nich, C., O'Connor, P. G., Eagan, D., Frankforter, T. L., Triffleman, E. G., Shi, J., & Rounsaville, B. J. (2001). Targeting behavioral therapies to enhance naltrexone treatment of opioid dependence: Efficacy of contingency management and significant other involvement. *Archives of General Psychiatry, 58*, 755–761.

Carroll, K. M., Sinha, R., Nich, C., Babuscio, T., & Rounsaville, B. J. (2002). Contingency management to enhance naltrexone treatment of opioid dependence: A randomized clinical trial of reinforcement magnitude. *Experimental and Clinical Psychopharmacology, 10*(1), 54–63.

Centers for Disease Control and Prevention (1992). Comparison of the cigarette brand preferences of adult and teenage smokers—US, 1989, and ten communities, 1988 and 1990. *Morbidity and Mortality Weekly Report, 41*, 169–173.

Corby, E. A., Roll, J. R., Ledgerwood, D. W., & Schuster, C. R. (2000). Contingency management interventions for treating the substance abuse of adolescents: A feasibility study. *Experimental and Clinical Psychopharmacology, 8,* 371–376.

Donatelle, R. J., Prows, S. L., Champeau, D., & Hudson, D. (2000). Randomized controlled trial using social support and financial incentives for high risk pregnant smokers: Significant other supporter (SOS) program. *Tobacco Control, 9*(Suppl. III), iii67–iii69.

Downey, K. K., Helmus, T. C., & Schuster, C. R. (2000). Treatment of heroin-dependent poly-drug abusers with contingency management and buprenorphine maintenance. *Experimental and Clinical Psychopharmacology, 8*(2), 176–184.

Floyd, R. L., Rimer, B. K., Giovino, G. A., Mullen, P. D., & Sullivan, S. E. (1993). A review of smoking in pregnancy: Effects on pregnancy outcomes and cessation efforts. *Annual Review of Public Health, 14,* 379–411.

Griffith, J. D., Rowan-Szal, G. A., Roark, R. R., & Simpson, D. D. (2000). Contingency management in outpatient methadone treatment: A meta-analysis. *Drug and Alcohol Dependence, 58,* 55–66.

Griffiths, R. R., Bigelow, G. E., & Henningfield, J. E. (1980). Similarities in animal and human drug taking behavior. In N. K. Mello (Ed.), *Advances in substance abuse: Behavioral and biological research, vol. I* (pp. 1–90). Greenwich, CT: JAI Press.

Higgins, S. T. (1997). The influence of alternative reinforcers on cocaine use and abuse: A brief review. *Pharmacology, Biochemistry and Behavior, 57*(3), 419–427.

Higgins, S. T. (1999). Potential contributions of the community reinforcement approach and contingency management to broadening the base of substance abuse treatment. In J. A. Tucker, D. M. Donovan, & G. A. Marlatt (Eds.), *Changing addictive behavior: Bridging clinical and public health strategies* (pp. 283–306). New York: Guilford Publications.

Higgins, S. T. (2001). A promising intervention for a daunting problem: Comment on Silverman et al. (2001). *Experimental and Clinical Psychopharmacology, 9*(1), 27–28.

Higgins, S. T., Badger, G. J., & Budney, A. J. (2000). Initial abstinence and success in achieving longer-term cocaine abstinence. *Experimental and Clinical Psychopharmacology, 8*(3), 377–386.

Higgins, S. T., Budney, A. J., Bickel, W. K., Badger, G. J., Foerg, F. E., & Ogden, D. (1995). Outpatient behavioral treatment for cocaine dependence: One-year outcome. *Experimental and Clinical Psychopharmacology, 3,* 205–212.

Higgins, S. T., Budney, A. J., Bickel, W. K., Foerg, F. E., Donham, R., & Badger, G. J. (1994). Incentives improve outcome in outpatient behavioral treatment of cocaine dependence. *Archives of General Psychiatry, 51,* 568–576.

Higgins, S. T., Budney, A. J., Bickel, W. K., Hughes, J. R., Foerg, F., & Badger, G. (1993). Achieving cocaine abstinence with a behavioral approach. *American Journal of Psychiatry, 150*(5), 763–769.

Higgins, S. T., Delaney, D. D., Budney, A. J., Bickel, W. K., Hughes, J. R., Foerg, F., & Fenwick, J. W. (1991). A behavioral approach to achieving initial cocaine abstinence. *American Journal of Psychiatry, 148*(9), 1218–1224.

Higgins, S. T., Heil, S. H., Plebani Lussier, J., Solomon, L., Abel, R. L., Lynch, M. E., & McHale, L. (in press). Effects of abstinence-contingent vouchers on cigarette smoking among pregnant women [Abstract]. *Drug and Alcohol Dependence.*

Higgins, S. T., & Wong, C. J. (1998). Treating cocaine abuse: What does research tell us? In S. T. Higgins, & J. L. Katz (Eds.), Cocaine abuse: Behavior, pharmacology, and clinical applications (pp. 343–361). San Diego: Academic Press.

Higgins, S. T., Wong, C. J., Badger, G. J., Ogden, D. E., & Dantona, R. L. (2000). Contingent reinforcement increases cocaine abstinence during outpatient treatment and one year of follow-up. *Journal of Consulting and Clinical Psychology, 68*(1), 64–72.

Hunt, G. M., & Azrin, N. H. (1973). A community-reinforcement approach to alcoholism. *Behaviour Research and Therapy, 11*(1), 91–104.

Kang, S.-Y., Kleinman, P. H., Woody, G. E., Millman, R. B., Todd, T. C., Kemp, J., & Lipton, D. S. (1991). Outcomes for cocaine abusers after once-a-week psychosocial therapy. *American Journal of Psychiatry, 148*, 630–635.

Kirby, K. C., Marlowe, D. B., Festinger, D. S., Lamb, R. J., & Platt, J. J. (1998). Schedule of voucher delivery influences initiation of cocaine abstinence. *Journal of Consulting and Clinical Psychology, 66*(5), 761–767.

Mendelson, J. H., & Mello, N. K. (1996). Management of cocaine abuse and dependence. *New England Journal of Medicine, 334*(15), 965–972.

Meyers, R. J., Miller W. R. (Eds.) (2001). A community reinforcement approach to addiction treatment. Cambridge, UK: Cambridge University Press.

Meyers, R. J., & Smith, J. E. (1995). *Clinical guide to alcohol treatment: The Community Reinforcement Approach.* New York: Guilford Press.

Mullen, P. D. (1999). Maternal smoking during pregnancy and evidence-based intervention to promote cessation. *Primary Care, 26*, 577–589.

Petry, N. M., & Martin, B. (2002). Lower-cost contingency management for treating cocaine and opioid abusing methadone patients. *Journal of Consulting and Clinical Psychology, 70*, 398–405.

Petry, N. M., Martin, B., Cooney, J. L., & Kranzler, H. R. (2000). Give them prizes, and they will come: Contingency management for treatment of alcohol dependence. *Journal of Consulting and Clinical Psychology, 68*(2), 250–257.

Piotrowski, N. A., Tusel, D. J., Sees, K. L., Reilly, P. M., Banys, P., Meek, P., & Hall, S. M. (1999). Contingency contracting with monetary reinforcers for abstinence from multiple drugs in a methadone program. *Experimental and Clinical Psychopharmacology, 7*(4), 399–411.

Preston, K. L., Silverman, K., Umbricht, A., DeJesus, A., Montoya, I. D., & Schuster, C. R. (1999). Improvement in naltrexone treatment compliance with contingency management. *Drug and Alcohol Dependence, 54*(2), 127–135.

Preston, K. L., Umbricht, A., Wong, C. J., & Epstein, D. H. (2001). Shaping cocaine abstinence by successive approximation. *Journal of Consulting and Clinical Psychology, 69*(4), 643–654.

Rawson, R. A., McCann, M. J., Huber, A., & Shoptaw, S. (1999). Contingency management and relapse prevention as stimulant abuse treatment interventions. In S. T. Higgins, & K. Silverman (Eds.), *Motivating behavior change among illicit-drug abusers: Research on contingency management interventions* (pp. 57–74). Washington, DC: American Psychological Association.

Rawson, R. A., McCann, M. J., Huber, A., Thomas, C., & Ling, W. (2000). Reducing cocaine use in methadone patients: Contingencies vs. counseling [Abstract]. In L. S. Harris (Ed.), Problems of Drug Dependence, 1999: Proceedings of the 61st Annual Scientific Meeting of the College on Problems of Drug Dependence. National Institute on Drug Abuse Research Monograph Series, vol. 180, p. 144.

Regier, D. A., Farmer, M. E., Rae, D. S., Locke, B. Z., Keith, S. J., Judd, L. L., & Goodwin, F. K. (1990). Comorbidity of mental disorders with alcohol and other drug abuse. Results from the Epidemiologic Catchment Area (ECA) Study. *Journal of the American Medical Association, 264*(19), 2511–2518.

Rigsby, M. O., Rosen, M. I., Beauvais, J. E., Cramer, J. A., Ralney, P. M., O'Malley, S. S., Dieckhaus, K. D., & Rounsaville, B. J. (2000). Cue-dose training with monetary reinforcement: Pilot study of an antiretroviral adherence intervention. *Journal of General Internal Medicine, 15*, 841–847.

Roll, J. M., Higgins, S. T., Steingard, S., & McGinley, M. (1998). Use of monetary reinforcement to reduce the cigarette-smoking of persons with schizophrenia: A feasibility study. *Experimental and Clinical Psychopharmacology, 6*, 157–161.

Shaner, A., Roberts, L. J., Eckman, T. A., Tucker, D. E., Tsuang, J. W., Wilkins, J. N., & Mintz, J. (1997). Monetary reinforcement of abstinence from cocaine among mentally ill patients with cocaine dependence. *Psychiatric Services, 48*(6), 807–810.

Shoptaw, S., Dow, S., Frosch, D. L., Ling, W., Madsen, D. C., & Jarvik, M. E. (1999). Reducing cigarette smoking in methadone maintenance patients. In S. T. Higgins, & K. Silverman (Eds.), *Motivating behavior change among illicit-drug abusers: Research on contingency management interventions* (pp. 243–264). Washington, DC: American Psychological Association.

Sigmon, S. C., Steingard, S., Badger, G. J., Anthony, S. L., & Higgins, S. T. (2000). Contingent reinforcement of marijuana abstinence among individuals with serious mental illness: A feasibility study. *Experimental and Clinical Psychopharmacology, 8*(4), 509–517.

Silverman, K., Chutuape, M. A., Bigelow, G. E., & Stitzer, M. L. (1999). Voucher-based reinforcement of cocaine abstinence in treatment-resistant methadone patients: Effects of reinforcement magnitude. *Psychopharmacology, 146,* 128–138.

Silverman, K., Higgins, S. T., Brooner, R. K., Montoya, I. D., Cone, E. J., Schuster, C. R., & Preston, K. L. (1996). Sustained cocaine abstinence in methadone maintenance patients through voucher-based reinforcement therapy. *Archives of General Psychiatry, 53,* 409–415.

Silverman, K., Robles, E., Bigelow, G. E., & Stitzer, M. L. (2000). Long-term abstinence reinforcement in methadone patients [Abstract]. In L. S. Harris (Ed.), *Problems of Drug Dependence, 1999: Proceedings of the 61st Annual Scientific Meeting of the College on Problems of Drug Dependence. National Institute on Drug Abuse Research Monograph Series, vol. 180,* p. 144.

Silverman, K., Svikis, D., Robles, E., Stitzer, M. L., & Bigelow, G. E. (2001). A reinforcement-based therapeutic workplace for the treatment of drug abuse: Six-month abstinence outcomes. *Experimental and Clinical Psychopharmacology, 9*(1), 14–23.

Silverman, K., Wong, C. J., Higgins, S. T., Brooner, R. K., Montoya, I. D., Contoreggi, C., Umbricht-Schneiter, A., Schuster, C. R., & Preston, K. L. (1996). Increasing opiate abstinence through voucher-based reinforcement therapy. *Drug and Alcohol Dependence, 41,* 157–165.

Silverman, K., Wong, C. J., Umbricht-Schneiter, A., Montoya, I. D., Schuster, C.R., & Preston, K. L. (1998). Broad beneficial effects of cocaine abstinence reinforcement among methadone patients. *Journal of Consulting and Clinical Psychology, 66*(5), 811–824.

Simpson, D. D. (1984). National treatment system evaluation based on the drug abuse reporting program (DARP) follow-up research. In F. M. Tims, & J. P. Ludford (Eds.), *Drug abuse treatment evaluation: Strategies, progress, and prospects* (National Institute on Drug Abuse Research Monograph No. 51; DHHS Publication No. ADM 84-1329, pp. 29–41). Washington, DC: U.S. Government Printing Office.

Simpson, D. D., Joe, G. W., & Brown, B. S. (1997). Treatment retention and follow-up outcomes in the Drug Abuse Treatment Outcome Study (DATOS). *Psychology of Addictive Behaviors, 11,* 294–307.

Stitzer, M. L., & Higgins, S. T. (1995). Behavioral treatment of drug and alcohol abuse. In F. E. Bloom, & D. J. Kupfer (Eds.), *Psychopharmacology: The fourth generation of progress* (pp. 1807–1819). New York: Raven Press.

Substance Abuse and Mental Health Services Administration (SAMHSA). (2000). *National household survey on drug abuse: Main findings 1998* (DHHS Publication No. SMA 00-3381). Washington, DC: U.S. Government Printing Office.

Tidey, J. W., O'Neill, S. C., & Higgins, S. T. (in press). Contingent monetary reinforcement of smoking reductions, with and without transdermal nicotine, in outpatients with schizophrenia. *Experimental and Clinical Psychopharmacology.*

Tseng, M., Yeatts, K., Millikan, R., & Newman, B. (2001). Area-level characteristics and smoking in women. *American Journal of Public Health, 91*(11), 1847–1850.

Wise, R. A. (1998). Drug-activation of brain reward pathways. *Drug and Alcohol Dependence, 51*(1–2), 13–22.

Chapter 7

A Comparison of Contingency Management and Cognitive-Behavioral Approaches During Methadone Maintenance Treatment for Cocaine Dependence

Richard A. Rawson, Ph.D.
Alice Huber, Ph.D.
Michael McCann, M.A.
Steven Shoptaw, Ph.D.
David Farabee, Ph.D.
Chris Reiber, Ph.D.
Walter Ling, M.D.

Background. This study compared two psychosocial approaches for the treatment of cocaine dependence: contingency management (CM) and cognitive-behavioral therapy (CBT).

Methods. Patients with cocaine dependence who were receiving methadone maintenance treatment (n = 120) were randomly assigned to one of four conditions: CM, CBT, combined CM and CBT (CBT + CM), or treatment as usual (i.e., methadone maintenance treatment program only [MMTP only]) (n = 30 per cell). The CM procedures and CBT materials were comparable to those used in previously published research. The active study period was 16 weeks, requiring three clinic visits per week. Participants were evaluated during treatment and at 17, 26, and 52 weeks after admission.

Results. Urinalysis results during the 16-week treatment period show that participants assigned to the two groups featuring CM had significantly superior in-treatment urinalysis results, whereas urinalysis results from participants in

the CBT group were not significantly different from those of the MMTP-only group. At week 17, self-reported days of cocaine use were significantly reduced from baseline levels for all three treatment groups but not for the MMTP-only group. At the 26-week and 52-week follow-up points, CBT participants showed substantial improvement, resulting in equivalent performance with the CM groups as indicated by both urinalysis and self-reported cocaine use data.
Conclusions. *Study findings provide solid evidence of efficacy for CM and CBT. Although the effect of CM is significantly greater during treatment, CBT appears to produce comparable long-term outcomes. There was no evidence of an additive effect for the two treatments in the CM + CBT group.* (Archives of General Psychiatry 2002;59:817–824)

INTRODUCTION

Cocaine dependence is an important public health problem in the United States.[1] During the past decade, progress has been made in the area of psychological/behavioral treatments for individuals with cocaine dependence.[2] The two approaches with the strongest empirical support are contingency management, based on the principles of operant conditioning,[3] and cognitive-behavioral strategies, based on social learning principles.[4–6]

Stitzer et al.[7–8] have documented the efficacy of establishing a contingent relationship between a desired response (frequently a urine sample free of drug metabolites) and the delivery of a positively reinforcing event (e.g., money or some desired item) as a method for reducing illicit drug use. The delivery of a reward that is contingent on reduced drug use has become known as contingency management (CM). Higgins et al.[9–12] have demonstrated that the use of CM contributes to a significant reduction in cocaine use when used as part of a behavioral treatment package. These investigators also found that CM had sustained positive effects at 6 and 12 months after admission.[13–14] Their work, and the work of Petry et al.,[15] has established CM as a powerful technique for reducing cocaine use.

Marlatt and Gordon[16] introduced the concept that cognitive-behavioral strategies can be effective in treating substance use disorders. Carroll et al.[17–18] established the efficacy of a manualized protocol for treating cocaine dependence with cognitive-behavioral therapy (CBT). These studies demonstrated that use of their CBT manual reduced cocaine use over 1 year. In fact, their report suggests that CBT is more efficacious at follow-up points than during treatment. These and other studies have provided solid empirical support for the use of CBT in treating cocaine dependence.[19–20]

The approximately 180,000 patients who are in methadone maintenance treatment programs (MMTPs) for opiate addiction are severely affected by the use of cocaine.[21–22] Studies have documented the efficacy of CM and CBT in reducing cocaine use among these patients.[23–26] However, little is known about the comparative efficacy of the two approaches.

The purpose of the present study is to compare the efficacy of CM and CBT, alone and in combination, for the treatment of cocaine dependence in patients receiving methadone maintenance and to explore whether reductions in cocaine use are sustained at posttreatment follow-up. The a priori hypotheses for this study were that all three treatment conditions would produce a reduction in cocaine use, whereas the MMTP-only condition would not, and that although CM may promote a more substantial reduction in cocaine use during treatment, CBT will produce a sustained reduction of cocaine use at follow-up points. Furthermore, it was predicted that the combined CM and CBT condition (CM + CBT) would produce better outcomes than either the CM or CBT conditions alone.

PARTICIPANTS AND METHODS

Participants

Candidates for this study were required to be in an MMTP for opiate use at one of two Los Angeles, CA, clinics for a minimum of 90 days, to meet *DSM-IV* criteria for cocaine dependence, and to show evidence of cocaine use (at least one urine sample positive for cocaine metabolites) during the month prior to study enrollment. Individuals were ineligible if they were also dependent on alcohol or benzodiazepines to the point of requiring medical withdrawal or if their treatment was court mandated. The study clinics serve a disadvantaged population and employ a high-tolerance approach (i.e., emphasis is on treatment retention, and no sanctions are applied for illicit drug use). The clinics charge patients $120 per month.

During the 2-year study recruitment period, approximately 1100 individuals were receiving methadone maintenance in the two clinics, and approximately 500 to 600 met eligibility criteria for study participation. Of those 500 to 600, however, only 180 volunteered for the study, and of this group, only 120 met study eligibility criteria, enrolled in the study, completed all baseline measures, and were randomly assigned to a study condition. This modest rate of study recruitment attests to the minimal interest these patients had in stopping cocaine use. In fact, a $40 per month methadone program fee reduction over the 16-week study period was necessary to promote study participation.

Procedures

All research activities were reviewed and approved by the Institutional Review Board of Friends Research Institute, Los Angeles. Following informed consent procedures and baseline data collection, the 120 participants were randomly assigned to one of four study conditions: CM, CBT, CM + CBT, or treatment as usual (i.e., MMTP only) (n = 30 per cell). All interventions lasted 16 weeks. Participants in all conditions received identical methadone treatment services, as described below. The methods for this study were previously reported[27] and are summarized here.

Treatment Condition Descriptions

MMTP-Only Group

Individuals assigned to this treatment condition participated in the clinics' standard methadone treatment. This treatment comprised daily clinic visits for methadone, twice-monthly counseling sessions, and medical care and case-management services as needed. The mean daily methadone dosage in the clinics during this period was 82 mg (range, 58–110 mg). The only characteristics that distinguished the MMTP-only patient group from the general clinic population were that the study participants were required to give three urine samples per week (compared with one per month for the general clinic population) and provide baseline, weekly, and follow-up data. In return, their clinic fees were reduced by $40 per month, and they received a $25 gift certificate at each follow-up interview.

Contingency Management Group

Participants in the CM group were required to provide three urine samples per week and meet briefly (2–5 minutes) with the CM technician while reviewing their methadone treatment. The meetings with the CM technician covered four topics: (1) a review of the results of the urine test (tested immediately using EMIT [enzyme-multiplied immunoassay technique]; Syva; Dade Behring, Deerfield, IL); (2) the delivery of a voucher, if earned; (3) a discussion of how the voucher or accumulated voucher account could be redeemed; and (4) the delivery of the earned items when the vouchers were redeemed. On occasions when vouchers were earned, the CM technician provided praise and encouragement.

The voucher value was based upon an escalating schedule.[9–10] The voucher value started at $2.50 per cocaine-negative urine sample and increased in value by $1.25 with each successive negative sample; patients received a $10 bonus for three consecutive cocaine-negative urine samples. The maximum voucher value was $20 per sample. When samples were missed or were positive for cocaine, the value of the voucher was reset to a lower level.[9–10] The maximum possible earning (48 consecutive cocaine-free samples) was $1277.50. Participants were never given cash, and they were encouraged to "spend" their savings on items that supported drug-free activities.

Cognitive-Behavioral Therapy Group

The CBT procedure consisted of 48 group sessions (3 per week for 16 weeks) concurrent with participation in methadone treatment. The 90-minute groups had

4 to 8 participants, and each session was guided by a worksheet from a manual.[28] Each worksheet presented a concept or a brief exercise that explained or illustrated an aspect of CBT. Each session was led by a master's degree-level therapist in a standardized manner. Study counselors only delivered CBT and were not members of the methadone maintenance program counseling staff. All study counselors received 120 to 180 hours of didactic and experiential training in the CBT method prior to their study participation. All sessions were audiotaped and reviewed by a counseling supervisor on a weekly basis, and feedback was given to the therapist to ensure consistency with the protocol. Although there was no quantitative measure of therapist adherence, the session taping and supervision appeared to produce a standardized treatment experience.

Contingency Management and Cognitive-Behavioral Therapy Group

Individuals in this treatment condition participated in both the CM and CBT groups while they continued their methadone maintenance treatment. The CBT and CM procedures were delivered in parallel, and no attempt was made to integrate CM techniques with CBT.

Termination from the study could be a result of study completion, missing two consecutive weekly data collection visits, or missing either six consecutive CBT groups or six consecutive urine samples. Therefore, a consistent 2-week absence from protocol participation was the criterion for study termination across all study conditions. Study termination had no effect on methadone maintenance treatment.

Study Measures

Baseline data were collected with the Structured Clinical Interview for *DSM-IV* (SCID),[29] the Beck Depression Inventory (BDI),[30] and the Addiction Severity Index (ASI).[31] All participants completed a BDI (to monitor safety) and provided a self-report of drug use weekly. All participants were required to give three monitored urine samples per week throughout the treatment intervention phase (16 weeks) and at three follow-up interviews 17, 26, and 52 weeks after study participation began. All samples were analyzed immediately for metabolites of cocaine (300 ng of benzoylecgonine was the cutoff), using EMIT reagent test procedures. In addition, one urine sample per participant per week and all follow-up urine samples were also analyzed for metabolites of illicit opiates, amphetamine, benzodiazepines, barbiturates, and cannabinoids. Although we were initially concerned about substitution of amphetamine for cocaine, only 8 of the weekly samples collected during the study were positive for amphetamine, suggesting that amphetamine was not substituted for cocaine among these patients. If participants missed or refused to give a urine sample, the sample was considered positive for the purposes of the CM intervention procedures.

Two trained PhD-level staff persons administered the SCID during the first 30 days of study participation. The SCID is a semistructured interview for making Axis I and II diagnoses, based on the *DSM-IV*. The SCID administrators were trained in a 1-week program based on the guidelines established by the developers of the SCID, and both passed proficiency tests.

Data Analysis

An α level of .05 was used for all statistical tests presented in this article. The distribution of demographic and drug-use characteristics across the experimental interventions was evaluated using Pearson χ^2 and multivariate factorial analysis of variance (MANOVA) tests.

The differential effects on cocaine use were assessed using several measures. The primary outcome measure was based on the number of urine samples free of cocaine metabolite provided during the trial. Because study participants were tested for cocaine use thrice weekly throughout the 16-week intervention, the total number of cocaine-free samples could range from 0 to 48. Study participants were also tested weekly for opiates and several other drugs, making 16 the maximum possible number of urine samples negative for opiates. Inspection of the distribution of data revealed neither significant skewness nor extreme kurtosis for cocaine or opiate urinalysis measures. Thus, in-treatment drug-use measurements were analyzed using MANOVA techniques. To control for experiment-wise error rates that can result from multiple least-squares mean comparisons, Tukey–Kramer honestly significant difference statistical tests were used for all post hoc comparisons.

The second method for toxicological evaluation of urine samples employed a criterion of whether study participants achieved 3 consecutive weeks of cocaine abstinence during the active treatment intervention period. Percentages for each group achieving this criterion were compared using χ^2 tests.

To assess the results of toxicological examinations for cocaine following active treatment conditions, separate χ^2 analyses compared the percentages of participants who produced cocaine-negative urine samples at follow-up evaluations. Pairwise contrasts between groups were conducted with χ^2 tests using α levels determined by dividing the conventional α of .05 by the number of pairwise comparisons made.

Lastly, self-reported data from the ASI were also examined. Specifically, the mean numbers of days in which the participants reported using cocaine and opiates during the preceding month were contrasted between study groups. Similarly, other domains of functioning as measured by the ASI were compared using the previously mentioned procedures. Four retrospective 30-day reporting periods, occurring at baseline and at the 17-week, 26-week, and 52-week follow-up points, were analyzed via repeated-measures MANOVA and subsequent Tukey–Kramer tests.

RESULTS

Participant Characteristics

Slightly more than half of the participants (55%) were men. The mean age was 43.6 years. Whites accounted for 39% of the sample; African Americans, 32%; Hispanics, 26%; and other ethnicity, 3%. None of the between-group differences in participant characteristics presented in Table 7.1 were statistically significant, nor were there significant between-groups differences in the methadone dosage during treatment.

We evaluated 108 clients using the SCID Axes I and II diagnostic interviews (antisocial personality disorder module only). Table 7.2 displays the prevalence

TABLE 7.1 Participant Characteristics by Study Condition*

Characteristic	Condition			
	CBT	CM	CBT+CM	MMTP only (control)
Age, mean, y	45.2	42.0	44.6	42.5
Male	63	67	50	40
Race				
White	40	27	47	43
African American	33	40	33	20
Hispanic	23	33	20	26
Other	3	0	0	10
Education, mean, y	11.7	12.0	12.5	12.4
Usually Unemployed Past 3 y	53	27	33	33
Married	17	20	30	27
Probation/parole	20	20	20	17
Methadone dosage, Mean, mg	82	78	83	82
ASI composite scores At admission, Mean (SD)				
Medical	0.30 (0.4)	0.40 (0.4)	0.44 (0.4)	0.29 (0.4)
Employment	0.75 (0.3)	0.67 (0.3)	0.70 (0.3)	0.71 (0.2)
Alcohol	0.17 (0.2)	0.10 (0.1)	0.08 (0.2)	0.07 (0.1)
Drug	0.37 (0.1)	0.31 (0.1)	0.33 (0.1)	0.36 (0.1)
Legal	0.19 (0.2)	0.06 (0.1)	0.13 (0.2)	0.17 (0.2)
Family/social	0.21 (0.2)	0.16 (0.2)	0.26 (0.2)	0.27 (0.2)
Psychiatric	0.26 (0.2)	0.24 (0.2)	0.25 (0.3)	0.27 (0.2)

*Data are presented as the percentage of participants unless otherwise indicated. Sample size was 30 participants for each group. None of the between-group comparisons are significant. CBT indicates cognitive-behavioral therapy; CM, contingency management; MMTP, methadone maintenance treatment program; and ASI, Addiction Severity Index.

TABLE 7.2. SCID Axis I and II Diagnoses by Study Condition (n = 108)*

| Diagnosis† | Condition, % of Participants | | | |
	CBT (n = 28)	CM (n = 27)	CBT + CM (n = 26)	MMTP Only (Control) (n = 27)
SCID Axis I				
Substance Use Disorder	100	100	100	100
Mood Disorder	18	33	23	19
Anxiety Disorder	18	37	27	19
SCID Axis II				
Antisocial Personality Disorder (ASPD)	50	56	27	44
Combinations of Disorders				
Substance Use Disorder only	29	23	50	36
Substance use disorder And other Axis I Disorders but no ASPD	21	22	23	19
Substance Use Disorder And only ASPD	36	22	12	26
Substance Use Disorder, ASPD, and other Axis I disorders	14	33	15	19

*Sample sizes vary slightly because of missing data. SCID indicates Stuctured Clinical Interview for *DSM-IV*; CBT, cognitive-behavioral therapy; CM, contingency management; and MMTP, methadone maintenance treatment program.
† Only diagnoses prevalent in 5% or more of the sample are shown.

of substance use disorder, other SCID Axis I psychiatric disorders, and antisocial personality disorder by study condition. Only those diagnoses prevalent in more than 5% of the sample are shown. There were no differences between groups in the prevalence of psychiatric disorders. The frequency of antisocial personality disorder among participants is consistent with other reports on individuals receiving methadone maintenance.[32]

Treatment Participation and Compliance

Retention

The value of treatment retention as a dependent measure was severely compromised in this study by the necessity of a $40 monthly incentive to promote study enrollment. As a consequence, there were no significant retention differences between conditions (Figure 7.1). The mean numbers of weeks in the protocol for participants in all 4 conditions were between 12 and 15 weeks out of a maximum of 16 weeks.

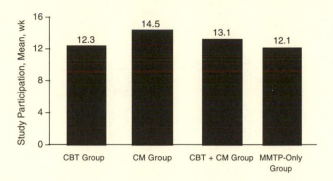

FIGURE 7.1. Retention of study participants by group ($F_3 = 1.37$; $P = .26$). CBT indicates cognitive-behavioral therapy; CM, contingency management; and MMTP, methadone maintenance treatment program.

Participation in Study Interventions and Follow-Up

Over the course of the study, 48 CBT group sessions were scheduled for individuals in the CBT and CBT + CM groups. As illustrated in Figure 7.2, individuals in the CBT + CM group attended more sessions than those in the CBT intervention ($P = .04$). There were no significant differences between the earnings of the CM group and the CM + CBT group (Figure 7.3).

At each of 3 time points, follow-up interview rates in the four intervention groups met or exceeded 80% (range, 80%–90%). There were no statistically significant differences in follow-up rates overall or at any of the 3 time points.

In-Treatment Cocaine Use

Figure 7.4 illustrates the mean number of cocaine-free urine samples by group assignment. Individuals in the two groups that received the CM procedure gave more cocaine-free urine samples during the trial than did individuals in the two

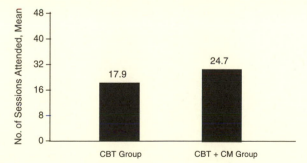

FIGURE 7.2. Attendance at cognitive-behavioral therapy (CBT) sessions by group ($F_1 = 4.39$; $P = .04$). CM indicates contingency management.

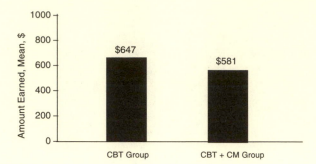

FIGURE 7.3. Earnings from contingency management (CM) vouchers by group (F_1 = 0.22; P = .64). CBT indicates cognitive-behavioral therapy.

groups that did not have access to the CM procedures. The number of cocaine-negative urine samples given was our most direct, reliable, and valid measure of in-treatment performance. A MANOVA comparing the mean number of cocaine-free urine samples in each intervention during the active treatment phase was statistically significant (n = 120; F_3 = 6.8; P < .001). Tukey-Kramer post hoc comparisons revealed that the least-squares means for both the CM and CBT + CM treatment interventions were significantly higher than for the MMTP-only condition. Although the CBT participants provided more cocaine-negative urine samples on average than did those in the MMTP-only group, the differences were not statistically significant. In support of this analysis, the same statistical relationship resulted from analysis of cocaine-positive urine samples and analysis of the percentages of cocaine-negative samples during the study period.

The percentage of participants achieving abstinence from cocaine for three consecutive weeks was significantly associated with treatment intervention (n = 120; χ^2_3 = 9.9; P = .02). Figure 7.5 depicts the percentage of participants from

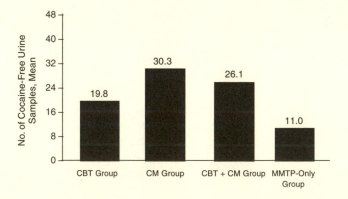

FIGURE 7.4. Number of cocaine-free urine samples provided during the study by group (F3 = 6.8; P < .001). CBT indicates cognitive-behavioral therapy; CM, contingency management; and MMTP, methadone maintenance treatment program.

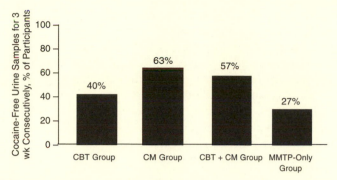

FIGURE 7.5. Percentage of patients achieving three consecutive weeks of cocaine-free urine samples by group $\chi^2_3 = 9.9$; $P = .02$). CBT indicates cognitive-behavioral therapy; CM, contingency management; and MMTP, methadone maintenance treatment program.

each group who had urine samples free of cocaine metabolites for three consecutive weeks. Comparisons of the percentages of patients achieving 3-week abstinence revealed significant contrasts between interventions. Significant group differences were found between the CM (63%) and MMTP-only (27%) groups (n = 60; $\chi^2_1 = 8.2$; $P = .004$) and the CBT + CM (57%) and MMTP-only groups (n = 60; $\chi^2_1 = 5.6$; $P = .02$). The percentages of CBT (40%) and MMTP-only group participants achieving 3-week abstinence were not statistically significant (n = 60; $\chi^2_1 = 1.2$; $P = .27$).

We were also interested in whether the techniques used to reduce cocaine use had any influence on participants' use of illicit opiates. The mean (SD) number of opiate-free urine samples across interventions was 5.7 (5.3) of 16 possible samples taken. There was no evidence that the groups differed in opiate use during the intervention period (n = 120; $F_3 = 0.26$; $P = .86$).

Cocaine Use at Week 17

Study participants were asked to provide urine samples at each follow-up assessment. At the end of active treatment intervention (week 17), urinalysis results were similar to the in-treatment results (n = 101; $\chi^2_3 = 10.2$; $P = .01$). The two treatment interventions that featured CM had the highest percentages of cocaine-free samples (CM group, 60%; CBT + CM group, 47%), followed by the CBT intervention (40%), and, lastly, the MMTP-only group (23%). After controlling for inflated α error associated with conducting five pairwise contrasts ($\alpha = .05/5$ = .01), the only significant pairwise contrast was between the CM and MMTP-only groups (n = 50; $\chi^2_1 = 9.7$; $P = .002$).

Self-Reported Cocaine Use

Although the urinalysis results offered the most reliable picture of in-treatment performance, a comparison of the self-reports of previous-month cocaine use taken from the ASI at baseline with those taken at the end of treatment (week 17) shows significant changes among study participants' cocaine use (within-group paired t test; n = 107; t_{106} = 6.0; P < .001). The MANOVA results indicate a significant main effect for all three treatment groups with regard to the reduction in the mean number of days subjects reported using cocaine from the month preceding admission to the month preceding the end-of-treatment interviews (n = 107; F_3 = 3.9; P = .01). However, post hoc comparisons revealed that none of the observed differences between treatment groups were statistically significant. All participants within each treatment modality reported significantly fewer days of cocaine use than were reported at baseline. There was no significant reduction for the MMTP-only group.

Other Measures of In-Treatment Effects

In addition to comparing the baseline with week-17 cocaine-use measurements, seven ASI composite scores were compared for reductions. Results showed that the reductions in ASI composite scores, if any, were not significant. The absence of a significant reduction in the ASI drug composite score despite significant reductions in cocaine use indicates the extent to which other drug use included in the ASI drug composite score continued. Further, with this group of older, chronically addicted individuals, the cessation of cocaine use did not produce significant change in other domains of functioning.

Week 26 and 52 Follow-Up Comparisons

Urinalysis Results

Figure 7.6 shows the percentage of subjects in each intervention with cocaine-free urine samples at the three follow-up points. Because the number of individuals

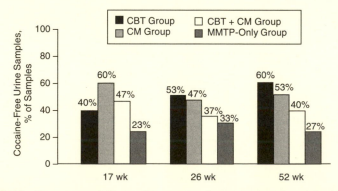

FIGURE 7.6. Percentage of 30 possible cocaine-free urine samples at the 17-week, 26-week, and 52-week follow-up points. CBT indicates cognitive-behavioral therapy; CM, contingency management; and MMTP, methadone maintenance treatment program.

contacted at each of the follow-up points was similar across the four conditions, the percentages of cocaine-free urine samples were calculated using 30 as the denominator for each condition. An analysis of the results using the number of samples collected as the denominator produced comparable statistical findings (data not shown).

At the time of the 26-week follow-up, the percentage of CBT group participants with cocaine-free urine samples (53%) exceeded the percentages of those in the CM (47%), CM + CBT (37%), and MMTP-only (33%) groups. This result, although not statistically significant (n = 94; χ^2_3 = 2.7; P = .43), marks an interesting shift that became more pronounced at the 52-week follow-up. As shown in Figure 7.6, 60% of those assigned to the CBT group had urine samples that tested negative for cocaine at this time, compared with 53% in the CM group, 40% in the CM + CBT group, and 27% in the MMTP-only group (n = 96; χ^2_3 = 8.3; P = .04). Pearson χ^2 pairwise comparisons of this omnibus effect, using an α criterion of .01, revealed that the only statistically significant difference was between the CBT and MMTP-only interventions (n = 46; χ^2_1 = 7.0; P = .008). The changes by groups over time are illustrated in Figure 7.7.

In summary, it appears that at the 26-week and 52-week follow-up points, the cocaine use of CBT group participants improved from their end-of-treatment (17-week) usage, in that the percentage of cocaine-free urine samples matched or exceeded that of the two groups who had received the CM procedures. As illustrated in Figure 7.6, the CBT group was the only treatment group to exceed the performance of the MMTP-only group at the final follow-up.

Self-Reported Cocaine Use in the Previous 30 Days

The mean number of days of self-reported cocaine use (of the previous 30 days) by treatment group at baseline and week 52 as measured by the ASI is illustrated

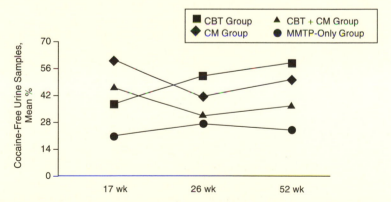

FIGURE 7.7. Mean percentage of cocaine-free urine samples at the 17-week, 26-week, and 52-week follow-up points (F_3= 2.85; P = .04). CBT indicates cognitive-behavioral therapy; CM, contingency management; and MMTP, methadone maintenance treatment program.

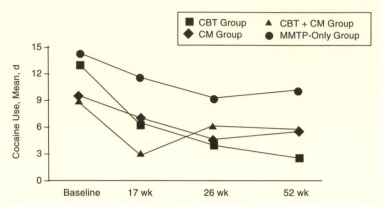

FIGURE 7.8. Number of self-reported days of cocaine use according to the Addiction Severity Index at baseline and three follow-up points ($F_3 = 4.92$; $P = .03$). CBT indicates cognitive-behavioral therapy; CM, contingency management; and MMTP, methadone maintenance treatment program.

in Figure 7.8. The MANOVA of the self-report data suggests a pattern of cocaine use similar to that seen in the data from the urinalysis results. Tukey–Kramer post hoc tests revealed that subjects in both the CBT and CM groups self-reported significantly fewer days of cocaine use than the MMTP-only group at the time of the 26-week follow-up and only the CBT subjects self-reported significantly fewer days of cocaine use than the MMTP-only group at the time of the 52-week follow-up. Therefore, self-reported data provide additional support for the persistence of CBT intervention effects at the posttreatment periods seen in our analyses of urine data.

To explore the specificity of this effect, the urinalysis results for opiates were analyzed across the three follow-up points. There were no group differences at any follow-up point, which was consistent with the in-treatment analyses for opiates. Furthermore, there were no significant changes in ASI composite scores from baseline to any follow-up point.

COMMENT

The purpose of this study was to compare the effectiveness of two promising interventions for the treatment of cocaine dependence, CM and CBT, alone and in combination in a randomized clinical trial. Because the selection of patients in opiate-dependence treatment with methadone allowed for a no-cocaine treatment condition, this study enabled comparison of these treatments with a control group.

The results of the study provide strong support for CM and CBT as treatments for cocaine dependence. Our data suggest that the impacts of the two interventions during treatment and at distant follow-up points are quite different. During the study and at the end of the 16-week study period, the CM procedure was associated with significantly more cocaine-free urine samples than was the control intervention. These urinalysis data were supported by self-reported data, although self-reported data suggested that CBT and CM, alone and in combination, produced significant reductions in cocaine use from baseline to week 17, whereas there was no reduction for the control group (MMTP-only group).

At the more distant follow-up points (weeks 26 and 52), the superiority of the CM procedure over the CBT procedure disappeared. By contrast, at both of these follow-up points an apparent improvement in the performance of the CBT group brought their cocaine use to a level comparable with that of the CM group. Although CM appeared to produce abstinence from cocaine that was sustained at follow-up, the performance of CBT group participants appeared to improve over time. This finding was supported by both the urinalysis data and the self-reported data collected in the ASI.

The mechanisms underlying the therapeutic benefit of the CM and CBT interventions may be quite different. It appears that positive reinforcement for cocaine-free urine samples (CM) produces an immediate and profound suppression of cocaine use. While CM treatment is in effect, this approach produces a greater reduction in cocaine use than does the CBT approach. When CM is applied for 16 weeks, this effect generally appears to be sustained for at least one year after admission.

The CBT approach did not produce as substantial a suppression of cocaine use during its implementation. However, individuals treated with this approach appeared to derive a benefit that became more pronounced during the follow-up period. Although this delayed effect was not systematically measured in this study, one possible explanation for it is that skills learned during treatment were successfully applied by the time of the follow-up interviews.

One consistent finding throughout the study was that the CBT + CM group did not demonstrate an additive effect. In fact, at week 17 and at the 26-week and 52-week follow-up interviews, both single-treatment groups had superior results compared with the combined group. The reason for the lack of an additive effect is not clear. It may be that delivering the two interventions in parallel is not useful. However, a combination of the procedures in some more carefully integrated manner might create a better synergy. Furthermore, it is interesting to speculate on the possible value of sequencing these treatments in such a manner that the immediate and profound suppression of cocaine use resulting from CM might be followed by the enduring benefit provided by CBT.

One final point of interest is the lack of impact of all treatments on opiate use or ASI composite scores during and following the trial. These treatments did not produce a change in overall illicit drug use or related psychosocial performance domains indicative of broad-based lifestyle or personality alterations; rather, these techniques produced reductions in cocaine use only. As with addiction pharmacotherapies, it is possible for an efficacious psychosocial intervention to be extremely effective for one type of drug use but to not produce a generalized reduction in use of all harmful psychoactive substances.

ACKNOWLEDGMENTS

We thank Steven Higgins, Ph.D., and Alan Budney, Ph.D., for design and implementation assistance, Christie Thomas, B.A., and Vikas Gulati, B.S., for data collection, David Parent, BS, and Anthony Ramirez, B.A., for data preparation and preliminary statistical analyses, and Dorynne Czechowicz, Ph.D., for National Institute on Drug Abuse project support.

This study was supported by grants DA09419, DA11972, DA12755, DA13045, and DA10429 from the National Institute on Drug Abuse, Bethesda, MD.

The opinions expressed in this article are those of the authors and are not necessarily shared by the National Institute on Drug Abuse.

REFERENCES

1. Office of National Drug Control Policy. (1998). *The National Drug Control Strategy, 1998: A 10-Year Plan.* Washington, DC: Office of National Drug Control Policy.
2. Ling, W., & Shoptaw, S. (1997). Integration of research in pharmacotherapy for addictive disease: Where are we? Where are we going? *Journal of Addictive Disorders, 16,* 83–102.
3. Skinner, B. (1938). *The behavior of organisms: An experimental analysis.* Englewood Cliffs, NJ: Prentice-Hall.
4. Bandura, A. (1977). Self-efficacy: Toward a unifying theory of behavioral change. *Psychology Review, 84,* 191–215.
5. Bandura, A. (1981). Self-referent thought: A developmental analysis of self-efficacy. In J. H. Flavell & L. Ross (Eds.), *Social cognitive development: Frontiers and possible futures* (pp. 122–149). Cambridge, MA: Cambridge University Press.
6. Bandura, A. (1984). Self-efficacy mechanism in human agency. *American Psychologist, 37,* 122–147.
7. Stitzer, M., Bigelow, G., & Liebson, I. (1980). Reducing drug use among methadone maintenance clients: Contingent reinforcement for morphine-free urines. *Addictive Behaviors, 5,* 333–340.
8. Stitzer, M., Bigelow, G., Leibson, I., & Hawthorne, J. (1982). Contingent reinforcement for benzodiazepine-free urines: Evaluation of a drug abuse treatment intervention. *Journal of Applied Behavior Analysis, 15,* 493–503.
9. Higgins, T., Budney, J., Bickel, K., Hughes, R., Foerg, F., & Fenwick, W. (1991). A behavioral approach to achieving initial cocaine abstinence. *American Journal of Psychiatry, 148,* 1218–1224.
10. Higgins, T., Budney, J., Bickel, K., Hughes, R., Foerg, F., & Badger, J. (1993). Achieving cocaine abstinence with a behavioral approach. *American Journal of Psychiatry, 150,* 763–769.
11. Higgins, T., & Budney, J. (1993). Treatment of cocaine dependence via the principles of behavior analysis and behavioral pharmacology. In L. S. Onken, J. D. Blaine, & J. Boren (Eds.), *Behavioral treatments for drug abuse and dependence* (pp. 97–121). NIDA Research Monograph 137.
12. Higgins, T., Budney, J., Bickel, K., Foerg, F., Donham, R., & Badger, J. (1994). Incentives improve outcome in outpatient behavioral treatment of cocaine dependence. *Archives of General Psychiatry, 51,* 568–576.
13. Higgins, S. T., Budney, A. J., Bickel, W. K., Foerg, F. E., Ogden, D., & Badger, J. (1995). Outpatient behavioral treatment for cocaine dependence: 1-year outcome. *Experimental and Clinical Psychopharmacology, 3,* 205–212.
14. Higgins, S. T., Wong, C. J., Badger, G. J., Ogden, D. E., & Dantona, R. L. (2000). Contingent reinforcement increases cocaine abstinence during outpatient treatment

and 1 year of follow-up. *Journal of Consulting and Clinical Psychology, 68,* 64–72.
15. Petry, N. M., Petrakis, I., Trevisan, L., Wiredu, G., Boutros, N. N., Martin, B., & Kosten, T. R. (2001). Contingency management interventions: From research to practice. *American Journal of Psychiatry, 158,* 694–702.
16. Marlatt, A., & Gordon, R. (1985). *Relapse prevention: Maintenance strategies in the treatment of addictive behaviors.* New York: Guilford Publications.
17. Carroll, K. M., Rounsaville, B. J., Gordon, L. T., Nich, C., Jatlow, P., Bisighini, R. M., & Gawin, F. H. (1994). Psychotherapy and pharmacotherapy for ambulatory cocaine abusers. *Archives of General Psychiatry, 51,* 177–187.
18. Carroll, K. M., Rounsaville, B. J., Nich, C., Gordon, L. T., Wirtz, P. W., & Gawin, F. H. (1994). One year follow-up of psychotherapy and pharmacotherapy for cocaine dependence: Delayed emergence of psychotherapy effects. *Archives of General Psychiatry, 51,* 989–997.
19. Rawson, R., Shoptaw, S., Obert, J., McCann, M., Hasson, A., Marinelli-Casey, P., Brethen, P., & Ling, W. (1995). An intensive outpatient approach for cocaine abuse treatment: The Matrix model. *Journal of Substance Abuse Treatment, 12,* 117-127.
20. Huber, A., Ling, W., Shoptaw, S., Gulati, V., Brethen, P., & Rawson, R. (1997). Integrating treatments for methamphetamine abuse: A psychosocial perspective. *Journal of Addictive Disorders, 16,* 41–50.
21. Condelli, W. S., Fairbank, J. A., Dennis, M. L., & Rachal, J. V. (1991). Cocaine use by clients in methadone programs: Significance, scope, and behavioral interventions. *Journal of Substance Abuse Treatment, 8,* 203–212.
22. Magura, S., Siddiqui, Q., Freeman, C., & Lipton, S. (1991). Changes in cocaine use after entry to methadone treatment. *Journal of Addictive Disorders, 10,* 31–45.
23. Foote, J., Seligman, M., Magura, S., Handelsman, L., Rosenblum, A., Lovejoy, M., Arrington, K., & Stimmel, B. (1994). An enhanced positive reinforcement model for the severely impaired cocaine abuser. *Journal of Substance Abuse Treatment, 11,* 525–539.
24. Silverman, K., Higgins, T., Brooner, K., Montoya, D., Cone, J., Schuster, R., & Preston, L. (1996). Sustained cocaine abstinence in methadone maintenance patients through voucher-based reinforcement therapy. *Archives of General Psychiatry, 53,* 409–415.
25. Silverman, K., Chutuape, M. A., Bigelow, G. E., & Stitzer, M. L. (1999). Voucher-based reinforcement of cocaine abstinence in treatment-resistant methadone patients: Effects of reinforcement magnitude. *Psychopharmacology (Berl), 146,* 128–138.
26. Robles, E., Silverman, K., Preston, K. L., Cone, E. J., Katz, E., Bigelow, G. E., & Stitzer, M. L. (2000). The brief abstinence test: Voucher-based reinforcement of cocaine abstinence. *Drug and Alcohol Dependence, 58,* 205–212.
27. Rawson, R. A., McCann, M., Huber, A., & Shoptaw, S. (1999). Contingency management and relapse prevention as stimulant abuse treatment interventions. In S. T. Higgins & K. Silverman (Eds.), *Motivating behavior change among illicit drug abusers* (pp. 57–74). Washington DC: American Psychological Association.
28. Rawson, R. A., Obert, J. L., McCann, M. J., Smith, D. P, & Scheffey, E. H. (1989). *The neurobehavioral treatment manual.* Beverly Hills, CA: Matrix.
29. Spitzer, R. L., Williams, J. B., Gibbon, M., & First, M. B. (1995). *The structured clinical interview for DSM-IV.* Washington, DC: American Psychiatric Association.
30. Beck, A. (1967). *Depression: Causes and treatment.* Philadelphia: University of Pennsylvania Press.
31. McLellan, A. T., Kushner, H., Metzger, D., Peters, R., Smith, I., Grissom, G., Pettinati, H., & Argeriou, M. (1992). The fifth edition of the Addiction Severity Index. *Journal of Substance Abuse Treatment, 9,* 199–213.
32. Brooner, R. K., Kidorf, M., King, V. L., & Stoller, K. (1998). Preliminary treatment response in antisocial drug abusers. *Drug and Alcohol Dependence, 49,* 249–260.

Chapter 8

Self-Help Strategies Among Patients with Substance Use Disorders

Joseph Westermeyer, M.D., Ph.D.
Sarah Myott, B.S.
Rembrant Aarts, B.S.M.
Paul Thuras, Ph.D.

The objective of this study was to determine (1) the type and extent of self-help efforts among patients presenting for treatment of substance use disorders, and (2) the association of self-help with demographic and clinical characteristics. A retrospective report of life self-help methods, current demographic characteristics, and current and lifetime clinical characteristics was used. Six hundred and forty-two patients in treatment for substance use disorder were interviewed at one of two university medical centers with Alcohol-Drug Programs located within departments of psychiatry. A research associate (RA) interviewed patients regarding seven types of self-help involving specific, mutually exclusive behaviors and rated the patient's lifetime self-help methods. The patient, RA, and addiction psychiatrists provided demographic, familial, and clinical information. Most patients (78%) had tried one or more types of self-help, with a mean of 2.7 methods per patient. They more frequently chose methods related to the substance (decreasing amounts or frequency, or changing substance type) or joining a self-help group than methods that involved changing friends, residence, or occupation/job/school. Certain patterns of self-help tended to occur together (e.g., changing substance frequency and dose), whereas others appeared more independent (e.g., joining a self-help group). Some self-help approaches occurred mostly in association with other methods rather than alone (e.g., changing occupation/job/school). More self-help was associated with higher socioeconomic class, more relatives with substance use disorder, greater severity of substance use disorder, and more treatment for substance use disorder. Self-help tends to occur more often after exposure to addicted relatives or addiction treatment. Clinicians and public adult education should promulgate self-help methods in the general population. (American Journal on Addictions 2001;10:249–257)

Self-help in relation to addiction consists of those strategies employed by addicted persons to extricate themselves from addiction, part of a process that has been referred to as natural recovery.[1] For purposes of this report, we define self-help as those self-initiated behaviors to reduce, control, or cease alcohol or drug use. The method of self-help perhaps most widely known is affiliation with sobriety-oriented groups, such as Alcoholics Anonymous[2,3] and Women for Sobriety.[4] Although some self-help methods primarily may involve cognitive methods,[5,6] we were interested in those approaches that were aimed at a behavioral outcome that could be assessed as to its success or failure. We are not addressing those events apt to initiate or motivate self-help efforts, although others have studied that dimension of recovery.[5,7–9]

Knowledge regarding self-help may be useful in educating people at risk to various methods that might help in overcoming substance use disorder on their own. Knowledge regarding self-help is also relevant to treated persons who must develop methods of helping themselves if they are to benefit from treatment. For example, in two Canadian surveys of the general population, 78% of recovering alcoholics mentioned self-help as their predominant pathway to recovery.[10]

Other behavioral approaches besides joining a self-help group can aid the person attempting to recover from substance use disorder. For example, women involved in a self-help group for alcoholism identified reducing the amount of alcohol use, changing when and where they drank, and changing what they drank as often used methods of self-help.[4] Kadushin found that making a change in the quality of one's environment reduced the level of alcohol or drug use.[11] Certain demographic characteristics have been found in association with self-help. For example, cigarette smokers have been more apt to attempt smoking cessation on their own if they belong to a higher socioeconomic status or if peers or close family members had quit or never smoked.[12]

In an ethnographic study of opiate addicts,[13] the first author identified the following methods of self-help as most often reported:

1. reducing frequency of use;
2. reducing dosage or amount used per time;
3. changing the type or form of substance (e.g., substituting marijuana for alcohol or beer for whiskey);
4. changing place of residence (i.e., moving to a new neighborhood or community);
5. changing type of job or place of employment (if a worker) or school (if a student);
6. changing friends (especially, avoiding friends who used alcohol or drugs heavily or regularly);
7. joining a self-help group.

Thus, we undertook the current study to assess the frequency of these methods in a large sample of patients presenting for alcohol and drug use disorders. Our first goal was to assess the relative frequency of these self-help methods, their association with each other, and the number of self-help methods employed by patients. Our second goal was to relate these frequencies (employing all seven methods in a single Self-Help Scale) to demographic and clinical characteristics of the patients. Based on reports from the literature, we hypothesized the following:

- More types of self-help would be associated with higher socioeconomic status.
- People with a family history of substance use disorder would employ more types of self-help.
- Other demographic and clinical characteristics would not be associated with number of self-help methods.

METHOD

Patients

A total of 642 patients was studied at two Alcohol-Drug Programs located in psychiatry departments at two university settings (Minnesota and Oklahoma). Upon entry into the Alcohol-Drug Program for assessment, the patients provided informed consent to the scientific use of these data in an anonymous and confidential fashion. Among these 642 patients, 32% had never been admitted previously to treatment for substance use disorder; for 14%, the current admission was their second treatment for substance use disorder.

Definition, Data Collection, Research Instruments

For purposes of this study, we defined the term "self-help" as being self-initiated, voluntary activities to overcome problems related to alcohol and/or drug use. Trained interviewers queried patients about the use of the seven self-help strategies listed above, recording them if the patient had (1) a conscious intent to undertake the particular strategy, and (2) made a conscientious effort to implement the strategy. Trained research associates completed forms regarding the following: (1) demographic information: age, sex, education, marital status, current residence, employment status, and socioeconomic status; (2) the Minnesota Substance Abuse Problem Scale, a lifetime scale of substance-related problems,[14] and (3) lifetime history of treatment for substance use disorder (i.e., number of types of treatment facilities, such as detoxification, general hospital inpatient, state hospital inpatient, residential, therapeutic community, outpatient; number of lifetime admissions; and number of days spent in treatment). Patients completed the Modified Michigan Alcohol-Drug Screening Test.[15] The addiction psychiatrist (1) identified comorbid psychiatric disorders, and (2) determined whether the patient had

TABLE 8.1. Percentage Use of More Than One Self-Help Method

	ΔFreq.	ΔDose	Join Group	ΔDrug	ΔFriend	ΔHome	ΔJob
ΔFreq		94%	67%	86%	81%	82%	84%
ΔDose	90%		66%	85%	80%	81%	83%
Join group	55%	56%		59%	71%	69%	71%
ΔDrug	64%	66%	53%		66%	75%	81%
ΔFriend	50%	52%	54%	56%		75%	81%
ΔHome	38%	39%	38%	47%	56%		78%
ΔJob	24%	24%	25%	31%	37%	48%	

Start with method described at the top of the column. Percentages of methods in the rows depict the proportion of all people who used the method in that column (e.g., in the first column, for all those who reduced frequency of use, 90% also reduced their dose per use).

substance abuse or dependence based on the traditional criteria of tolerance and dependence (rather than the latter-day *DSM* criteria for dependence). The protocol for detecting comorbid psychiatric disorders required that the patient be neither intoxicated nor in withdrawal. In addition to an open-ended interview regarding psychiatric symptoms and psychosocial problems and a formal mental status exam, the addiction psychiatrist completed the following scales: Global Assessment Scale, Brief Psychiatric Rating Scale, Hamilton Anxiety Scale, and Hamilton Depression Scale. A biomedical evaluation was conducted (review of systems, medical history, current or recent physical exam, CBC, LFT, UA, serological tests of renal function) to assess the presence of an Axis 3 Biomedical Condition.

Statistical Analyses

The data were analyzed using the following statistical measures:

- Mann–Whitney test for two-group comparisons of ordinal non-parametric data;
- Kruskal–Wallace test for ordinal non-parametric data involving more than two variables;
- correlation coefficient for comparison of two variables with ordinal distributions.

In order to correct for the Meehl effect in large samples, the level of statistical significance was set at .01. No significant relationships would be expected by chance among the comparisons in the study.

RESULTS

Frequency of Self-Help Categories

The distribution of self-help for each category by these 642 patients for their addiction was as follows:

- reducing frequency of use 56%
- reducing dosage or amount used per time 54%
- joining a self-help group 46%
- changing the substance form 41%
- changing friends 35%
- changing place of residence 26%
- changing job, work place, or school 16%.

The number of patients versus the number of types of self-help were as follows:

- none: 143 (22%);
- one: 96 (15%);
- two: 78 (12%);
- three: 91 (14%);
- four: 82 (13%);
- five: 62 (10%);
- six: 42 (7%);
- seven: 48 (8%).

The mean for number of self-help categories was 2.7 (standard deviation 2.2) with a skewness of .38. Each of the seven self-help items was highly associated with the entire Self-Help Scale at $p < .001$, with z scores on the Mann–Whitney, respectively, of 19.55, 19.85, 18.18, 16.21, 13.69, 17.61, and 13.69 (using the order of items as listed in the introduction).

The pattern of using various combinations of self-help is shown in Table 8.1. Percentages in each column are, among those who endorsed that particular item, the percentage who endorsed each of the other items. For example, among those who endorsed changing the frequency of use (Δ Freq), 90% also changed the amount used (D Dose). Note the following trends in the table: the high co-occurrence of changing frequency and dose (90 and 94%) and the high occurrence of all other methods among those who have made an occupation/job/school change (i.e., 71% to 84%).

Demographic Characteristics

As shown in Table 8.2, the only demographic characteristic associated with extent of self-help was the Hollingshead and Redlich socioeconomic status ($p < .002$). Among middle class patients, higher class was associated with more self-help methods. (Upper class and lower class subjects did not follow this trend; they resembled the middle-middle class in their use of self-help.) Demographic factors not correlated with self-help included age ($r = -.05$), years of education ($r = +.02$), number of individuals in the social network ($r = +.03$), sex, marital status, employment status, and residence.

TABLE 8.2. Number of Self-Help Methods vs. Demographic, Familial, and Clinical Characteristics

Characteristics	N	Mean (SD)	Statistics
Demographic Characteristics			
Socioeconomic Status			
Upper	12	2.6 (1.9)	F ratio = 4.36,
Upper middle	55	2.1 (1.9)	$p < .002$
Middle middle	100	2.4 (2.1)	
Lower middle	273	3.1 (2.3)	
Lower	133	2.5 (2.3)	
Minors, missing data*	69		
Gender			
Men	365	2.7 (2.2)	z = 0.49,
Women	277	2.8 (2.3)	$p = .63$
Employment			
Employed, student	237	2.6 (2.1)	K-W X2 = 3.70,
Homemaker	36	2.4 (2.4)	$p = .16$
Not employed	369	2.9 (2.3)	
Residence			
With family, friends	305	2.7 (2.2)	z = .62
Alone, none, institution	307	2.8 (2.2)	$p = .54$
Unknown*	30		
Marital Status			
Single	359	2.7 (2.3)	K-W X2 = 1.07
Married, common law	93	2.5 (2.1)	$p = .35$
Other	190	2.9 (2.2)	
Family History of Substance Use Disorder			
Nuclear Family			
Absent	213	2.3 (2.1)	z = 3.06
Present	429	2.9 (2.3)	$p < .002$
Extended Family			
Absent	140	2.1 (2.0)	z = 3.93
Present	502	2.9 (2.2)	$p < .0001$
Clinical Characteristics			
Substance Diagnosis			
Abuse	308	2.4 (2.2)	z = 2.85,
Dependence	332	2.9 (2.2)	$p < .005$
Uncertain* 2			
Comorbid Psychiatric Disorder			
Absent	309	2.7 (2.3)	z = 0.51,
Present	333	2.8 (2.2)	$p = .61$
Biomedical Condition			
Absent	430	2.6 (2.2)	z = 1.30,
Present	212	2.9 (2.3)	$p = .19$

*Excluded from the statistical analysis.

Family History

As shown in Table 8.2, the existence of more nuclear family members (consisting of father, mother, and sibling; scale range 0 to 3) with a substance use disorder is strongly related to more self-help categories at $p < .002$. Likewise, having more extended family (including the nuclear family, plus grandparents and aunts/uncles scale range 0 to 5) was even more strongly associated with more self-help at $p < .0001$.

Clinical Characteristics

As shown in Table 8.2, patients with substance dependence (i.e., tolerance and/or withdrawal) had used 0.5 more self-help methods than those with substance abuse ($p < .005$). Strong correlations were also found between the number of self-help types and two measures of substance use disorder severity: the patient-scored Modified Michigan Alcohol-Drug Screening Test ($r + .42$, $p < .01$) and the interview-based Minnesota Substance Abuse Problem Scale or M-SAPS ($r + .50$, $p < .01$). We also analyzed the seven subscales of the Minnesota SAPS and found significant correlations between self-help and several subscales as follows:

- Pharmaco-behavioral subscale, $r = +.44$, $p < .01$
- Interpersonal problem subscale, $r = +.42$, $p < .01$
- Psychological problems subscale, $r = +.41$, $p < .01$
- Occupation-academic subscale, $r = +.39$, $p < .01$
- Financial problems subscale, $r = +.35$, $p < .01$
- Family problems subscale, $r = +.34$, $p < .01$
- Legal problems subscale, $r + .18$, $p < .01$

Positive correlations were also found between number of self-help methods and three lifetime indicators of previous treatment for substance use disorder, as follows:

- types of facilities in which treatment was sought, including detoxification, general hospital substance treatment, state hospital substance treatment, residential substance treatment, halfway house, therapeutic community, and outpatient clinic or partial hospital, range 0 to 7 ($r = +.40$, $p < .01$);
- the lifetime number of admissions to the substance treatments described above ($r = +.40$, $p < .01$);
- the lifetime number of days in all substance treatment ($r = +.29$, $p < .01$).

Presence of a current comorbid psychiatric condition did not bear any relationship to self-help seeking for substance use disorder. Current Axis 3 Biomedical Condition likewise was not associated with self-help. These data are shown in Table 8.2.

DISCUSSION

In our patient group, we found that 78% of 642 people had tried some form of self-help. This percentage closely replicates that reported by recovering people in a general population survey.[10] Of interest, three of the four most commonly reported methods required only a decision about one's own substance-related behavior (i.e., reducing frequency, reducing dosage, changing substance) and these were highly apt to co-occur. The remaining four self-help methods involved planning and involvement of other people or resources (i.e., joining a self-help group, changing friends, changing residence, changing occupation/job/school). The three methods that involved appreciable changes in one's social network (changing friends, residence, occupation/job/school) were tried less often than self-help involving substance use or affiliation with a recovery group. Those making an occupational/job/school change were most apt to also have tried a few other approaches. This high rate of self-help efforts supports Satel's opinion that we can and should expect that an addicted person will become his or her "agent of recovery."[16]

Our data on middle class patients confirmed the finding of Wilcox and coworkers among cigarette smokers,[12] in which those from a higher socioeconomic status were more apt to employ self-help methods. However, upper- and lower-class patients did not follow this trend. Parenthetically, Wilcox and coworkers did not have any explanations for this finding. Additional work would be needed to clarify this unexpected but apparently replicable relationship.

Wilcox also found that cigarette smokers were more likely to quit on their own if family members had quit smoking or never smoked.[12] Our finding supports this notion in part and disagrees with it in part. Our patients used more types of self-help in direct proportion to the number of relatives with substance use disorder. In fact, the association was stronger when more relatives were added (i.e., in the extended family, compared to the nuclear family). We surmise that people with more affected relatives may have observed or received information regarding more types of self-help from their relatives, perhaps an example of "learned resourcefulness" as described by Rosenbaum.[17] Some disparity between the Wilcox finding and our finding suggests that recovery from cigarette dependence may differ from recovery involving other substances.

The number of self-help methods was strongly and directly correlated with lifetime severity of substance use disorder as measured by substance-dependent vs. -abuse and by two scales (the Modified Michigan Alcohol-Drug Screening Test and the Minnesota Substance Abuse Problem Scale). This finding is bolstered by the fact that three methods of data collection were employed: physician assessment of tolerance, patient self-rating on the MMADST, and research interview-based rating on the M-SAPS. Tuchfeld found that alcoholics who spontaneously quit drinking often ascribed their change to problems associated with their alcoholism, especially financial problems created by drinking, alcohol-related legal problems, and illness or accident associated with drinking.[18] Our research results linking severity and self-help appear to confirm Tuchfeld, with the exception that comorbid psychiatric and biomedical problems did not increase the likelihood of more self-help seeking in our study.

Tuchfeld also found that three factors besides the person's own substance-related problems could lead to spontaneous sobriety: the alcohol-related illness or death of a friend, confrontation by others, and education regarding alcoholism. It seems likely that these "external" factors (e.g., death of a friend, confrontation) would need to produce some "internal" or patient-centered response (e.g., an insight, an emotional crisis) in order to result in sobriety, which might then result in a "behavioral" or self-help effort. Thus, Tuchfeld emphasized motivational source vis-a-vis self-help, as have other investigators.[7,19,20] We ignored self-reported motivation and focused on the methods of self-help in this study.

Extent of previous treatment was related to extent of self-help approaches in this study. This finding suggests that people with substance use disorders may not necessarily exhaust self-help methods before seeking treatment, but rather they may try additional self-help concurrently with treatment. As another example of this phenomenon, among 600 California women in a self-help group, 89% had been or were currently in treatment. This co-use or sequential use of self-help and treatment is a different process from that described in Canada, where recoveries without treatment "seem to be the predominant pathway to recovery."[20] Perhaps national differences affect the treatment/self-help relationship, although sampling and data collection differences could also produce different results.

The categories of self-help addressed in this study are mutually exclusive but not all-inclusive. Other approaches have included prayer and participation in religious institution,[11] over-the-counter medication, willpower,[4] and a "cognitive appraisal process" weighing the pros and cons of continuing substance use.[20] These methods were not commonly reported in our original pilot work, but they might be relevant at other times and places. In this regard, Tucker and coworkers have also cogently observed that the self-help factors associated with early sobriety are not necessarily the same factors that help in maintaining long-term sobriety.[21] For example, "reduced use" strategies may be more appropriate if the individual is using substances excessively but not yet abusing or dependent on them; "total sobriety" strategies would be more relevant to cases reaching greater clinical severity (i.e., those cases warranting a diagnosis of substance abuse or dependence). For example, in a community survey from England, continued but reduced drinking was apt to accompany self-help alone, whereas abstinence was more apt to ensue following treatment.[7]

Although self-help has been described for many years, careful studies have been relatively few until the last decade. Investigators have employed a variety of methods and categories. For example, one team used three of our categories (i.e., change in friends, change in job, self-help group), a single category that included three of our drug use items (i.e., change in drug use), and a large number of other categories that involved recent crises support by others and a variety of behavioral changes that would not necessarily involve substances (e.g., dietary change).[22] At some point, it might be well to develop a list or scale of items in several categories: e.g., precipitants leading to self-help, outside supports to self-help, "reducing usage" methods, sobriety-oriented methods, and "social network change" methods.

The orientation of some self-help research has demonstrated that treatment is not a *sine qua non* for recovery, a message that can sometimes contain an anti-treatment bias. By the same token, attempts to "match" people to professional vs. self-help approaches have not revealed any scientific basis for such matching.[22,23] Increasingly in mental health, the goal has been for as complete a restoration to full health as is possible, rather than simply a lessening of symptom severity.[24] These data, as well as other reports in the literature, suggest that neither treatment nor self-help alone may be sufficient for all patients at all times. Future research should address the optimal integration of both treatment activities and self-help activities so as to produce maximum recovery.

ACKNOWLEDGMENTS

Partial support for this project was obtained from the Laureate Foundation of Tulsa, Okla. James Halikas, M.D., John Neider, B.A., and Greg Carlson, M.A., collaborated in the collection of these data. Carl Isenhart, Psy.D., and Roger Struck, M.A., provided useful comments during earlier drafts.

REFERENCES

1. Granfield, R., & Cloud, W. (1996). The elephant that no one sees: Natural recovery among middle-class addicts. *Journal of Drug Issues, 26*(1), 45–61.
2. Dumont, M. P. (1974). Self-help treatment programs. *American Journal of Psychiatry, 131*(6), 631–635.
3. Godlaski, T. M., Leukefeld, C., & Cloud, R. (1997). Recovery: With and without self-help, *Substance Use and Misuse, 32*(5), 621–627.
4. Kaskutas, L. A. (1996). Pathways to self help among Women for Sobriety. *American Journal of Drug and Alcohol Abuse, 22*(2), 259–280.
5. Ludwig, A. M. (1985). Cognitive processes associated with "spontaneous" recovery from alcoholism. *Journal on the Study of Alcohol, 46*(1), 53–58.
6. Burman, S. (1997). The challenge of sobriety: Natural recovery without treatment and self-help groups. *Journal of Substance Abuse, 9*, 4–61.
7. Saunders, W. M., & Kershaw, P.W. (1979). Spontaneous remission from alcoholism: A community study. *British Journal of Addiction, 74*, 251–265.
8. Mariezcurrena, R. (1996). Recovery from addictions without treatment: An interview study. *Scandinavian Journal of Behaviour Therapy, 25*(2), 57–84.
9. Klingemann, H. K. H. (1991). The motivation for change from problem alcohol and heroin use. *British Journal of* Addiction, 86, 72–744.
10. Sobell, L., Cunningham, J., & Sobell, M. (1996). Recovery from alcohol problems with and without treatment. *American Journal of Public Health, 86*(7), 966–972.
11. Kadushin, C., Reber, E., Saxe, L., & Livert, D. (1998). The substance use system: Social and neighborhood environments associated with substance use and misuse. *Substance Use and Misuse, 33*(8), 1681–1710.

12. Wilcox, N., Prochaska, J., & Velicer, W. (1985). Subject characteristics as predictors of self change in smoking. *Addictive Behavior, 10*, 407–412.
13. Westermeyer, J. (1982). *Poppies, pipes, and people: Opium and its use in Laos*. Berkeley, CA: University of California Press.
14. Westermeyer, J., Crosby, J., & Nugent, S. (1998). The Minnesota Substance Abuse Problem Scale: Psychometric analysis and validation in a clinical population. *American Journal on Addiction, 7*, 24–24.
15. Westermeyer, J., & Neider, J. (1988). Social networks and psychopathology among substance abusers. *American Journal of Psychiatry, 145*(10),1265–1269.
16. Satel, S. L. (1999). What should we expect from drug abusers? *Psychiatric Services, 50*(7), 861.
17. Rosenbaum M. (1990). *Learned resourcefulness in coping skills, self-control and adaptive behaviors*. New York: Springer.
18. Tuchfeld, B. (1981). Spontaneous remission in alcoholics: Empirical observations and theoretical implications. *Journal on the Study of Alcohol, 42*(7), 626–641.
19. McMurran, M., & Whitman, J. (1990). Strategies of self-control in male young offenders who have reduced their alcohol consumption without formal intervention. *Journal of Adolescence, 13*, 115–128.
20. Sobell, L. C., Sobell, M. B, Toneatto, T., & Leo, G. I. (1993). What triggers the resolution of alcohol problems without treatment? *Alcoholism, Clinical and Experimental Research,17*, 217–224.
21. Tucker, J. A., Vuchinich, R. E., & Gladsjo, J. A. (1994). Environmental events surrounding natural recovery from alcohol-related problems. *Journal of Studies on Alcohol, 55*, 401- 411.
22. Miller, W. R. (1989). Matching individuals with interventions. In R. K. Hester & W. R. Miller (Eds.), *Handbook of alcoholism treatment approaches* (pp. 261–272). New York: Pergamon Press.
23. Group PMR. (1997). Matching alcoholism treatments to client heterogeneity: Project MATCH posttreatment drinking outcomes. *Journal of Studies on Alcohol, 58*, 7–29.
24. Stahl, S. M. (1999). Why settle for silver when you can go for the gold? Response vs. recovery as the goal of antidepressant therapy. *Journal of Clinical Psychiatry, 60*(4), 213–214.

Chapter 9

Residential Treatment for Dually Diagnosed Homeless Veterans

A Comparison of Program Types

Wesley J. Kasprow, Ph.D., M.P.H.
Robert Rosenheck, M.D.
Linda Frisman, Ph.D.
Diane DiLella, M.P.H.

This study compared two types of residential programs that treat dually diagnosed homeless veterans. Programs specializing in the treatment of substance abuse disorders (SA) and those programs addressing both psychiatric disorders and substance abuse problems within the same setting (DDX) were compared on (1) program characteristics, (2) clients' perceived environment, and (3) outcomes of treatment. The study was based on surveys and discharge reports from residential treatment facilities that were under contract to the Department of Veterans Affairs Health Care for Homeless Veterans program, a national outreach and case management program operating at 71 sites across the nation. Program characteristics surveys were completed by program administrators, perceived environment surveys were completed by veterans in treatment, and discharge reports were completed by VA case managers. DDX programs were characterized by lower expectations for functioning, more acceptance of problem behavior, and more accommodation for choice and privacy, relative to SA programs after adjusting for baseline differences. Dually diagnosed veterans in DDX programs perceived these programs as less controlling than SA programs, but also as having lower involvement and less practical and personal problem orientations. At discharge, a lower percentage of veterans from DDX than SA programs left without staff consultation. A higher percentage of veterans from DDX than SA programs were discharged

to community housing rather than to further institutional treatment. Program
effects were not different for psychotic and non-psychotic veterans. Although
differences were modest, integration of substance abuse and psychiatric treat-
ment may promote a faster return to community living for dually diagnosed
homeless veterans. Such integration did not differentially benefit dually diag-
nosed veterans whose psychiatric problems included a psychotic disorder.
(American Journal on Addictions 1999; 8:34–43)

Dual diagnosis refers to the concurrent presence of a major psychiatric disorder and substance abuse disorder in the same individual. Historically, dually diagnosed individuals have been among the most difficult to treat of patient populations. Dual diagnosis has been associated with less compliance with treatment, a higher rate of treatment failures, and more adverse life outcomes. A substantial percentage of dually diagnosed individuals experience episodes of homelessness.[1]

Recent reviews have suggested that treatment systems must be modified to accommodate dual diagnosis patients. Historically, treatment of substance abuse and psychiatric illness have been implemented independently, with separate and sometimes conflicting philosophies and procedures. For example, substance abuse treatment has emphasized personal responsibility, abstinence, and confrontation of denial about substance use. Treatment of psychiatric illness, in contrast, has emphasized support, empathy, and pharmacological treatment.[2] Integration of substance abuse and psychiatric treatment in a single setting or clinical team have been suggested to minimize conflicting treatment goals.[2,3] In homeless individuals, assistance with housing dually diagnosed individuals have better outcomes (fewer days institutionalized, more days housed) following integrated psychiatric, substance abuse, and housing treatment.[3] Integrated treatment models may be especially important for those dually diagnosed patients who have psychotic disorders because they are least able to tolerate confrontive treatment.[4]

The present study investigated programmatic differences that are indicative of service integration in residential treatment of homeless dually diagnosed individuals. Specifically, we analyzed data from residential placements contracted by the Department of Veterans Affairs Health Care for Homeless Veterans (HCHV) program, which places approximately 3000 veterans a year.[5] Focusing on the difficult-to-treat dually diagnosed population, the present study compared treatment and outcome in residential-treatment facilities that specialize in substance abuse treatment and those that specialize in the combined treatment of both psychiatric and substance abuse disorders. First, these two nominal program types were described and compared using a survey completed by program administrators. Second, client perception of treatment environment in these two program types was compared via a survey of the dually diagnosed homeless veterans served by those facilities. Third, the program types were compared on several measures of the course of residential treatment and outcome at the time of discharge. The overall purpose of these comparisons was to assess whether dually diagnosed veterans benefit from incorporation of psychiatric treatment along with substance abuse treatment in the mission of residential treatment facilities. In particular, it was hypothesized that such integrated treatment would be particularly beneficial for those veterans who have a psychotic disorder and therefore are most in need of specialized integrated care.

METHODS

Study Samples

Programs. Programs were categorized on the basis of responses to a survey of residential treatment facilities that was conducted in 1996. During the period of data collection, 185 residential treatment facilities were under contract with the Veterans Health Administration (VHA). Administrators of these facilities were asked to complete a survey of policy and service characteristics, the Program and Services Characteristics Inventory (see below).[6] One hundred twenty-four (67%) facilities returned surveys. An item on the questionnaire asked the administrator to list the program type as (1) substance abuse, (2) psychiatric, (3) both substance abuse and psychiatric, or (4) other. The current analyses focused on the 43 programs that described themselves as "substance abuse" (SA) and 56 programs which described themselves as "both substance use and psychiatric" (DDX). (There were too few "psychiatric" ($n = 15$) and "other" ($n = 10$) programs to be included in the analyses). While the initial categorization of the programs was based on a single item, these programs were different along a variety of dimensions. Program differences are described in more detail below.

Perceived Environment Survey. A survey of perceived environment was conducted using the Community Oriented Perceived Environment Survey (see below).[7,8]

The client sample included 385 dually diagnosed veterans served by the facilities described above. Designation of dual diagnosis was made on the basis of a clinical assessment completed at the time of the veteran's entry to the program. Veterans who were diagnosed as having serious psychiatric problems (mood disorder, PTSD, schizophrenia, or other psychotic disorder) and a concurrent substance abuse disorder (alcohol or drug dependency/abuse) were included. The demographic characteristics of the survey sample are presented in the left panel of Table 9.1. These characteristics reflect the high level of psychiatric and substance abuse problems as well as severe economic disadvantage faced by these veterans.

Treatment Outcomes at Discharge. The sample for analysis of residential treatment outcomes included all dually diagnosed veterans discharged from the programs described in previous sections during 1995 and 1996 ($n = 1495$). The same definition of dual diagnosis was used. The demographic characteristics of this sample for the two program types are shown in the right panel of Table 9.1.

TABLE 9.1. Veteran Characteristics: Survey and Residential
Treatment Samples

	Survey Additional Res.		Treatment a	
Variable	SA ($n = 144$)	DDX ($n = 196$)	SA ($n = 388$)	DDX ($n = 755$)
Age (m ± sd)	43.3 ± 7.4	43.9 ± 7.6	42.6 ± 7.1	43.3 ± 7.0
Female (%)	0.7	3.0	4.3	1.3*
Black (%)	58.3	40.1*	50.5	42.4*
Hispanic (%)	0.7	7.8*	4.2	4.3
White (%)	41.0	50.5	43.7	51.5*
Other (%)	0.0	1.5	1.3	1.1
In 30 days prior to intake: (m ± sd):				
Days Worked	3.8 ± 6.8	2.4 ± 5.3*	3.3 ± 6.5	2.7 ± 5.9
Days Housed	7.4 ± 10.5	6.9 ± 10.8	7.6 ± 11.2	7.1 ± 10.8
Days Homeless	14.0 ± 12.8	17.4 ± 12.9*	15.2 ± 12.6	15.7 ± 12.6
Days Institutionalized	8.6 ± 11.5	5.6 ± 9.9*	7.1 ± 11.0	7.1 ± 10.7
Receive Public Support (%)	32.6	37.2	45.1	46.1
Combat Experience (%)	29.9	38.3	31.0	31.1
Dx of Alcohol Abuse/ Dependency (%)	90.3	90.8	86.1	89.5
Previous Hosp for Alcoholism (%)	79.2	70.4*	74.7	69.9
ASI Alcohol Scale (m ± sd)	0.25 ± 0.33	0.24 ± 0.33	0.28 ± 0.35	0.21 ± 0.30*
Dx of Drug Abuse/ Dependency (%)	76.4	60.7*	70.9	63.4*
Previous Hosp for Drug Dependency (%)	65.7	52.1	63.6	53.6*
ASI Drug Scale (m ± sd)	0.17 ± 0.28	0.10 ± 0.21*	0.16 ± 0.27	0.09 ± 0.19*
Both Alcohol and Drug Dependent (%)	66.7	51.5*	57.0	53.0
Dx of Mood Disorder (%)	84.7	76.5	77.8	75.8
Dx of PTSD (%)	16.7	25.5*	23.2	20.1
Dx of Psychotic Disorder (%)	8.3	14.3	12.6	22.0*
Multiple Psyc Dx (%)	9.7	16.3	12.6	16.7
ASI Psych Scale (m ± sd)	0.41 ± 0.22	0.46 ± 0.21*	0.41 ± 0.22	0.47 ± 0.22*

Notes: a = Veterans discharged from Residential Treatment survey facilities who did not take the survey.
* $p < .05$

Measures and Data Collection

Program Characteristics. Service providers completed a modified version of the Policy and Service Characteristics Inventory (PASCI).[6] The PASCI is a 140-item survey that forms nine subscales as follows:

1. Expectation for Functioning, which assesses minimum physical and psychological functioning that is necessary for admission to the program;
2. Acceptance of Problem Behavior, which assesses the extent to which uncooperative, aggressive, or other problem behavior is tolerated;
3. Policy Choice, which reflects the extent to which the program provides options from which residents can select individual patterns of daily living;
4. Resident Control, which measures the extent of formal structures that enable residents to influence program policies;
5. Policy Clarity, which measures the extent to which program policies are communicated clearly through formal mechanisms;
6. Provision for Privacy, which assesses the amount of privacy given to residents;
7. Availability of Health and Treatment Services;
8. Availability of Daily Living Assistance, which measures assistance with tasks like money management or grooming; and
9. Availability of Social-Recreational Activities, such as exercise or movies.[6]

In addition to these nine subscales, an additional scale of Substance Abuse Regulations was formed.

Perceived Environment. Veterans in the survey sample completed the Community-Oriented Program Environment Scale (COPES).[7,8] This well-validated 100-item instrument consists of 10 scales of perceived environment:

1. Involvement, which rates how active members are in the day-to-day functioning of the program;
2. Support, which rates how much members help and support each other, and how supportive the staff is toward members;
3. Spontaneity, which assesses how much the program encourages the open expression of feelings by members and staff;
4. Autonomy, which measures how self-sufficient and independent members are in decision making and how much they are encouraged to take leadership in the program;
5. Practical Orientation, which assesses the degree to which members learn practical skills and are prepared for release from the program;
6. Personal Problem Orientation, which measures the extent to which members are encouraged to understand their feelings and personal problems;
7. Anger and Aggression, which measures how much members argue with each other and with staff, become openly angry, and display aggressive behavior;
8. Order and Organization, which rates how important order and organization are in the program;
9. Program Clarity, which rates the extent to which members know what to expect in the day-to-day routine of the program and the explicitness of program rules and procedures; and

10. Staff Control, the extent to which the staff uses measures to keep members under necessary controls.

Veterans completed the COPES individually approximately two weeks following admission to the program. Data collection was coordinated by VA case managers. Survey results were collected during the calendar year 1996.

Background Characteristics and Residential Treatment Outcomes. Veteran background characteristics and clinical diagnoses were collected at the time of intake to the HCHV program in a structured interview conducted by trained program clinicians (predominantly social workers and nurses). Demographic characteristics included gender, ethnicity, military history, economic situation, and length of homelessness. The interview also included a section to record clinical psychiatric diagnoses based on *DSM-IV* criteria.[9] These diagnoses were derived from unstructured assessments and were therefore based on clinical judgment.

Measures of each veteran's participation in residential treatment were taken from discharge reports completed by the veterans' case managers. These measures included: (1) length of stay, (2) discharge status (successful discharge, discharge for rule violations, leaving the program without staff consultation), (3) housing status at discharge, (4) employment status at discharge, (5) clinical improvement in the areas of alcohol, drug, psychiatric, and social-vocational problems (improved/not improved rating by case manager), and (6) arrangements for follow-up treatment in these same areas.

Data Analysis

The purpose of statistical analyses was to assess differences across program types, as well as the differential outcomes by program type, for dually diagnosed veterans with and without a psychotic disorder. Therefore, the independent variable of interest in all analyses was program type (dummy variable coded 1 for SA program, 0 for DDX program), and an interaction term for program type and psychotic disorder (intake diagnosis of schizophrenia or other psychotic disorder) was included in all models, along with a main effect term for psychotic disorder. Linear multiple regression analyses were conducted on the PASCI and COPES scale scores, and on continuous measures of residential treatment (length of stay). Logistic regression was conducted on dichotomous (yes/no) measures of residential treatment participation (successful discharge from program; housed at discharge; employed at discharge; improved on alcohol, drug, psychiatric and social/vocational problems; follow-up arrangements made for alcohol, drug, psychiatric, and social/vocational problems). All models included several covariates: gender (coded 1 for females), age at time of interview (continuous), and ethnicity (separate dummy variables coded 1 for African American and Hispanic). Other control variables were included in the model for each dependent variable based on statistical significance following backward selection. Candidates for inclusion were: currently married, receiving public support payments, and previous combat experience (all dichotomous); days homeless, days institutionalized, and days worked within the last month before intake (all continuous); abbreviated ASI scores for alcohol use, drug abuse, and psychiatric symptoms (all continuous); veteran's report of alcohol dependence problems, drug dependence problems, and psychiatric problems (all dichotomous), prior hospitalization for alcohol dependence, drug dependence, or psychiatric problems (all dichotomous); and clinician rating of any of several psychiatric disorders (all dichotomous).

RESULTS

Characteristics of SA and DDX Program Types

There were several programmatic differences between nominal SA and DDX program types. As expected, a higher percentage of SA programs than DDX programs listed their primary treatment population as alcohol and drug abusers (66% vs. 35%). Almost half of DDX programs (49%) listed the mentally ill or homeless as their primary populations (as compared to 17% of the SA programs). While the majority of SA programs (69%) listed the Twelve-Step model as their primary treatment philosophy, only 28% of DDX programs did so. A greater percentage of DDX programs listed the Psychosocial Rehabilitation (34%) or Therapeutic Community model (19%) as their primary treatment philosophy.

A comparison of SA and DDX programs on policy and service characteristics scores from the PASCI is presented in Table 9.2. With respect to resident functioning, SA programs were higher than DDX programs on Expectations for Functioning and lower than DDX programs on Acceptance of Problem Behavior. With respect to program structures that relate to residents' individual freedom, SA programs were characterized by less policy choice and fewer provisions for

TABLE 9.2. Policy and Service Characteristics of Residential Treatment Facilities

PASCI Scale	SA ($n = 34$)	DDX ($n = 29$)	t value	prob t
Expect High Functioning	77.6	61.0	2.42	0.02
Accept Problem Behavior	22.8	40.0	3.01	0.0038
Policy Choice	37.9	52.4	4.12	0.0001
Resident Control	55.6	54.7	0.25	ns
Policy Clarity	75.2	76.5	0.36	ns
Provision for Privacy	36.8	51.0	3.38	0.002
Avail. Soc/Rec Activities	47.9	52.1	0.66	ns
Assist w/ Daily Living	47.9	54.1	1.10	ns
Avail. of Health Serv.	55.2	47.4	1.97	.051
SA Regulations	75.9	65.7	1.40	ns

privacy for residents. Provision of services was generally comparable between the two programs, with somewhat higher Availability of Health and Treatment Services scores at SA programs. Thus, as reported by program staff, SA and DDX programs were different along a variety of dimensions, as would be expected, given the different primary treatment populations. The differences observed in the present study are generally consistent with Timko's[6] comparison of substance abuse and psychiatric facilities using the PASCI.

Veterans' Perception of Treatment Environment

Mean COPES scales for the program types, and a test of program differences controlling for veteran characteristics, are presented in Table 9.3. Where differences between programs existed, SA programs generally scored higher. For example, SA programs had higher Involvement scores than DDX programs. The most consistent differences were along what Moos and Otto[8] have called the "Personal Growth" dimension: SA programs score higher on the Practical Orientation, Personal Problem Orientation, and Anger & Aggression scales. Likewise, Staff Control was higher in the SA programs.

Results from the COPES suggest that SA programs are perceived differently than DDX programs by the veterans served by them. As expected, SA programs are more controlling and problem oriented, involving increased expression of anger. Differences were observed even when controlling for veteran characteristics such as substance abuse and psychiatric symptom severity.

Residential Treatment Stays

Table 9.4 shows the results of regression analyses of the effects of program type, psychotic disorder, and the interaction of these variables on measures of residen-

TABLE 9.3. Veteran Report of Perceived Treatment Environment

Scale (m B sd)	SA ($n = 144$)	DDX ($n = 196$)	t value	prob t
Involvement	7.8 ± 2.4	6.3 ± 2.9	4.26	0.0001
Support	7.6 ± 2.3	7.5 ± 2.4	0.23	ns
Spontaneity	5.6 ± 2.0	5.8 ± 2.0	0.89	ns
Autonomy	5.1 ± 1.5	5.4 ± 1.6	1.30	ns
Practical Orientation	7.4 ± 2.2	6.8 ± 2.4	1.98	0.048
Personal Problem Orientation	7.0 ± 2.5	5.3 ± 2.7	4.43	0.0001
Anger & Aggression	4.9 ± 2.1	3.8 ± 2.1	4.20	0.0001
Order	8.2 ± 2.0	7.7 ± 2.2	1.87	.06
Policy Clarity	7.0 ± 1.9	7.1 ± 2.4	0.59	ns
Staff Control	7.5 ± 1.2	6.6 ± 1.6	5.13	0.0001

Note: Covariates for each measure differ, see text for full list.

TABLE 9.4. Measures of Residential Treatment

Measure	SA ($n = 538$) (m B sd) or %	DDX ($n = 957$) (m B sd) or %	Regression Model Effects		
			Program Type F or $x2$	Psychotic Dx F or $x2$	Interaction F or $x2$
Length of Stay			0.23	2.98	2.25
Psychotic	57.2 ± 47.9	70.4 ± 58.0			
Non-psychotic	73.4 ± 51.1	73.4 ± 57.8			
Status of Discharge					
Successful			0.00	5.05*	0.39
Psychotic	32.8	37.8			
Non-psychotic	49.1	49.1			
Rule Violation			1.17	9.32**	1.34
Psychotic	16.4	28.0			
Non-psychotic	15.6	17.6			
Left Without Consult			7.00**	0.49	0.06
Psychotic	32.8	22.3			
Non-psychotic	26.5	21.0			
Housed at Discharge			22.12***	7.46**	0.12
Psychotic	22.9	31.1			
Non-psychotic	29.9	43.1			
Discharged to Institution			28.29***	1.92	0.25
Psychotic	39.3	29.0			
Non-psychotic	38.3	23.7			
Employed at Discharge			0.00	5.72*	1.77
Psychotic	36.1	24.9			
Non-psychotic	48.0	46.2			
Clinical Improvement					
Alcohol Probs			0.05	5.20*	0.00
Psychotic	63.6	63.2			
Non-psychotic	74.4	74.6			
Drug Probs			0.51	6.69**	0.01
Psychotic	65.1	62.7			
Non-psychotic	75.9	75.0			
Psych Probs			0.11	2.74	0.58
Psychotic	61.2	66.3			
Non-psychotic	74.0	75.4			
Soc/Voc Probs			35.72***	0.21	0.43
Psychotic	47.8	61.3			
Non-psychotic	41.4	61.9			
Follow-up Treatment					
Alcohol Probs			3.95*	1.11	0.27
Psychotic	78.2	80.1			
Non-psychotic	78.1	82.8			
Drug Probs			5.48*	0.66	0.01
Psychotic	76.4	82.0			
Non-psychotic	78.8	84.7			

(Continued)

TABLE 9.4. Continued

Measure	SA (n = 538) (m B sd) or %	DDX (n = 957) (m B sd) or %	Regression Model Effects		
			Program Type F or $x2$	Psychotic Dx F or $x2$	Interaction F or $x2$
Psych Probs			6.17*	0.00	1.31
Psychotic	85.7	85.6			
Non-psychotic	77.6	85.1			
Soc/Voc Probs			56.89***	4.10*	1.03
Psychotic	69.6	81.9			
Non-psychotic	43.9	69.9			

Notes: A separate regression analysis was conducted for each measure. Covariates for each measure differ; see text for full list.
* $p < .05$ ** $p < .01$ *** $p < .001$

tial treatment participation. The primary focus of these analyses was the comparison of program types. A secondary focus was the assessment of differential outcomes by program type across veteran subgroups that were based on the presence or absence of a psychotic disorder at intake.

Length of stay did not differ between the program types, and both program types had a similar percentage of successful discharges. However, SA programs had a higher percentage of veterans leave the program without consulting the staff. There were no interactions of program type and psychotic disorder on these measures of status of discharge.

Housing outcomes were also different for the two programs. A higher percentage of veterans in DDX programs were in independent housing after discharge, while a higher percentage of veterans in SA programs were discharged to another institutional setting for further treatment. There was no difference between program types on employment measures. Veterans with a psychotic disorder had worse outcomes on several of these measures; however, there was no interaction between program type and psychotic disorder on these residential treatment outcomes.

Judgments of clinical improvement were generally similar across the programs, with the exception of improvements in social/ vocational problems, which was higher in DDX programs. A higher percentage of clinicians indicated that follow-up arrangements for drug, psychiatric, and social/vocational problems had been made for veterans in DDX programs.

DISCUSSION

The purpose of the current study was to compare treatment of dually diagnosed veterans in programs that specialize in substance abuse treatment and in those that address both psychiatric disorders and substance abuse problems within the same treatment setting. These comparisons were conducted in two areas: perceived environment and residential treatment outcomes.

With respect to the first comparison, it is apparent that veterans in substance abuse treatment programs view those programs as more controlling and feel that more anger is expressed by staff and residents than do veterans in combined psychiatric and substance abuse programs. At the same time, veterans in substance abuse programs view those programs as having more of a skill-oriented, practical problem approach, and they feel more involved in program function than do veterans in combined psychiatric and substance abuse programs. These differences were observed even after accounting for veteran characteristics, including symptom severity. These findings are consistent with the widely acknowledged differences in treatment philosophies of substance use and psychiatric programs that motivated this study.[2] In the current study, the differences in perceived environment show that the nominal program types were indeed experienced differently by the veterans served by them.

With respect to the second comparison, our results suggest somewhat better outcomes for these dually diagnosed veterans when treatment occurs in DDX programs; however, the differences are relatively modest. Specifically, veterans placed in DDX treatment programs were less likely to leave the program without staff consultation. They were also less likely to be discharged to another treatment setting and more likely to be discharged to independent housing, relative to veterans placed in specialized SA treatment programs. These results suggest better compliance in DDX programs as well as a faster return to independent community living. Yet, other basic outcomes, including employment at discharge and clinical improvement, were similar across the two program types (the sole exception being a greater improvement in social/vocational problems for those veterans treated in DDX programs).

Methodological limitations of the study must be noted. While our sample size was reasonably large and several differences for both program type and psychotic disorder were found, the outcome measures used were based on single-item ratings at time of discharge from the residential program. These measures may have been too coarse to detect changes in some of the areas addressed by this study (e.g., clinical improvement) compared to explicit measures taken at both baseline and discharge. Additionally, the current study does not address long-term outcomes. We doubt, however, that these methodological limitations affected the validity of our observations.

While our program characteristics and perceived environment results support the validity of the distinction between the nominal program types described here, it should be noted that all of the veterans in the current study were receiving comprehensive case management by HCHV staff. Thus, even those individuals in the specialized substance abuse programs had someone to facilitate connection to services other than those received in the residential program. The treatment of veterans in this study therefore may have been "integrated" to some degree, regardless of program type. This may have minimized differences in the current study.

The implementation of effective community based treatment models for dually diagnosed individuals is essential, particularly in public sector health care systems like VHA. There has been a substantial reduction in the availability of inpatient care for psychiatric and substance abuse problems recently, and this trend is likely to continue.[10] The current results provide limited endorsement for the integration of psychiatric and substance abuse as a desirable feature of such models.

REFERENCES

1. Minkoff. L., & Drake, R. E. (1991). *Dual diagnosis of major mental illness and substance abuse disorder: New directions for mental health services*. San Francisco: Jossey-Bass.
2. Ries, R. (1993). Clinical treatment matching models for dually diagnosed patients. *Psychiatric Clinics of North America, 16,* 167–175.
3. Drake, R. E., Yovetich, N. A., Bebout, R. R., et al. (1997). Integrated treatment for dually diagnosed homeless adults. *Journal of Nervous and Mental Diseases, 185,* 298–305.
4. Osher, F. C., & Kofoed L. L. (1989). Treatment of patients with psychiatric and psychoactive substance abuse disorders. *Hospital and Community Psychiatry, 40,* 1025–1030.
5. Kasprow, W. J., Rosenheck, R., & Chapdelaine, J. (1997). *Health care for homeless veterans programs: The tenth annual report*. West Haven, CT: Northeast Program Evaluation Center.
6. Timko, C. (1995). Policies and services in residential substance abuse programs: Comparisons with psychiatric programs. *Journal of Substance Abuse, 7,* 43–59.
7. Moos, R. (1988). *Community-oriented programs environment scale manual*. Palo Alto, CA: Consulting Psychologists Press Inc.
8. Moos, R., & Otto, J. (1972). The community-oriented programs environment scale: A methodology for the facilitation and evaluation of social change. *Community Mental Health Journal, 8,* 28–37.
9. American Psychiatric Association. (1994). *Diagnostic and statistical manual of mental disorders* (4th ed.). Washington, DC: Author.
10. Rosenheck, R., & DiLella, D. (1998). National Mental Health Program performance monitoring system: Fiscal Year 1997 Report. West Haven, CT: Northeast Program Evaluation Center.

Chapter 10

Psychotherapies for Adolescent Substance Abusers

15-Month Follow-Up of a Pilot Study

Yifrah Kaminer, M.D.
Joseph A. Burleson, Ph.D.

In order to test the hypothesis that adolescent substance abusers could be matched to effective treatments on the basis of their comorbid psychopathology, 32 dually diagnosed adolescents were randomized into two short-term outpatient group psychotherapies: cognitive-behavioral treatment (CBT), and interactional treatment (IT). Two follow-up assessments were conducted at three and 15 months after planned treatment completion. As reported recently, at the three-month follow-up, no patient-treatment matching effects were identified. However, adolescents assigned to CBT demonstrated a significant reduction in severity of substance abuse compared to those assigned to IT. At 15-month follow-up, there were no differential improvements as a function of therapy type. However, subjects in general maintained significant treatment gains on the substance abuse, family function, and psychiatric status domains of the Teen-Addiction Severity Index (T-ASI), and both CBT and IT were associated with similar long-term gains. Large scale, randomized, controlled treatment studies are further recommended to examine the findings of this small-scale pilot study. (American Journal on Addictions 1999;8:114–119)

Few studies have examined treatment outcomes of substance use disorders (SUD) in adolescents compared to adults.[1,2] Cognitive-behavioral treatment (CBT) and interactional treatment (IT) have been utilized in the treatment of adult substance abusers.[3] The cognitive-behavioral perspective views substance abuse as a maladaptive way of coping with problems or meeting certain needs.[4] According to

this view, substance use involves a sequence of learned behaviors that are suscep-
tible to alteration (relapse prevention) through the application of behavior modi-
fication interventions.[5]

In contrast to relapse prevention approaches, IT is based on the work of
Yalom as adapted for use with groups of outpatient alcoholic patients.[6] The goal
was to explore participants' interpersonal relationships, foster insight, and regulate self-care, affect, and self-esteem as manifested in "here and now" interactions within the group.

Two significant adult studies compared CBT to IT in an outpatient group
setting. Stephens and colleagues conducted a randomized study comparing CBT
to IT in adults with primary marijuana dependence.[7] Both treatments resulted in
similar reductions of marijuana intake and related problems at 12-month follow-up.

Kadden and colleagues conducted a randomized patient-treatment matching
study comparing CBT to IT. Patients' characteristics were specified through matching variables on the basis of prior indications of their prognostic significance in
alcoholism: sociopathy and global psychopathology. CBT was seen to be more
effective for adult alcoholics higher in sociopathy, while IT was more effective
for subjects lower in sociopathy. Generally, both treatments appeared equally effective for patients lower in psychopathology, while 2-year follow-up data showed
durability for these matching effects.[8]

The purpose of this pilot study was to attempt to evaluate the generalizability
of Kadden's[3] patient-treatment matching effects at 3- and at 15-month posttreatment completion follow-up in dually diagnosed adolescents. The goal was to
evaluate potential matching effects of patient type and treatment type.

The study hypotheses were that:

1. the general efficacy of CBT and IT will be similar for adolescent substance
   abusers,
2. patients with externalizing disorders (e.g., disruptive disorders) will fare better in CBT, and
3. subjects with internalizing disorders (e.g., mood and anxiety disorders) without comorbid externalizing disorders will respond more favorably to IT.

This pilot study also examined the feasibility of manual guided group psychotherapies for adolescent substance abusers as well as therapist adherence and treatment discriminability (reported elsewhere).[9]

METHODS

Subjects

Thirty-two dually diagnosed consenting adolescents were randomized for treatment with an intent to treat design. Youths were recruited for an outpatient after-

care treatment from a partial hospitalization program (PHP). Inclusion criteria were: subjects ages 13–18 years and meeting *DSM-III-R* criteria[10] for psychoactive substance use disorders. Exclusion criteria were: required a more intensive treatment setting or menu, current acute psychosis, reading level and comprehension below sixth grade, refusal to consent for either randomization to treatment conditions or for session videotaping, no permanent address, and transportation difficulties for treatment program.

Of the 32 assigned to condition (nCBT = 17; nIT = 15), the baseline T-ASI was administered to all 32, with 29 providing complete data on all subscales and 31 on Alcohol and Drug subscales. Of these 32, 15 completed the treatment program (seven of 15 IT, and eight of 17 CBT, $x 2(1) = 0.00, p = .98$, as well as 10 of 20 males, five of 12 females, $x 2(1) = 0.21, p = .65$). Completion was defined as having completed a valid Baseline and End-of-Treatment assessment and being present at the final therapy session. Treatment type and gender were not significant, $x 2(1) = 1.01, p = .31$. Regardless of program completion status, 22 of the 32 original subjects completed the 3-month follow-up assessment procedures, while 14 completed the 15-month follow-up. Of the 22 who followed up at three months, eight were not interviewed at 15 months because of incarceration (one), having moved out of state (three), refusal (two), and failure to locate (two). Data of two adolescents who were interviewed at 15 months are not included in the data analysis because their baseline data could not be retrieved.

Instruments

Intake assessment battery included: the Diagnostic Interview Schedule for Children (DISC),[11] the Child Behavior Checklist (CBCL),[12] the Youth Self Report (YSR),[13] the Situational Confidence Questionnaire (SCQ),[14] The Teen Addiction Severity Index (T-ASI),[15,16] and the Teen Treatment Services Review (T-TSR).[17] The T-ASI, TTSR, and SCQ were also administered at 3- and 15-month follow-up. The T-ASI Chemical Scale, while listed as such in Table 10.1, was divided into its two subcomponents, an Alcohol and a Drug subscale, for purposes of this investigation. An operational definition of an internalizing disorder was that the subject had either anxiety disorder or depressive disorder as determined by the DISC. An operational definition of an externalizing disorder was that the subject had either attention deficit hyperactivity disorder or conduct disorder as determined by the DISC. The instruments as well as the CBT and IT manuals were recently described in the paper reporting the 3-month follow-up results.[18] The measurement of the differential treatment process between CBT and IT is being detailed elsewhere.[9]

Data Analysis

Hierarchical multiple regression was used to analyze the six T-ASI scales, each in a univariate manner. The original T-ASI substance abuse scale was split into an

TABLE 10.1. Baseline and 15-Month Follow-Up Means (and SDs)
on Teen-Addiction Severity Index Subscales for CBT and IT Subjects

Measure	CBT ($n = 5$)		IT ($n = 7$)		Total ($n = 12$)	
	Baseline	Follow-Up	Baseline	Follow-Up	Baseline	Follow-Up
Alcohol	1.40	0.86	1.71	1.86	1.58	1.36
	(1.67)	(0.90)	(1.25)	(1.35)	(1.38)	(1.22)
Drugs	1.70	1.00	2.43	1.86	2.13	1.43
	(1.20)	(1.15)	(0.53)	(1.57)	(0.91)	(1.40)
Chemical	3.10	1.86	4.14	3.71	3.71	2.79
	(2.61)	(2.04)	(1.35)	(2.50)	(1.94)	(2.39)
School	0.75	1.33	2.14	2.00	1.64	1.60
	(0.96)	(1.51)	(1.35)	(1.41)	(1.36)	(1.43)
Family	1.75	1.43	1.86	0.71	1.82	1.07
	(0.96)	(1.62)	(1.07)	(1.25)	(0.98)	(1.44)
Peer	1.00	0.29	1.57	0.57	1.36	0.43
	(1.41)	(0.49)	(0.98)	(0.53)	(1.12)	(0.51)
Legal	2.50	1.43	1.29	1.29	1.73	1.36
	(0.58)	(1.62)	(1.38)	(1.50)	(1.27)	(1.50)
Psychiatric	2.00	0.14	2.14	0.57	2.09	0.36
	(1.63)	(0.38)	(1.07)	(0.98)	(1.22)	(0.74)

Alcohol and a Drug subscale. After baseline T-ASI scores were entered first (in order to produce an analysis of change from baseline to follow-up), the demographic covariates (gender, age) were entered into the equations, followed by a dichotomous Completion status, then by individual difference measures (internalizing or externalizing), and finally by Treatment Type.

RESULTS

Alcohol

While there were no significant baseline, Treatment Group, or Gender main effects, there was a significant effect of Negative Affect, $F(1, 6) = 46.22$, $\Delta R^2 = .88$, $p < .001$—the higher Negative Affect, the lower the alcohol use. There was also a trend toward a Completion main effect, $F(1, 5) = 4.08$, $\Delta R2 = .05$, $p = .099$, such that those who completed treatment were somewhat higher on alcohol use. There was a trend toward a Treatment Group X Completion interaction, $F(1, 3) = 8.21$, $\Delta R2 = .04$, $p = .064$ (with too few subjects per cell for interpretation).

Psychiatric

While there were no significant baseline or Treatment Group main effects, there was a significant Gender effect, $F(1, 10) = 6.67$, $\Delta R2 = .40$, $p = .027$, such that girls showed higher psychiatric severity than boys at intake as well as at the two points of time in follow-up. There were no Completion or individual difference main effects, nor any interactions.

Peer

While there were no significant baseline nor Treatment Group main effects, there was a significant effect of Externalizing Disorders, $F (1, 8) = 6.03$, $\Delta R2 = .43$, $p = .04$, such that the higher the score on Externalizing, the higher the peer relations dysfunction. There were no Completion or Gender main effects, nor any interactions.

Other Subscales

There were no significant baseline, main, or interactive effects for T-ASI Drug, School, Legal, or Family subscales.

DISCUSSION

This pilot study combined feasibility and preliminary efficacy as its specific aims. Manual guided psychotherapies for adolescent substance abusers were tested, and therapists adherence and treatment discriminability were examined.[9] The pilot study hypotheses were that:

1. the general efficacy of CBT and IT will be similar for adolescent substance abusers,
2. patients with externalizing disorders (e.g., disruptive disorders) will fare better in CBT, and
3. subjects with internalizing disorders (e.g., mood and anxiety disorders) without comorbid externalizing disorders will respond more favorably to IT.

Overall, participants exhibited substantial pre-post treatment gains at 15-month follow-up, as measured by the T-ASI domains of substance abuse, family function, and psychiatric status. However, there were neither matching effects nor differential improvements as a function of psychopathology and therapy type, as reported in adult alcoholics by Kadden and colleagues[3] at treatment completion and by Cooney and colleagues[8] with the same cohort at 2-year follow-up.

The findings regarding the comparison between the long-term effectiveness of CBT to IT and 15-months are similar to those reported by Stephens and colleagues[7] in marijuana abusers at 12-month follow-up. In general, the treatment gains seen at 3-month are maintained (T-ASI Chemical and Family scales) or, on some scales, continue to show improvement (T-ASI Psychiatric and Peer scales), while on some scales, the changes from baseline to 3-month to 15-month were not appreciable (T-ASI Legal and School scales). The difference between the 3-month[18] and 15-month follow-up results could be attributed to CBT working sooner than IT because CBT substance focused (i.e., drug refusal skills) sessions constituted a more specific intervention for relapse prevention than did those of IT. At a follow-up period longer than three months, however, CBT superiority proved not to be enduring. Similarly, Hoffman and colleagues reported that the nature of psychosocial treatment provided to adult cocaine abusers did not have a differential impact on treatment outcome at 12-month follow-up.[19]

Our findings are also in the same direction of three groups of investigators who reported that delayed effects of psychotherapy in adult substance abusers may emerge from six months to a year after completion of treatment[20,21] and may be maintained even after two years of post-treatment follow-up.[22] Aside from the analysis of treatment effects, it is noteworthy that females were higher than males on psychiatric severity, as reported also at 3-month follow-up.[18]

The influence of comorbid psychopathology on treatment outcome has received increased attention.[2] Therefore, the persistent gender difference reported here regarding a higher severity of psychopathology among females, which is based on the evaluation of the global psychopathological impairment of the respondent according to the T-ASI, deserves further investigation, and its implications regarding treatment outcome should be probed in a larger sample.

Although this pilot study was not based on a large sample size, the resultant variance accounted for by the significant factors was quite high, in that significant findings from small studies reflect higher proportions of variance than from large studies. Several shortcomings of this pilot study should be considered in evaluating the results and in planning future studies.

These include a lack of control condition, such as Waiting List, No Treatment, Non Specific Treatment (Attention Group), or Minimal Treatment; a low follow-up rate; and lack of objective measures of urinalysis during the follow-up period. These limitations have been addressed in an ongoing study that includes a control group and aggressive retention and follow-up procedures.

CONCLUSION

To the best of our knowledge, this is the first study reporting long-term follow-up of the psychosocial treatment outcome of adolescent substance abusers. It is concluded that:

1. treatment positively impacted post-treatment gains;
2. manual guided CBT has a potential as an effective short-term intervention for adolescents in an outpatient group setting; and
3. both CBT and IT were associated with similar long-term gains.

Large scale, randomized, controlled treatment studies are further recommended to examine the findings of this small-scale, feasibility, and preliminary efficacy pilot study and to explore the potential importance of patient-treatment matching effects in adolescents.

ACKNOWLEDGMENTS

This study was supported by grants from NIDA DA00262-01 (Dr. Kaminer) and P50 DA09241-02 (Dr. Rounsaville).

REFERENCES

1. Catalano, R. F., Hawkins, J. D., Well, E. A., et al. (1990–91). Evaluation of the effectiveness of adolescent drug abuse treatment, assessment of risks for relapse, and promising approaches for relapse prevention. *International Journal of Addictions, 25,* 1085 –1130.
2. Kaminer, Y. (1994). *Adolescent substance abuse: A comprehensive guide to theory and Practice.* New York: Plenum.
3. Kadden, R. M., Cooney, N. L., Getter, H., et al. (1989). Matching alcoholics to coping skills or interactional therapies: Posttreatment results. *Journal of Consulting and Clinical Psychology, 57,* 698 –704.
4. Mackay, P. W., Donovan, D. M., & Marlatt, G. A. (1991). Cognitive and behavioral approaches to alcohol abuse. In R. J. Frances & S. I. Miller (Eds.), *Clinical textbook of addictive disorders* (pp. 452–481). New York: Guilford.
5. Marlat, G. A., & Gordon, J. R. (Eds.). (1985). *Relapse prevention.* New York: Guilford.
6. Brown, S., & Yalom, I. D. (1977). Interactional group therapy with alcoholics. *Journal of Studies on Alcohol, 38,* 426–456.
7. Stephens, R. S., Roffman, R. A., & Simpson, E. E. (1994). Treating adult marijuana dependence: A test of the relapse prevention model. *Journal of Consulting and Clinical Psychology, 62,* 92–99.
8. Cooney, N. L., Kadden, R. M., Litt, M. D., et al. (1991). Matching alcoholics to coping skills or interactional therapies: Two-year follow-up results. *Journal of Consulting and Clinical Psychology, 59,* 598–601.
9. Kaminer, Y., Blitz, C., Burleson, J. A., et al. (1998). Measuring treatment process in cognitive-behavioral and interactional group therapies for adolescent substance abusers. *Journal of Nervous and Mental Diseases, 186,* 407-413.
10. American Psychiatric Association. (1987). *Diagnostic and statistical manual of mental disorders* (3rd ed.) Washington, DC: Author.
11. Fisher, P. W., Shaffer, D., Piacentini, J. C., et al. (1993). Sensitivity of the Diagnostic Interview Schedule for Children (2nd ed.) (DISC-2.1) for specific diagnoses in children and adolescents. *Journal of the American Academy of Child and Adolescent Psychiatry, 32,* 666–673.
12. Achenbach, T. M., & Edelbrock, C. S. (1983). *Manual for the Child Behavior Checklist and Revised Child Behavior Profile.* Burlington, VT: University of Vermont, Department of Psychiatry.
13. Achenbach, T. M., & Edelbrock, C. S. (1987). *Manual for Youth Self Report and Profile.* Burlington, VT: University of Vermont, Department of Psychiatry.

14. Annis, H. M. (1987). *Situational Confidence Questionnaire (SCQ-39)*. Toronto: Addiction Research Foundation.

15. Kaminer, Y., Bukstein, O. G., & Tarter, T. E. (1991). The Teen Addiction Severity Index: Rationale and reliability. *International Journal of Addictions, 26,* 219–226.

16. Kaminer, Y., Wagner, E., Plummer, B., et al. (1993). Validation of the Teen Addiction Severity Index: Preliminary findings. *American Journal on Addictions, 2,* 221–224.

17. Kaminer, Y., Blitz, C., Burleson, J. A., et al. (1998). The Teen Treatment Services Review (T-TSR): Rationale and reliability. *Journal of Substance Abuse Treatment, 15,* 291–300.

18. Kaminer, Y., Burleson, J. A., Blitz, C., et al. (1998). Psychotherapies for adolescent substance abuse: A pilot study. *Journal of Nervous and Mental Diseases, 186,* 684–690.

19. Hoffman, J. A., Caudill, B. D., Koman, J. J., et al. (1996). Psychosocial treatments for cocaine abuse: 12-month treatment outcomes. *Journal of Substance Abuse Treatment, 13,* 3–11.

20. Carroll, K. M., Rounsaville, B. J., Nich, C., et al. (1994). One year follow up of psychotherapy and pharmacotherapy for cocaine dependence. *Archives of General Psychiatry, 51,* 989–997.

21. Woody, G. E., McLellan, A. T., Luborsky, L., et al. (1995). Psychotherapy in community methadone programs: A validation study. *American Journal of Psychiatry, 152,* 1302–1308.

22. Jerreli, J. M., & Ridgely, M. S. (1995). Comparative effectiveness of three approaches to serving people with severe mental illness and substance abuse disorders. *Journal of Nervous and Mental Diseases, 183,* 566–576.

Chapter 11

The Links Between Alcohol, Crime and the Criminal Justice System

Explanations, Evidence and Interventions

Susan E. Martin, Ph.D.

*Many studies indicate that alcohol abuse and dependence are closely linked
with the criminal justice system (CJS). Alcohol was consumed prior to about
half of all homicides and assaults, and nearly 40 percent of state prisoners
report committing their current offense under the influence of alcohol. Alcohol abuse cost approximately $13 billion in 1992 non-health related costs.
This article seeks to address this burden on the CJS and society. It presents a
conceptual framework for explaining the alcohol-crime nexus, reviews empirical evidence of the complex associations between alcohol consumption
and crime, and links these with promising intervention strategies to reduce
alcohol-related crime.* (American Journal on Addictions 2001;10:136–158)

Hundreds of articles and studies have shown that alcohol abuse is closely associated with violent and other criminal offenses. For example, alcohol was found to
have been used in more than half of homicides and assaults,[1] about 40% of violent
offenders in state and local jails in the United States had been drinking at the time
of the offense for which they have been incarcerated,[2] and about a quarter of state
prisoners were found to be alcohol dependent.[3] Nevertheless, there is a gap between alcohol-related research on crime, violence, and the criminal justice system and other research addressing these issues. The former seeks to determine
whether the association of alcohol and violence is causal or models the mechanisms through which alcohol affects criminal behavior. Other alcohol researchers
evaluate interventions designed to delay the onset or reduce the amount of drinking

(particularly among youth), with little attention to the broader impact of these programs. Criminal justice system (CJS) research, conversely, largely ignores the contributions of alcohol. Rather, it emphasizes the connection between illicit drugs and crime or describes the drug-related treatment needs in the offender population. Consequently, important issues related to assessing and reducing the burden of alcohol-related crime often are not addressed by either the criminal justice or public health communities, and there is limited communication and cooperation between them.

This article seeks to bridge that gap. In the first section, the scope and costs of alcohol-related crime and offenders' alcohol dependence are briefly noted. These data clearly indicate the heterogeneous nature of alcohol-related crimes and their perpetrators and victims, and thus the need for a wide range of interventions to address these problems. The next section provides a conceptual framework for examining the multiple factors that may contribute to an incident of alcohol-related crime. Because most drinking does not result in crime or violence and most criminal offenses involve persons that have not consumed alcohol, there does not appear to be a single or simple direct pharmacological effect of alcohol that "causes" alcohol-related crime. Rather, multiple factors at several levels of analysis are involved in a variety of combinations. The framework identifies and links these factors, including the characteristics of the individual (i.e., physical, psychological, attitudinal, and social factors) as these interact with the effects of alcohol in a specific drinking context. These in turn are located within and influenced by the larger societal and cultural context. Based on this conceptual framework, the next section explores the empirical evidence supporting the diverse associations between drinking and crime. It reviews research focused primarily on the association of alcohol with violent crime and explores how the pharmacological effects of alcohol might increase the likelihood of aggression by interacting with personal, situational, and cultural factors in which drinking occurs. The final section identifies promising intervention strategies and specific programs that might reduce and prevent alcohol-related crime, based on the conceptual model and research findings. It also suggests additional research on the alcohol-crime nexus that may serve as a basis for the next generation of interventions.

Given the number of reviews of the vast literature on alcohol and aggression and/or violence (the form of behavior most closely associated with crime),[1,4-8] these will not be duplicated here. Instead, the present article focuses on linking these findings with their implications for interventions, drawing on findings from a wide variety of disciplines and methodologies.

THE CRIMINAL JUSTICE SYSTEM'S BURDEN OF ALCOHOL ABUSE AND DEPENDENCE

Several recent reports make clear the enormous burden of alcohol abuse and dependence on the criminal justice system. That burden arises both from high rates of intoxication at the time of the offense (including many offenses that probably would not otherwise have occurred if the offender, victim, or both had not been drinking) and from high rates of alcohol dependence among criminal offenders. The burden of alcohol includes costs incurred by victims, by offenders and their families, and by the larger society, including the criminal justice system expenses.

The Extent of Alcohol Involvement in Crime and Use of Alcohol by Criminal Offenders

Many studies have documented offenders' use of alcohol prior to the offense. For example, the National Crime Victimization Survey (NCVS) is an ongoing survey of a nationally representative sample of households in the United States. Based on aggregated NCVS data from 1993 through 1998, a recent report indicates that about one quarter of the approximately 10 million annual victims of violent crime perceive their offenders to have been drinking. This includes 26% of incidents where the offender used alcohol only, 7% where the offender was under the influence of both alcohol and other drugs, and 2% where the victim knew the offender to be under the influence but was unsure if the offender was using alcohol, another drug, or both. In contrast, victims reported that their assailant was solely under the influence of other drugs in only 8% of the incidents, and the remaining 60% were not believed to be using alcohol or drugs.[9] Even the presence of alcohol in about one third of violent offenses probably is an underestimate, because homicides, which are not included in the NCVS data, consistently show a higher proportion of alcohol involvement than less serious violent crimes.[1,5,7,8,10,11] There also is variation among these less serious offenses in the use of alcohol by offenders. Drinking offenders committed nearly 40% of the rapes or sexual assaults, more than a quarter of the aggravated and simple assaults, but only 16% of the robberies.[9]

Data compiled from surveys of adults on probation, inmates in local jails, and inmates in State and Federal correctional facilities indicate that 38% of the nearly 5.7 million convicted adult offenders under the jurisdiction of correctional authorities reported that they had been drinking at the time of the offense for which they were convicted. As shown in Table 11.1, this includes more than 40% of violent offenders, about one third of property offenders, a quarter of drug offenders, and more than half of public order offenders (including DWIs).[9]

Calculations of those offenders' blood alcohol concentrations (BACs) at the time of the offense, based on self-reports of the amount of alcohol consumed in the eight hours before their crime and the offender's weight, clearly indicate that most of the drinking offenders were quite intoxicated.[2] The average estimated BAC was 0.16 for probationers, 0.19 for jail inmates, and 0.27 for state prisoners. Interestingly, the BAC levels for property offenders were higher than those of violent offenders. The high BACs of the property offenders may have contributed to their apprehension for the crime (in contrast to the sober thieves who were less likely to be caught).

TABLE 11.1. Percent of Offenders Drinking at Time of Offense
by Offense Type

| Type of Offense | Percent of Offenders Drinking at the Time of Offense | | | |
| | Adults on Probation (N = 3,417,613) | Convicted Offenders in | | |
		Local Jails (N = 252,600)	State Prison (N = 1,178,978)	Federal Prison (N = 123,041)
All offenses	39.9%	39.5%	37.2%	20.4%
Violent	40.7%	40.6%	41.7%	24.5%
Murder	*	43.7	44.6	38.7
Rape/sexual assault	31.8	31.5	40.0	32.3
Robbery	*	37.6	37.4	18
Assault	45.5	45.6	45.1	46.0
Property	18.5%	32.8%	34.5%	15.6%
Burglary	38.5	38.2	37.2	*
Larceny	16.3	31.6	33.7	*
Fraud	9.7	21.6	25.2	10.4
Drug	16.3%	28.8%	27.4%	19.8%
Possession	14.4	28.6	29.6	21.3
Trafficking	16.2	28.4	25.5	19.4
Public order	75.1%	56.0%	43.2%	20.6%

*Too few cases for estimates to be made.
From Greenfeld, L. A. & Henneberg, M. A. Alcohol, crime, and the criminal justice system. Commissioned paper presented at Alcohol and Crime: Research and Practice for Prevention Conference, June 11–14, 2000.

Given these high BAC levels, it is not surprising that 24% of state prisoners were found to be alcohol dependent (i.e., gave three or four positive responses on the four-item CAGE screening instrument).[9]

Driving While Intoxicated (DWI): Arrestees and Offenders

Drunk driving often is considered a "junk" crime.[12] Nevertheless, in 1997, the nearly 1.5 million arrests for drunk driving or driving while intoxicated (i.e., DWI, the term that will be generically used for several alcohol-related driving offenses) accounted for about 10% of all police arrests nationwide. Although the number of DWI arrests has declined since peaking in 1983, the number of DWI offenders under correctional supervision has grown to an estimated 513,200 offenders in 1997. That year, DWI offenders accounted for nearly 14% of probationers, 7% of jail inmates, and 2% of state prisoners.[13]

Monetary Costs of Alcohol-Related Crime

The most recent estimate of the costs of crime attributed to alcohol abuse, based on 1992 data, is $12.8 billion. This includes total public expenditures of $6.2

billion for criminal justice system costs, including police protection, legal and judicial services, and correctional institutions at all levels of government. The remaining $6.6 billion in costs include lost productivity arising from offenders' reduced earnings due to incarceration and the costs to victims in the form of lost earnings, legal defense, and property damage. However, the figure does not include their medical costs and health consequences or the intangible costs from heightened fear of crime and changes in their quality of life.[14] Given the financial and other burdens that alcohol-related crime imposes on society, it is important to better understand the nature of the alcohol–crime connection in order to identify malleable targets and opportunities for intervention.

CONCEPTUAL FRAMEWORK FOR EXPLAINING THE ALCOHOL–CRIME CONNECTION

Despite ample evidence of the frequent association of alcohol consumption and criminal behavior, the ways in which drinking and crime are linked and the extent to which the association is a causal one is a matter of considerable debate. Disagreement over whether the alcohol-violence relationship is a causal one hinges, in part, on different meanings attributed to "causation." [4,8,10,11,15,16] In a meta-analysis of studies of alcohol and violence, despite evidence "consistent with a causal interpretation," Lipsey and colleagues conclude that "the causal issue is still cloudy and uncertain." [8 (p. 277)] In contrast, Room and Rossow[17] note that their epidemiological approach for attributing causality does not require a "main effect." Even in the absence of an overall causal association, there may be a causal relationship for some types of persons and/or in certain circumstances that need to be identified empirically. Fuller understanding of the relationship between alcohol consumption and crime, therefore, requires identifying those individuals, situations, and circumstances likely to increase the chance of violent or other criminal behaviors (i.e., mediators) and those that reduce their likelihood (i.e., moderators). It also requires examining how these factors interact with each other and the pharmacological effects of alcohol.

Figure 11.1 presents a multi-level framework for understanding the alcohol-crime connection, based on the model proposed by Graham and West.[18] In the figure, the outer dark rectangle represents the broad cultural context for drinking and criminal behavior. This includes sociocultural attitudes, expectations, and norms that shape how and how much people drink; how they behave when they drink; the frequency of crime; and the forms of social control over both drinking and crime, all of which vary across cultures.

Within any particular cultural or societal context, there remains wide variability in alcohol-related behavior, depending on the situational context in which drinking occurs. This is depicted in the figure by the nested smaller rectangle. For instance, people moderate their behavior depending on the norms of a particular drinking setting. Thus, the particular social and physical context within which people drink also affects behavior, including crime.

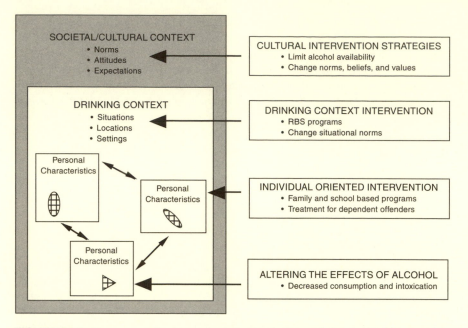

FIGURE 11.1. Factors contributing to alcohol-related crime and their implied intervention strategies. Graham, K., West, P., Alcohol and Crime. In N. Heather, T. J. Peters, T. Stockwell (Eds.), *Handbook of alcohol dependence and alcohol-related problems*. Sussex, England: John Wiley & Sons. In press. © John Wiley & Sons Limited. Reproduced with permission.

Within any given situation, location, or drinking context, the characteristics of individuals within that setting also affect whether crime will occur. As shown by the three smallest rectangles representing different individuals, people within a single drinking setting vary with respect to demographic characteristics, attitudes, expectations, and personality characteristics, such as impulsivity.

The effects of alcohol also play a role in that most people are likely to behave differently when intoxicated, as well as vary among themselves and intrapersonally under the effects of the same amount of alcohol depending on the situation or setting. The effects of alcohol interact with a person's characteristics and may affect the likelihood of the occurrence of a crime by altering his/her assessment of risks or judgment. In addition, as indicated by the double arrows between the individuals, alcohol-related violence involves the interaction of two or more individuals who act and react to each other within any given context.

In sum, the relationship between crime and alcohol is subject to many factors that operate simultaneously, although for any individual crime certain factors may contribute more than others. Based on this framework, the various aspects of drinking that may account for an increased likelihood of criminal behavior can be explored, and the avenues for intervening to prevent or treat this problem, which also are indicated on the right in the figure, can be explored.

The Effects of Alcohol

Where once a simple "pharmacological" theory competed with a "disinhibition" explanation of the effects of alcohol on behavior,[19] increasingly it is recognized that it is possible that alcohol intoxication may contribute to some portion of alcohol-related aggressive and criminal behavior through its mediating effects on the physiological, cognitive, affective, or behavioral functioning of the drinker. The extent of alcohol's effects also may vary, depending on the drinker and the amount of alcohol consumed.

Evidence supporting an intoxication effect comes from emergency room (ER) studies. Using representative samples of patients, several studies have found that persons with violence-related injuries are two to five times more likely to be intoxicated at the time of the ER visit than persons injured from other causes.[20,21] In addition, drinking prior to the event was a more powerful predictor of violent (as compared with non-violent) injuries seen in the emergency room than was the usual amount of alcohol consumed.[22] An overview of experimental studies also suggests that there is some basis for assuming that the effects of alcohol on the drinker contribute to the likelihood of engaging in violent behavior.[23]

Efforts to understand the effects of alcohol on aggression have suggested that it intensifies violence or contributes to its escalation. One study[4] found that more severe incidents (e.g., kicking and punching) were more likely than less severe incidents to involve alcohol. Another study[24] found women (but not men) were significantly more likely to sustain an injury in an assault by an intimate partner (but not in other assaults) if the man was drinking. Variation in the effect of alcohol on violence, depending on the victim-perpetrator relationship, also is found in NCVS data. According to those victims of violence who could describe the offender's substance use, between 1993 and 1998, 63% of persons victimized by an intimate (i.e., current or former spouse, intimate partner, or boyfriend/girlfriend), but only 37% victimized by an acquaintance, and 29% victimized by a stranger perceived the offender to be using alcohol alone or in combination with other drugs.[9]

One explanation for these findings is alcohol's effects on physiological processes. For example, alcohol has been found to affect the GABA-benzodiazepine receptor complex in the brain.[25,26] This may result in reduced anxiety about the consequences of aggressive behavior.[27] Alcohol also affects the dopaminergic system, leading to an increase in psychomotor stimulation, which, in turn, may increase the intensity and level of aggression.[28] Other studies have found that drinking initially increases serotonin but then decreases it, thereby increasing the effects of dopamine.[29] This then results in reduced impulse control, which increases the likelihood of aggression.[30]

Alcohol also affects perception and motor skills, which may in turn increase the likelihood of criminal behavior or victimization. Alcohol appears to reduce pain sensitivity, and thus may result in aggression due to reduced concern about painful consequences of action.[31] Impaired motor functioning may result in increasing the risk of provoking others by bumping into them and eliciting an aggressive response. It also increases the likelihood of erratic/dangerous driving observable by the police when intoxicated persons drive a car.

Consuming alcohol impairs cognitive functioning,[16,19,32] which may reduce the drinker's ability to think of peaceful solutions when difficult situations arise in a social setting, as well as affect attention and emotions. For example, alcohol consumption results in a narrowing of the perceptual field,[15] which subsequently was described as *alcohol myopia*, defined as "short sightedness in which superficially understood, immediate aspects of experience have a disproportionate influence on behavior and emotion."[33(p. 923)] This myopia tends to result in more extreme responses. It thus appears to prevent consideration of alternative inhibitory responses, as the individual both perceives fewer situational cues and is less aware of internal values and cues. One of the few studies to actually test the effects of cognitive impairment involved an experiment that used a balanced placebo design. Four groups of students were asked to respond to a videotaped situation involving a provocative interaction. The two groups of intoxicated individuals were less able to find a non-aggressive solution to the provocation than those in the non-alcohol groups.[34]

An observational study of naturally occurring incidents in bars frequented by young adults also supports both cognitive and attentional effects of alcohol.[35] Analyses of observational data that detailed aggressive incidents in bars found that being "focused on the present" was rated by observers as contributing to 84% of incidents, followed by reduced anxiety or fear (73% of incidents), and impaired problem-solving (more than 60% of incidents).

Studies of marital conflict also suggest that alcohol affects the cognitive-emotional aspects of couples' interaction processes.[36,37] For example, in an experimental study, maritally aggressive and nonaggressive couples first were asked to discuss an important conflict in their marriage (baseline). They then discussed their most serious conflict after the husbands had received either no alcohol, an active placebo, or an intoxicating dose (0.10 BAC) of alcohol. Alcohol led to increased husband and wife negativity over baseline, while the interactions in the couples in the placebo and no-alcohol conditions did not change. This suggests that alcohol had a deleterious effect on the husband's problem solving.[37]

Alcohol use also may increase concerns with power and dominance issues that have been linked to male violence generally[38] and to spousal violence in particular.[39] This may arise from gender role strain promoted by an unattainable masculine ideal[40] or from a male-dominated social structure that devalues feminine qualities and ideals.[41] In *The Drinking Man,* McClelland and his colleagues examined the fantasies of university students and working class men when they were sober and intoxicated.[42] They noted that the fantasies were more likely to have themes of power and domination when the men were under the influence of alcohol and that heavy drinkers were more likely to have power fantasies than men who were not heavy drinkers. The authors concluded that men drink to compensate for unconscious feelings of deficiency, avoid intimacy, and evade responsibility.

Comparative studies of alcohol-abusing wife assaulters support the power theory. Kantor and Straus[43] found that approval of violence interacted with a pattern of heavy drinking as a significant predictor of wife assault. In their bar observation study, Graham and colleagues[35] found empirical support for the proposition that alcohol increases the likelihood of aggression by increasing power concerns among some men. Power concerns may also interact with impaired cognitive function. For example, alcohol-impaired cognitive appraisal may result in an inappropriate sense of mastery, control, or power.[15]

The amount of alcohol consumed appears to influence the effects of drinking on cognitions and affect. Experimental studies have found that higher levels of aggression are related to higher doses of alcohol (BAC of .08 or more).[44] Husband-to-wife violence was found to be highest among husbands who were binge drinkers (i.e., consumed five or more drinks at one sitting), followed by "high" drinkers (i.e., those who consume from three times a week to daily and drink three or more drinks a day).[43] Dawson found that fighting after alcohol use in a representative sample of over 18,000 current drinkers was significantly associated with overall volume of alcohol consumption as well as the proportion of drinking days resulting in intoxication.[45] High quantity drinking additionally has been associated with drinking and driving. For example, Liu and associates[46] observe that persons who reported drinking five or more drinks in a day during the past month were 30 times more likely than other survey respondents to report driving after having "had perhaps too much to drink."

Characteristics of People Who Engage in Criminal Behavior When Drinking

The relationship between alcohol and crime varies with factors related to the characteristics of the drinker, including demographics (i.e., gender and age), the drinker's normative expectations, temperament, or personality predisposition, and general deviant attitudes. Most crimes, including alcohol-related offenses, clearly are committed by men. Bushman's[23] metaanalysis found larger effects of alcohol on aggression for men than women, suggesting that men may respond differently to alcohol than women. Similarly, age has been consistently related to crime,[47] marital violence,[48] and drinking and driving.[46] For example, although persons 13 through 29 years of age comprise 17 percent of the U.S. population, they made up 58% of the persons arrested in the United States in 1997.[47]

There are a number of general explanations for young people's deviance, including substance abuse, delinquency, and other behaviors among young persons defined as "problem behaviors" by the larger society.[49,50] For example, Jessor's problem behavior theory (PBT)[50] accounts for such deviant behaviors as substance use, aggression, delinquency, and precocious sexuality by addressing three systems of psychosocial influence: the personality system, the perceived environmental system, and the behavioral system. Within each, the explanatory variables reflect either instigations to problem behavior or controls against it. Jointly, these factors generate a dynamic state labeled "proneness" that specifies the likelihood of occurrence of normative violations or problem behavior. Thus, deviance arises through the joint role of personality and environmental systems in shaping the individual's propensity to be less controlled by social convention. Much empirical research, based on cross-sectional and longitudinal studies from both a community sample and national samples of adolescents (reviewed elsewhere[51–53]), supports PBT theory. These studies generally find substantial correlations among the various problem behaviors, suggesting that both alcohol use and aggression in adolescence are linked through common causes. Among the psychosocial risk factors that tend to correlate with measures of problem behavior are low value on academic achievement, high tolerance of deviance, high friends' approval for problem behaviors, and low parent-friend compatibility.[52] Which form of deviance is manifested, however, is less predictable. It is likely to be influenced by the number and specific combination of distal risk factors, the individual's stage of development, and proximal influences arising out of specific opportunities (e.g., alcohol being more readily available than marijuana or vice versa). The emergence of problem behaviors from combinations of risk factors in the personality and environment suggests that it would be advantageous to intervene as early as feasible with children by targeting malleable distal risk factors from several systems. For example, parent training programs when the children are young might improve family management practices, enhance parental and children's values on academic achievement, and increase the child's perception of parental support. These would be most appropriate for families in which there is an alcoholic parent and families in poverty and/or disorganized neighborhoods, and thus might subsequently have positive outcomes on a variety of deviant behaviors.

White's related common-cause model postulates that substance use and crime are not directly linked but are related because they share common causes.[50,54] Both are predicted by childhood risk factors, including hyperactivity, impulsivity, poor parenting, problems in school, and familial criminal behavior also identified by PBT. For example, young males account for a disproportionate share of crime and are the heaviest drinkers. Being male thus is a common link, regardless of whether this is due to biological or social factors or the subcultural norms that may reinforce both criminal behavior and substance use.

In a refinement of the common cause model, Zhang and colleagues[55] used the Buffalo Longitudinal Survey of Young Men to test the moderating role of alcohol use on four predictors of aggravated assault in adolescent males: deviant attitudes, aggression and hostility, impulsivity, and problem-solving abilities. They found that deviant attitudes and aggression were very strong predictors of the prevalence of assault in the predictive model. However, these two main effects became non-significant when interaction terms were added. Additional analyses showed that the relationships between deviant attitudes and the prevalence of assault were significant for heavy drinkers but not light drinkers. Similar findings were obtained for the interaction of aggression/hostility and alcohol consumption. These findings support the argument that alcohol is linked to violent crime through an interaction effect of heavy drinking with a deviant or hostile predisposition.

Attitudes and expectations also appear to be important factors in predicting violence after drinking. Leonard and Senchak[56] found that heavy drinking was associated with higher premarital aggression, but only for men who expected alcohol to facilitate aggression. Abbey[57] identified a number of attitudinal variables that might be implicated in male sexual violence against women. These include expectancies about the effects of alcohol on sexuality, the belief that intoxication can serve as an excuse, and the stereotype that women who drink alcohol invite sex. Kantor and Straus[43] found that alcohol consumption was more strongly associated with husband-to-wife violence among men who approved of violence than among those who did not.

Drinking Contexts and Situational Factors Associated with Alcohol-Related Violence

Some research has focused attention on the role that settings, situations, and circumstances play when violence occurs, and how these interact with the characteristics of the person, such as attitudes and personality factors. Experimental studies have found that some situational factors increase aggression among persons who have been drinking, whereas other situational factors reduce or moderate the likelihood of alcohol-related aggression. For example, situations involving high anxiety, frustration, and inhibition conflict increase aggressive responses.[58] Conversely, third-party interventions that provided an explicit nonaggressive norm[59] and those providing monetary incentives not to aggress[60] both reduced the likelihood of alcohol-related aggression.

Naturalistic studies provide evidence that other people in the drinking setting may play a key role in contributing to escalation of the violence through a dynamic interaction process. Particularly when both parties are intoxicated, the chances are increased that one will perceive the other's comment or look as a slight and react in a way that further escalates the tension or increases miscommunication.[6,61] These findings additionally support the observation that alcohol-related violent crimes often involve drinking by the victim as well as the perpetrator. Because the person who ends up being the "victim" often is the initiator of the aggressive interaction,[1] interventions need to reduce the likelihood of victimization without "blaming the victim."

Bars and other licensed premises have been identified as high risk drinking environments that foster both violence and drunk driving.[62] One review of factors associated with violence in public drinking contexts[44] found that the type of drinking establishment, the physical and social environment, the type of patrons, and the role of bar workers each are related to violence. For example, bars with a reputation for violence, skid row bars, and discotheques are more likely to experience violence than others,[63] as are bars that are unclean, poorly ventilated, dimly lit, and patronized primarily by groups of males rather than solo males and couples.[64]

Violence in barrooms also is more likely in those bars in which there is unrestricted swearing, sexual activity, prostitution, drug use and dealing, crowding,[65] and an "anything goes" atmosphere.[63] A lack of control by bar management and staff also affects violence, in that violence is more likely to occur when there is a low staff-to-patron ratio and a failure to engage in responsible serving practices.[62,64]

One theme found throughout the alcohol-related crime literature is the specific social context of young men drinking in bars.[6,44,62,66] For example, Stockwell and colleagues' household survey of alcohol-related harm found that both violent incidents and drunk driving occurred most commonly among heavy drinking young men who drank at licensed premises.[62] Pernanen linked this to power concerns among men, proposing that in certain settings frequented by groups of young men, "the greater proportion of people displaying power concerns and resulting attitudes and behavior, the smaller will be the probability of compliance with anyone's wishes."[15(pp. 406–407)]

Neighborhoods and communities also may be "hot spots" for violence. Initially, criminologists studying the geographic distribution of violence found that alcohol availability is a key factor in identifying such "hot spots." Roncek and Maier[67] found that in one medium-sized city, city blocks with bars had higher rates of assaults, robberies, and rapes than other blocks, even after accounting for the impact of unemployment, poverty, and racial composition. Three recent studies focusing on the effects of the physical availability of alcohol on violence have found that outlet density appears to have negative consequences on communities when measured at the neighborhood level. A study of 74 cities in Los Angeles County found that the rate of assaults reported to the police was significantly associated with the density of both on-sale and off-sale alcohol outlets. After controlling for a variety of neighborhood factors, a 1% increase in the density of outlets was associated with a 0.62% increase in the rate of violent offenses.[68]

Using the same methodology to analyze data from 223 municipalities in New Jersey with populations greater than 10,000, Gorman and colleagues[69] found no significant association between outlet density and violence after the introduction of sociodemographic control variables. Puzzled by the inconsistent findings, the investigators conducted another study limited to Newark, NJ. They examined the relationship between sociodemographic characteristics, alcohol outlet densities, and violent crime at two smaller levels of analysis: the census tract and census block group.[70] At each level, alcohol outlet densities were significantly related to violent crime rate. This led to their conclusion that alcohol outlet densities have negative consequences on communities that only can be detected at the neighborhood level. This finding is supported by the observation that if alcohol outlets dominate a location, this feature of the local environment stimulates crime by attracting certain types of people and activities, such as drug sales, prostitution, and gang activities.[71] Thus, it appears that "broken bottles" are symbolic of neighborhood social disorder and invite crime in much the same way as "broken windows."[72]

Cultural Norms and Expectations Affecting Alcohol-Related Violence

Alcohol consumption patterns, crime rates, and the extent to which drinking is associated with aggressive or criminal behavior all differ widely across cultures as well as among subcultures within them. Cross-cultural studies documenting this variability suggest that there is no simple causal association between alcohol and crime.[73,74] Two main aspects of cultural framing have been identified as being associated with a higher rate of alcohol-related aggression: defining a drinking occasion as a "time out" period in which controls are loosened from usual behavior[73] and a willingness to hold a person less responsible for their actions when drinking than when sober by attributing the blame to alcohol (termed "deviance disavowal").[75] Key elements in both time out and deviance disavowal are the belief that alcohol is a cause of violent behavior, the view that the individual who is violent while intoxicated is regarded as less deviant than one who is violent without drinking, and the expectation of lessened blame, all of which influence behavior.

Some expectancies research has sought to better understand the extent to which different cultures and subcultural groups accept alcohol as an excuse for aggression and as a way of mitigating blame for crimes committed while drinking. For example, several studies have found that people in North America believe that aggression is one effect of alcohol consumption, although there is variability in expectations depending on such factors as the type of drink and gender of the drinker.[76–78]

Public opinion polls suggest that there is a widespread belief that alcohol is causally related to aggression and crime. However, being intoxicated is not necessarily accepted by the general public as an excuse for violent behavior.[79] Ironically, although the general rule in our legal system is that "intoxication is no excuse" in the determination of guilt, the U.S. legal system allows several limited exceptions. Because intoxication may be taken into consideration in sentencing,[80] the result may not be very different from a "discount for drunkenness."[81] However, empirical data are lacking on the effects of intoxication on criminal justice system outcomes, including police willingness to make an arrest, prosecutorial decision making, and judicial sentencing for various types of offenses.

As the ample empirical evidence above suggests, multiple factors contribute to the complex pathways through which alcohol affects deviant or criminal behavior. These factors include the effects of alcohol, the characteristic of the person, the drinking situation, and the cultural framing of both drinking and deviant behaviors. How might understanding of the relationships among these factors guide the implementation of preventive and treatment interventions more effectively to reduce this burden? The next section briefly sketches directions for interventions, their evaluations, and other research.

INTERVENTION STRATEGIES TO REDUCE
THE BURDEN OF ALCOHOL-RELATED CRIME

Because many factors contribute to alcohol-related crime, effective interventions to reduce it need to include a broad spectrum of prevention and treatment programs. It is desirable to design preventive interventions that simultaneously aim at the environment (society or community), the drinking situation, and the individual at risk of offending. Such interventions need to specify which aspects of the culture/society, situations or settings, and individuals (or the entire population) they are targeting. A related issue that remains even when targets are identified is whether prevention efforts should give priority to changing particularly high-risk offenders involved in the CJS or the general population.

McClelland and Teplin[82] suggest focusing on those at highest risk, including the relatively small group of persons involved with the CJS. In contrast, others[7,83] point to the importance of general population approaches to prevention but note that within this broader framework locally oriented programs may be implemented. As Mosher and Jernigan observe, "interventions at the level of the entire population have the potential to address the multiple and interactive causes of alcohol-related violence."[83(p. 11)]

Population or environmental approaches rest on the understanding that drinking and alcohol-related problems occur along a continuum. At one end are the heaviest drinkers or individuals at highest risk of problems. This group is comprised of a relatively small number of individuals, each at very high risk. A much larger number of persons are found to be nearer the lower-risk light and moderate drinking end of the spectrum. Consequently, the latter may create a larger aggregate burden to society, depending both on the size of the group and level of group risk. When the contribution of the larger low/moderate risk group outweighs the relative contribution of the smaller high-risk group, the situation is referred to as the "prevention paradox."[84–86] As Skog[86] states:

> In survey data it has been found repeatedly that only a fairly modest part of alcohol-related problems can be attributed to heavy drinkers. Light and moderate consumers are responsible for the much larger fraction of the problems, as the large number of such drinkers make up for their smaller risk. On the basis of this "prevention paradox," the claim has been made that the population strategy of prevention is much more likely to produce tangible results than the risk-group strategy. (p. 751)

Support for this strategy was found for reducing drunk driving,[87] and several population survey studies suggest that the prevention paradox may be valid for violent behavior.[88,89] Since a substantial proportion of sexual assaults among acquaintances (i.e., "date rape"), domestic violence incidents, and public disorder offenses are attributable to light and moderate drinkers, a population-based strategy that reduces the overall level of drinking and intoxication may be the most effective way to lower rates of these types of alcohol-related crime. Such an approach also may affect those at highest risk because they, too, experience the benefits of prevention efforts that shift the risk curve to the left. Because much of the alcohol-related crime is the result of heavy drinking episodes of non-dependent drinkers, effective prevention efforts must work to reduce the risk of intoxication across the entire population of drinkers.[84]

Population prevention efforts hold great promise because they target the social structures, norms, and other aspects of the environment, thereby addressing the conditions that give rise to risky drinking practices. Nevertheless, selective intervention strategies that focus more narrowly on specific high-risk situations, groups and individuals, and interventions targeted at particular alcohol-related problems and the aggressive tendencies of convicted offenders also are needed. Since convicted offenders and dependent drinkers are at a disproportionately high risk of future alcohol-related violence, altering the drinking and criminal behavior patterns of even a fraction of these high risk groups is likely to have substantial benefits.

This section reviews some universal, selective, and targeted intervention strategies to reduce alcohol-related violence and other crimes. Although universal strategies tend to be directed at the changing cultural norms and drinking contexts, they also may be directed at individual drinkers and even at altering the effects of drinking. Strategies focusing on high-risk groups more often are directed at the individual or social context.

Since alcohol-related offenses are problems for both the criminal justice and public health system, greater communication and co-operation among practitioners and researchers in each system is likely to enhance the effectiveness of most interventions. Criminal justice and public health experts often are isolated from each other. They need to collaborate more closely in developing and implementing strategies to reduce the harm caused by the alcohol-crime nexus and to more effectively link existing data systems.

Universal or Environmental Intervention Strategies

Many studies document the links between both the social and physical availability of alcohol and alcohol-related problems, including crime.[84,85] Since this research provides strong evidence that increased alcohol availability increases rates of problems, a key to preventing alcohol-related crime involves implementing environmental policies that limit the social and physical availability of alcohol. Such policies may be public, institutional, or both. Public policies that regulate alcohol availability are found at federal, state, and local levels of government; institutional policies regulate alcohol availability and drinking patterns through their effects in such institutional settings as alcohol outlets and worksites. Public policies may include regulations on how, where, and when alcohol is sold; where and when alcohol is consumed; the price of alcohol; the social environment related to drinking; enforcement mechanisms; and regulations on access to alcohol by minors. Although many of these policy approaches have been implemented and evaluated, those evaluations rarely have examined their impact on alcohol-related crime in particular. Where alcohol-related crime has been studied will be indicated, as will other interventions that appear promising and require further study.

Reducing Alcohol's Physical Availability. One policy intervention, raising the minimum legal drinking age to 21 in the United States, has been found to reduce drinking and driving among both underage and young adult drivers,[90] and it probably reduced youth homicide rates as well.[91] Research cited in the previous section[67–70] confirms that alcohol outlet density at the neighborhood level is related to both violent assaults and drunk driving in the local community. Although all states and communities regulate alcohol sale and service, some communities have recently adopted a variety of zoning and planning initiatives to restrict new liquor licenses and challenge relicensing decisions, and the effectiveness of these efforts has rarely been evaluated.[92] The limited evidence to date, nevertheless, suggests that lowering outlet density in neighborhoods with "hot spots" of crime will reduce alcohol-related offenses, including DWI, in the surrounding area.

Several states have mandated policies targeting operational practices of alcohol retailers through Responsible Beverage Service (RBS) programs and server liability legislation.[84] In other states and communities, such programs have been implemented voluntarily. These programs put into effect in local settings to alter the immediate drinking context include training staff to identify and refuse sales to obviously intoxicated patrons, implementing policies such as limiting the number of drinks served to a customer per hour, and providing increased food service. Although there is some evidence that RBS reduces the risk of patron intoxication[93] and traffic crashes,[94] it has been less effective in cutting off service to intoxicated and underage patrons.[84] One Australian intervention program was designed specifically to provide violence prevention training for pub licensees and staff. The training program resulted in an improvement in serving practices and policies that resulted in a lower rate of aggressive incidents inside these venues.[63,64] Similarly, a recent pilot test of the Safer Bars Training program implemented in Ontario, Canada, increased knowledge and changed attitudes among bar staff about the prevention and reduction of violence in bars.[95] Thus, training bar staff to prevent and manage aggressive behaviors in licensed establishments, as well as the active involvement of management in these goals, not only may reduce intoxication rates but may also directly address alcohol-related violence. Such interventions may be most effective if they are accompanied by law enforcement monitoring of "hot spot" licensed establishments.

Strategies to reduce alcohol availability have been hampered by weak enforcement. For example, commercial suppliers routinely violate laws against providing alcohol to minors and intoxicated patrons.[65,84,92] Two studies observed decreases in intoxicated patrons after law enforcement agencies conducted highly publicized programs to enforce laws against sales to obviously intoxicated patrons.[96,97] Thus a promising avenue for reducing alcohol-related violence would be a combination of RBS training and enhanced law enforcement monitoring of the laws prohibiting service to intoxicated bar patrons, since these individuals are at greatly increased risk.

Despite the 21-year minimum legal drinking age laws, minors have little difficulty gaining access to alcohol,[98] although they are less likely to drink in bars and licensed establishments.[84] Since adolescents and young adults are responsible for a disproportionate amount of alcohol-related violence, universal strategies designed to reduce alcohol availability to youth also are likely to have an impact on their law-related problems. Policies designed to reduce youth access include keg registration, enhancement of drivers' licenses, and penalties for having a false ID. These have been found to reduce DWI,[84] and their effects on alcohol-related violence, though unknown, are potentially large.

Increasing the Price of Alcohol. A convincing body of research shows that increasing alcohol prices by raising alcohol excise taxes reduces alcohol consumption as well as alcohol problems, including violence[99] and motor vehicle fatalities.[100] State and federal excise taxes on alcoholic beverages have been largely static over the last five decades. The effect of inflation during the same period has resulted in a relative drop in the price of alcoholic beverages. One analysis examined the effects on crime rates of a hypothetical 10% increase in state excise taxes. It used data on state excise taxes for the 48 contiguous states from 1979 to 1988 and rates of violent crimes from the FBI's Uniform Crime reports. It estimated that an increase of 10% in state beer tax would reduce rape by 1.3%, assaults by 0.3% and robberies by 0.9% by reducing per capita consumption.[73] Both increases in excise taxes to reduce alcohol-related crime and studies of the impact of such changes on various types of crime are desirable.

Altering the Social Environment. Both alcohol advertising and public health messages to counter advertising's effect are important aspects of a universal strategy. For example, a combination of effective laws, highly publicized enforcement, and public information and education were effective in reducing alcohol-related traffic fatalities in the United States from 25,165 in 1982 to an estimated 15,794 in 1999.[101] Alcohol advertising and promotion send powerful messages regarding alcohol use, implying that it brings social and sexual success, relief from stress, and adult status. According to a recent Federal Trade Commission (FTC) report, the beer, wine, and distilled spirits industries spend at least $4 billion annually on promotional activities.[102] The research regarding the impact of alcohol marketing on alcohol-related consumption and problems is equivocal and limited by methodological problems.[103] Nevertheless several studies[104,105] have found that alcohol advertising does have a measurable impact on consumption and problems. Even without research demonstrating a direct link to consumption, there is evidence of the influence of alcohol advertising on the norms and values of the society,[106] which suggests the need to carefully monitor advertisements and study their effects.

To limit the effects of alcohol advertising and promotion and the norms and attitudes that they foster, public health activists have sought to use the media and other information sources to provide accurate information and challenge misperceptions. They have implemented initiatives involving media advocacy[107] and other media-based counter advertising approaches. For example, to address the observation that youths overestimate the amount of alcohol consumed by their peers,[108] an initiative to reduce college alcohol-related problems using social norms marketing has been implemented. Preliminary findings from a media campaign to correct students' perceptions of how much their peers drink shows decreases in rates of high-risk drinking.[109] Although social norms marketing still has not been rigorously evaluated, this approach may also reduce the high rates of date rape and vandalism in the student population that frequently are associated with binge drinking.

An Example of a Universal Intervention: The Community Prevention Trial

Multiple strategies were combined in a coordinated Community Prevention Trial (CPT) study designed to reduce alcohol-related trauma through the synergistic effects of simultaneously implementing a number of intervention strategies in three experimental communities.[107] The CPT's intervention components included community mobilization, media advocacy, increased drinking/driving enforcement, initiation of RBS, and police monitoring and enforcement of responsible service and underage drinking laws.[107] In one of the three experimental communities and its matched control community, surveys were conducted in emergency rooms and hospital records were examined on a monthly basis to determine assault rates. Relative to the control community, assaults seen in the hospital in the experimental community declined 43% and hospitalized assault cases fell by 2%, suggesting an overall reduction in violence that is consistent with reduction in heavy drinking. There also was a 10% decrease in nighttime injury crashes and a 6% reduction in DWI crashes.[110] The demonstrated greater effectiveness of the combination of intervention strategies in reducing assaults suggests the desirability of replicating the study in communities in different regions and/or with different racial/ethnic and economic mixes.

Selective Interventions with High-Risk Groups and in High-Risk Environments

Preventive interventions also may target populations that are at high risk for alcohol-related violence but have not been identified in a criminal justice setting. Interventions also may focus on changing high-risk locations and settings in which such individuals are found. Ideally, a selective prevention strategy should identify risky settings, groups, and individuals before violence occurs or at the first instance of violent behavior and tailor interventions to the developmental stage of the designated person's or setting's particular problems. High-risk groups for subsequent alcohol-related violence for whom interventions might be designed include young children with criminal and/or substance-abusing parents, hyperactive pre-school children, victims of violence who are seen in emergency rooms, newly married couples in which one partner is a heavy drinker, first-time domestic violence offenders, members of college fraternities, and persons in alcoholism treatment.

For example, interventions might focus on victims of violence who appear in emergency rooms. These may be beneficial because injured persons are at elevated risk for further victimization and because suffering an injury may provide a "teachable moment," given the recency of the event and the patient's emotional state. Findings from a number of interventions in medical settings with adult problem drinkers[111] and older adolescents[112] suggest the utility of both routine alcohol assessments and the implementation of brief interventions in that setting with this high-risk population. In one study, a brief motivational interview for reducing the harm associated with drinking was implemented among alcohol-positive adolescents who were ER patients. The intervention was found to be effective in reducing both subsequent alcohol-related injuries and drinking and driving[113] and thus also may reduce assaultive behavior.

Men in treatment for alcoholism constitute another high-risk group because they have been found to have high rates of domestic violence. One program that involved behavioral marital therapy along with the alcoholism treatment found that participants' domestic violence rates were reduced from the year before to the year after treatment.[113] O'Farrell and Murphy[114] replicated this finding but observed that only alcoholics who were in remission reduced partner violence; those who relapsed after treatment did not.

Feminists and service providers often resist incorporating alcohol treatment into programs for domestic batterers to avoid providing them with an excuse for such violence. However, it may be time to reconsider this position. Although successful alcohol treatment does not necessarily lead to reduced partner violence, failure to address abusers' alcohol problems is likely to undermine positive effects of batterers' treatment that may occur. Thus, it is desirable for the criminal justice response to domestic violence to include alcohol assessment and mandatory treatment as an additional condition of a sentence, not as an alternative to a sanction. In addition, linkages between domestic violence and alcohol treatment programs, which now are infrequent, need to be expanded through efforts to address the philosophical, structural, and practical impediments to such linkage, and the effects of such changes should be evaluated.[115]

Treatment Interventions with Persons Involved with the CJS

A wide variety of alcohol treatments currently is available, including cognitive behavioral therapy, motivational enhancement therapy, 12-Step programs, and pharmacotherapy. These treatment approaches also may be used in combination, depending on the individual's treatment needs. The first step is determining the offender's treatment needs. Surveys of probation and correctional populations indicate that those are enormous.[116] For example, about 40% of adult male and 29% of female jail inmates were drinking at the time of their offense; about a third of convicted inmates in local jails described themselves as having been daily drinkers at the time of their offense.[9] Among state prisoners, nearly 30% were daily drinkers during the period preceding their incarceration, and about a quarter of both men and women fit the standard diagnostic profile of alcohol dependence.[9] Given the magnitude of the alcohol problem for the CJS, arrestees routinely should be screened for alcohol and other drug problems. For those that appear to have abuse or dependence problems, fuller assessment of substance abuse involvement and inclusion of appropriate treatment should be included as part of, not as a substitute for, the sentence imposed by the court.

Although most interventions with offenders will focus on changing the effects of alcohol (through pharmacotherapy) and offenders' expectancies and behaviors (through behavioral treatments), other interventions may be undertaken at the community or policy level. These include policies that increase government funding for CJS treatment programs and personnel. This would permit more careful monitoring of offenders in the community, greater oversight by the courts of the quality of programs in which alcohol-abusing offenders sentenced to probation participate, more attention to offenders' compliance with court-ordered sanctions, and imposition of further sanctions for failure to comply with program requirements.

Other policies include the recent development of innovative specialized courts. Based on positive preliminary findings in drug courts[117] and the Dade County Domestic Violence Court experiment,[118] it would be desirable to expand such innovative programs to DWI offenders, alcohol-involved spouse abusers, and even to first offenders convicted of a violent offense in which no weapon is involved. Non-incarcerative sentences for these offenders would be based on the drug court and Dade County models that combine treatment with close supervision.

There is ample evidence that treatment of substance-abusing offenders is both effective and cost effective.[117,119] Yet only 62% of probationers and 39% of state prison inmates who were drinking at the time of their offense received any treatment after being put on probation or entering prison, respectively.[9] Most of the offenders participated in self-help groups or peer counseling; a far smaller proportion received treatment or professional counseling.[9] Funding to expand substance abuse treatment programs in the correctional system requires both policy changes and program implementation. Nevertheless, these programs, accompanied by post-release planning, increased monitoring, and more after-care services for those who need them, also are likely to decrease subsequent alcohol-related crime.

CONCLUSIONS

The costs of alcohol-related crime in lives and dollars are enormous. The burden falls on both the abuser and his/her household, the victims, and the public through criminal justice system expenses. Despite falling crime rates, the number of persons under correctional supervision with alcohol problems has grown in the past decade. This suggests the need to combine population-wide approaches to further reduce overall rates of intoxication, more targeted intervention approaches to change the drinking behavior and/or the drinking environment of high-risk groups, and increased availability of alcoholism treatment for dependent offenders in order to reduce alcohol-related crime. Rigorous evaluations of the implementation and effectiveness of these efforts also are needed.

A comprehensive agenda of research on all aspects of alcohol-related crime is beyond the scope of this article. Nevertheless, additional survey, experimental, and observation studies can serve as the basis for further interventions if they elaborate on how the various risk and protective factors mediate and moderate alcohol-related violence for certain groups and the specific contexts in which they occur. Among the issues to be explored in surveys is an explanation of the recent decrease in alcohol-related crime. An analysis of recent NCVS data covering 1993 through 1998 found that although there was an overall decrease of 23% in violent crimes, alcohol-related violent offenses decreased by 31%, whereas crimes not involving a drinking offender fell by only 20%.[9] It is unclear to what extent these decreases are due to community policing programs, the changing demographics of the American population, decreases in drinking among high-risk groups, or other factors. To address questions related to the changing role of alcohol in crime, however, requires the expansion of the survey instruments currently being used in several national data collection efforts (e.g., NCVS and prisoner surveys) and/or much larger samples in new surveys focused on alcohol use and abuse.

Observational studies of violence might be conducted in bars and informal drinking settings, such as parks and fraternity houses. These could help pinpoint the situational factors that contribute to alcohol-related violence and the mechanisms through which escalation of incidents occurs. Given the limits of studying alcohol-related violence in a natural setting, additional experimental research on alcohol-related aggression in controlled settings also might explore how the effects of alcohol on aggressive behavior are mediated by cognitive and affective factors. In-depth interviews with victims and perpetrators might probe their experiences with violent and threatening situations to better understand the incident escalation process. Incidents that involve or do not involve alcohol might be compared with respect to the interaction processes and outcomes and how these are mediated by individual personality factors and victim-assailant relationships. Additionally, the effect of alcohol intoxication on criminal justice decision-making merits further examination.

There are many ongoing intervention studies designed to reduce alcohol availability, consumption, and problem drinking. Too often, however, the outcome measures being used are limited to determining the quantity and frequency of drinking and/or patterns of alcohol consumption. It would be desirable if more investigators expanded their measures to include the effects of their interventions on a range of alcohol-related problems, including crime and injuries.

The role of alcohol in criminal behavior is not yet fully understood. Nevertheless, there are a number of promising population strategies and individual-oriented treatment approaches identified in this article. Expanded efforts to systematically implement and rigorously evaluate these approaches is likely to reduce alcohol-related crime and the burden of alcohol on the criminal justice system, the victims of crime, and the society at large.

REFERENCES

1. Murdoch, D., Phil, R. O., & Ross, D. (1990). Alcohol and crimes of violence. *International Journal of Addictions, 25,* 1065–1081.
2. Greenfeld, L. A. (1998). *Alcohol and crime: An analysis of national data on the prevalence of alcohol involvement in crime.* NCJ 168632. Washington, DC: U.S. Department of Justice.
3. Mumola, C. J. (1999). *Substance abuse and treatment, state and federal prisoners, 1997.* NCJ 172871. Washington, DC: Bureau of Justice Statistics.
4. Pernanen, K. (1991). *Alcohol and human violence.* New York: Guilford Press.
5. Collins, J. J., & Messerschmidt, P. M. (1993). Epidemiology of alcohol-related violence. *Alcohol Health and Research World, 17,* 93–100.
6. Graham, K., Wells, S., & West, P. (1997). A framework for applying explanations of alcohol-related aggression to naturally occurring aggressive behavior. *Contemporary Drug Problems, 24,* 625–666.
7. Graham, K., Leonard, K. E., Room, R., et al. (1998). Current directions in research on understanding and preventing intoxicated aggression. *Addiction, 93*(5), 659–676.
8. Lipsey, M. W., Wilson, D. B., Cohen, M. A., et al. (1997). Is there a causal relationship between alcohol use and violence? A synthesis of the evidence. In M. Galanter (Ed.), *Recent developments in alcoholism,* vol. 13 (pp. 245–283). New York: Plenum Press.
9. Greenfeld, L. A., & Henneberg, M. A. (2000). Alcohol, crime, and the criminal justice system. Commissioned paper presented at *Alcohol and Crime: Research and Practice for Prevention Conference.*
10. Roizen, J. (1993). Issues in the epidemiology of alcohol and violence. In S. E. Martin (Ed.), *Alcohol and interpersonal violence: Fostering multidisciplinary perspectives* (pp. 3–36). Rockville, MD: National Institutes of Health.
11. Roizen, J. (1997). Epidemiological issues in alcohol-related violence. In M. Galanter, (Ed.), *Recent developments in alcoholism,* vol. 13 (pp. 7–40). New York: Plenum Press.
12. Ross. H. L. (1984). Social control through deterrence: Drinking-and-driving laws. *Annual Review of Sociology, 10,* 21–35.
13. Maruschak, L. M. (1999). *DWI offenders under correctional supervision.* NCJ172212. Washington, DC: Bureau of Justice Statistics.
14. Harwood, H., Fountain, D., & Livermore, G. (1998). *The economic costs of alcohol*

and drug abuse in the United States, 1992. NIH Pub. No. 98-4327. Rockville, MD: National Institutes of Health.

15. Pernanen, K. (1976). Alcohol and crimes of violence. In B. Kassin & H. Begleiter (Ed.), *The biology of alcoholism: Social aspects of alcoholism* (pp. 351–444). New York: Plenum Press.

16. Pernanen, K. (1981). Theoretical aspects of the relationship between alcohol use and crime. In J. J. Collins (Ed.), *Drinking and crime: Perspectives on the relationship between alcohol consumption and criminal behavior* (pp. 1–69). New York: Guilford Press.

17. Room, R., & Rossow, I. (2000). The share of violence attributable to drinking: What do we need to know and what research is needed? In *Alcohol and crime: Research and practice for prevention* (pp. 41–54). Washington, DC: National Crime Prevention Council.

18. Graham, K., & West, P. (in press). Alcohol and crime: Examining the link. In N. Heather, T. J. Peters, & T. Stockwell (Eds.), *Handbook of alcohol dependence and alcohol-related problems.* Sussex, England: John Wiley & Sons.

19. Pernanen, K. (1993). Research approaches in the study of alcohol-related violence. *Alcohol and Health Research World, 17,* 101–107.

20. Cherpitel, C. J. (1994). Alcohol and injuries resulting from violence: A review of emergency room studies. *Addiction, 89,* 157–165.

21. Cherpitel, C. J. (1997). Alcohol and violence-related injuries in the emergency room. In M. Galanter (Ed.), *Recent developments in alcoholism,* vol. 13 (pp. 105–122). New York: Plenum Press.

22. Borges, G., Cherpitel, C. J., & Rosovsky, H. (1998). Male drinking and violence-related injury in the emergency room. *Addiction, 93,* 103–112.

23. Bushman, B. J. (1997). Effects of alcohol on human aggression: Validity of proposed explanations. In M. Galanter (Ed.), *Recent developments in alcoholism,* vol. 13 (pp. 227–244). New York: Plenum Press.

24. Martin, S. E., & Bachman, R. (1997). The relationship of alcohol to injury in assault cases. In M. Galanter (Ed.), *Recent developments in alcoholism,* vol. 13. (pp. 42–56). New York: Plenum Press.

25. Miczek, K. A., DeBold, J. F., van Erp, A. M., & Tornatzky, W. (1997). Alcohol, GABAa-benzodiazepine receptor complex, and aggression. In M. Galanter (Ed.), *Recent developments in alcoholism,* vol. 13 (pp. 139–171). New York: Plenum Press.

26. Miczek, K. A., Weerts, E. M., & DeBold, J. F. (1993). Alcohol, benzodiazepine-GABA receptor complex and aggression: Ethological analysis of individual differences in rodents and primates. *Journal of Studies on Alcohol,* September (suppl. 11), 170–179.

27. Pihl, R. O., Peterson, J. B., & Lau, M. A. (1993). A biosocial model of the alcohol-aggression relationship. *Journal of Studies on Alcohol,* September (suppl. 11), 128–139.

28. Pihl, R. O., & Peterson, J. B. (1992). Etiology. *Annual Review of Addictions Research and Treatment,* 153–175.

29. Virkkunen, M., & Linnoila, M. (1993). Brain serotonin, type II alcoholism, and impulsive violence. *Journal of Studies on Alcohol,* September (suppl 11), 163–169.

30. Linnoila, M., & Virkkunen, M. (1992). Aggression, suicidality, and serotonin. *Journal of Clinical Psychology, 53,* 46–51.

31. Cutter, H. S. G., Jones, W. C., Maloof, B. A., & Kurtz, N. R. (1979). Pain as a joint function of alcohol intake and customary reasons for drinking. *International Journal of Addictions, 14,* 73–182.

32. Peterson, J. B., Rothfleisch, J., Zelazo, P. D., et al. (1990). Acute alcohol intoxication and cognitive functioning. *Journal of Studies on Alcohol,* 51, 114–122.

33. Steele, C. M., & Josephs, R. A. (1990). Alcohol myopia: Its prized and dangerous effects. *American Psychologist,* August, 921–933.
34. Sayette, M. A., Wilson, T., & Elias, M. J. (1993). Alcohol and aggression: A social information processing analysis. *Journal of Studies on Alcohol,* 54, 399–407.
35. Graham, K., West, P., & Wells, S. (2000). Evaluating theories of alcohol-related aggression using observation of young adults in bars. *Addiction, 95,* 847–864.
36. Leonard, K. E. (1993). Drinking patterns and intoxication in marital violence: Review, critique, and future directions for research. In S. E. Martin (Ed.), *Alcohol and interpersonal violence: Fostering multidisciplinary perspectives.* Research Monograph No. 24 (pp. 253–281). Rockville, MD: NIH.
37. Leonard, K. E., & Roberts, L. J. (1998). The effects of alcohol on the marital interactions of aggressive and nonaggressive husbands and their wives. *Journal of Abnormal Psychology, 107,* 602–615.
38. Archer, J. (1994). Power and male violence. In J. Archer (Ed.), *Male violence* (pp. 310–331). London: Routledge.
39. Gondolf, E. (1995). Alcohol abuse, wife assault, and power needs. *Social Service Review, 69,* 276–284.
40. Pleck, J. (1981). *The myth of masculinity.* Cambridge, MA: MIT Press.
41. Dobash, R. E., & Dobash, R. P. (1992). *Women, violence, and social change.* New York: Routledge.
42. McClelland, D. C., Davis, W. N., Kalin, R., et al. (1972). *The drinking man: Alcohol and human motivation.* Toronto: Collins-Macmillan Canada.
43. Kantor, G., & Straus, M. (1987). The "drunken bum" theory of wife beating. *Social Problems, 34,* 213–230.
44. Graham, K., Schmidt, G., & Gillis, K. (1996). Circumstances when drinking leads to aggression: An overview of research findings. *Contemporary Drug Problems, 23,* 493–557.
45. Dawson, D. A. (1997). Alcohol, drugs, fighting, and suicide attempt/ideation. *Addiction Research, 5,* 451–472.
46. Liu, S., Siegel, P., Brewer, R., et al. (1997). Prevalence of alcohol impaired driving. *JAMA, 277,* 122–125.
47. Pastore, A. L., & Maguire, K. (Eds.) (1999). *Sourcebook of criminal justice.* Washington, DC: Bureau of Justice Statistics. Available at: http://www.albany.edu/sourcebook/indx.html
48. Stets, J. E., & Straus, M. A. (1990). Gender differences in reporting marital violence and its medical and psychological consequences. In M. A. Straus & R. J. Gelles (Eds.), *Physical violence in American families* (pp. 151–165). New Brunswick, NJ: Transaction Publishers.
49. White, H. R. (1997). Longitudinal perspectives on alcohol use and aggression during adolescence. In M. Galanter (Ed.), *Recent developments in alcoholism,* vol. 13 (pp. 81–103). New York: Plenum Press.
50. Jessor, R., & Jessor, S. L. (1977). *Problem behavior and psychosocial development. A longitudinal study of youth.* San Diego, CA: Academic Press.
51. Donovan, J. E. (1997). Young adult drinking-driving: Behavioral and psychosocial correlates. *Journal of Studies on Alcohol, 58,* 600–613.
52. Donovan, J. E. (1996). Problem-behavior theory and the explanation of adolescent marijuana use. *Journal of Drug Issues, 26,* 379–404.
53. Donovan, J. E., Jessor, R., & Costa, F. M. (1999). Adolescent problem drinking: Stability of psychosocial and behavioral correlates across a generation. *Journal of Studies on Alcohol, 60,* 352–361.
54. White, H. R., Brick, J., & Hansell, S. (1993). A longitudinal investigation of alcohol use and aggression in adolescence. *Journal of Studies on Alcohol,* September (suppl. 11), 62–77.

55. Zhang, L., Wieczorek, W. F., & Welte, J. W. (1997). The nexus between alcohol and violent crime. *Alcohol Clinical and Experimental Research, 21,* 1264–1271.
56. Leonard, K. E., & Senchak, M. (1993). Alcohol and premarital aggression among newlywed couples. *Journal of Studies on Alcohol, 54,* 96–108.
57. Abbey, A. (1991). Acquaintance rape and alcohol consumption on college campuses: How are they linked? *Journal of American College Health, 39,* 165–169.
58. Ito, T. A., Miller, N., & Pollock, V. E. (1996). Alcohol and aggression: A meta-analysis on the moderating effects of inhibitory cues, triggering events, and self-focused attention. *Psychological Bulletin, 120,* 60–82.
59. Jeavons, C. M., & Taylor, S. P. (1985). The control of alcohol-related aggression: Redirecting the inebriate's attention to socially appropriate conduct. *Aggressive Behavior, 11,* 93–101.
60. Hoaken, P., Assaad, J., & Pihl, R. O. (1998). Cognitive functioning and the inhibition of alcohol-induced aggression. *Journal of Studies on Alcohol, 59,* 599–607.
61. Fagan, J. (1993). Set and setting revisited: Influences of alcohol and illicit drugs on the social context of violent events. In S. E. Martin (Ed.), *Alcohol and interpersonal violence: Fostering multidisciplinary perspectives.* NIAAA Monograph Vol. 24 (pp. 160–192). Rockville, MD: NIH.
62. Stockwell, T., Lang, E., & Rydon, P. (1993). High risk drinking settings: The association of serving and promotional practices with harmful drinking. *Addiction, 88,* 1519–1526.
63. Homel, R., & Clark, J. (1994). The prediction and prevention of violence in pubs and clubs. *Crime Prevention Studies, 3,* 1–46.
64. Homel, R., Hauritz, M., Wortley, R., et al. (1994). *The impact of the Surfers Paradise Safety Action Project. Key findings of the evaluation.* Queensland, Australia: Griffith University Centre for Crime Policy and Public Safety.
65. Graham, K. (1985). Determinants of heavy drinking and drinking problems: The contribution of the bar environment. In *Public Drinking and Public Policy.* Toronto: Addiction Research Foundation.
66. Burns, T. F. (1980). Getting rowdy with the boys. *Journal of Drug Issues, 10,* 273–286.
67. Roncek, D. W., & Maier, R. A. (1995). Bars, blocks, and crimes revisited: Linking the theory of routing activities to the empiricism of "hot spots." *Criminology, 29,* 725–754.
68. Scribner, R. A., MacKinnon, D. P., & Dwyer J. H. (1995). Relative risk of assaultive violence and alcohol availability in Los Angeles County. *American Journal of Public Health, 85,* 335–340.
69. Gorman, D. M., Speer, P. W., Labouvie, E. W., & Subaiya, A. P. (1998). Risk of assaultive violence and alcohol availability in New Jersey. *American Journal of Public Health, 88,* 97–99.
70. Speer, P. W., Gorman, D. M., Labouvie, E. W., et al. (1998). Violent crime and alcohol availability: Relationships in an urban community. *Journal of Public Health Policy, 19,* 303–318.
71. Alaniz, M. L., Cartmill, R. S., & Parker, R. N. (1998). Immigrants and violence: The importance of context. *Hispanic Journal of Behavioral Sciences, 20,* 155–174.
72. Wilson, J. Q., & Kelling, G. L. (1982). Broken windows: The police and neighborhood safety. *Atlantic Monthly, 249,* 29–38.
73. MacAndrew, C., & Edgerton, R. B. (1969). *Drunken comportment: A social explanation.* Chicago: Aldine.
74. Health, D. B. (1975). A critical review of ethnographic studies of alcohol use. In R. J. Gibbins, Y. Israel, H. Kalant, et al. (Eds.), *Research advances in alcohol and drug problems,* vol. 2 (pp. 1–92). Toronto: John Wiley & Sons.
75. McCaghy, C. H. (1968). Drinking and deviance disavowal: The case of child molesters. *Soc Forces, 16,* 43–49.

76. Brown, S., Goldman, M., Inn, A., et al. (1980). Expectations of reinforcement from alcohol: Their domain and relation to drinking patterns. *Journal of Consulting and Clinical Psychology, 48,* 419–426.

77. Leigh, B. C. (1987). Beliefs about the effects of alcohol on self and others. *Journal of Studies on Alcohol, 48,* 467–475.

78. Lindeman, R. E., & Lang, A. R. (1994). The alcohol-aggression stereotype: A cross-cultural comparison of beliefs. *International Journal on Addictions, 29,* 1–13.

79. Wild, T. C., Graham, K., & Rehm, J. (1998). Blame and shame for intoxicated aggression: When is the perpetrator culpable? *Addiction, 93,* 677–688.

80. Mosher, J. (1983). Alcohol: Both blame and excuse for criminal behavior. In R. Room & G. Collins (Eds.), *Alcohol and disinhibition: Nature and meaning of the link* (pp. 437–460). Rockville, MD: NIAAA.

81. Room, R. (1996). Drinking, violence, gender, and causal attribution: A Canadian case study in science, law, and policy. *Contemporary Drug Problems, 23,* 294–297.

82. McClelland, G. M., & Teplin, L. A. (2001). Alcohol intoxication and violent crime: Implications for public health policy. *American Journal on Addictions, 10*(suppl), 70–85.

83. Mosher, J. F., & Jernigan, D. J. (2000). Making the link: A public health approach to preventing alcohol-related violence and crime. In *Alcohol and crime: Research and practice for prevention* (pp. 1–22). Washington, DC: National Crime Prevention Council.

84. Toomey, T. L., & Wagenaar, A. C. (1999). Policy options for prevention: The case of alcohol. *Journal of Public Health Policy, 20*(2), 192–213.

85. Edwards, G., Anderson, P., Babor, T. F., et al. (1994). *Alcohol policy and the public good.* New York: Oxford University Press.

86. Skog, O. J. (1999). The prevention paradox revisited. *Addiction, 94,* 751–757.

87. Preusser, D., McCartt, A., & Martin, S. E. (1999). *Impaired driving research needs and priorities.* Paper presented at Committee on Alcohol and Other Drugs and Transportation Meeting, Irvine, CA.

88. Room, R., Bondy, S. J., & Ferris, J. (1995). The risk of harm to oneself from drinking: Canada 1989. *Addiction,* 90, 499–513.

89. Rossow, I., Pape, H., & Wichstrom, I. (1999). Young, wet, and wild? Associations between alcohol intoxication and violent behaviour in adolescence. *Addiction, 94,* 1017-1031.

90. O'Malley, P., & Wagenaar, A. C. (1991). Effects of minimum drinking age laws on alcohol use, related behaviors, and traffic crash involvement among American youth, 1976–1987. *Journal of Studies on Alcohol, 52,* 478–491.

91. Parker, R. N., & Rebhun, L. A. (1995). *Alcohol and homicide: A deadly combination to two American traditions.* Albany, NY: State University of New York Press.

92. Wittman, F. (1997). Local control to prevent problems of alcohol availability. In M. Plant, E. Single, & T. Stockwell (Eds.), *Alcohol: Minimizing the harm. What works?* (pp. 43–71). New York: Free Association Books Ltd.

93. Saltz, R. F. (1987). The roles of bars and restaurants in preventing alcohol-impaired driving: An evaluation of server intervention. *Evaluation and the Health Professions, 10,* 5–27.

94. Holder, H. D., & Waganaar, A. C. (1994). Mandated server training and reduced alcohol-involved traffic crashes: A time series analysis of the Oregon experience. *Accident Analysis and Prevention, 26,* 89–97.

95. Coutts, M. C., Graham, K., Braun, K., & Wells, S. (2000). Results of a pilot program for training bar staff in preventing aggression. *Journal of Drug Education, 30,* 171–191.

96. McKnight, A., & Stref, F. (1994). The effect of enforcement upon service of alcohol to intoxicated patrons of bars and restaurants. *Accident Analysis and Prevention, 26,* 79–88.

97. Jeffs, B., & Saunders, W. (1983). Minimizing alcohol related offences by enforcement of the existing licensing legislation. *British Journal of Addiction, 78*, 67–77.
98. Johnston, L. D., O'Malley, P. M., & Bachman, J. G. (1998). *National survey results on drug use from the Monitoring the Future Study, 1975–1997.* Volume 1: Secondary School Students. NIH Publication No. 98-4345. Rockville, MD: National Institute on Drug Abuse.
99. Cook, P. J., & Moore, M. J. (1993). Economic perspectives on reducing alcohol-related violence. In S. E. Martin (Ed.), *Alcohol and interpersonal violence: Fostering multidisciplinary perspectives.* NIAAA Research Monograph No. 24 (pp. 193–212). Department of Health and Human Services. NIH # 93-3496. Washington, DC.
100. Chaloupka, F. (1993). Effects of price on alcohol-related problems. *Alcohol Health and Research World, 17*, 46–53.
101. Fell, J. C. (2000). Keeping us on track: A national program to reduce impaired driving in the United States. In *Alcohol and crime: Research and practice for prevention* (pp. 55–68). Washington, DC: National Crime Prevention Council.
102. Federal Trade Commission. (1999). *Self-regulation in the alcohol industry: A review of industry efforts to avoid promoting alcohol to underage consumers.* Washington, DC: Author.
103. Martin, S. E., & Mail, P. (Eds.). (1995). *The effects of the mass media on the use and abuse of alcohol.* Research Monograph #28. Bethesda, MD: National Institute on Alcohol Abuse and Alcoholism.
104. Saffer, H. (1997). Alcohol advertising and motor vehicle fatalities. *Review of Economics and Statistics, 79*, 431–431.
105. Atkin, C. (1995). Survey and experimental research on effects of alcohol advertising. In S. E. Martin & P. Mail (Eds.), *The effects of the mass media on the use and abuse of alcohol.* Research Monograph #28 (pp. 39–68). Bethesda. MD: National Institute on Alcohol Abuse and Alcoholism.
106. Kilbourne, J. (1999). *Deadly persuasion: Why women and girls must fight the addictive power of advertising.* New York: Free Press.
107. Holder, H. D., Saltz, R. F., Grube, J. W., Voas, R. B., et al. (1997). A community prevention trial to reduce alcohol involved accidental injury and death. *Addiction, 92*(suppl. 2), S155–S172.
108. Perkins, H. W., & Berkowiz, A. D. (1986). Perceiving the community norms of alcohol use among students: Some research implications for campus alcohol education programming. *International Journal on Addictions, 21*, 961–976.
109. DeJong, W., & Linkenbach, J. *Telling it like it is: Using social norms marketing campaigns to reduce student drinking.* Available at http://\www.edc.org/hec/pubs/articles/tellingit.txt
110. Holder, H. D., Gruenewald, P. J., & Treno, A. J. (2000). Effects of community-based interventions on high-risk drinking and alcohol-related injuries. *JAMA, 84*, 2341–2347.
111. Wilks, A. I., Jensen, N. M., & Havinghurst, T. C. (1997). Meta-analysis of randomized control trials addressing brief interventions in heavy alcohol drinkers. *Journal of General Internal Medicine, 12*, 274–283.
112. Monti, P. M., Spirito, A., Myers, M., et al. (1999). Brief intervention for harm reduction with alcohol-positive older adolescents in a hospital emergency department. *Journal of Consulting and Clinical Psychology, 67*, 989–994.
113. O'Farrell, T. J., & Choquette, K. (1991).Marital violence in the year before and after spouse-involved alcoholism treatment. *Family Dynamics of Addiction Quarterly, 1*, 32–40.
114. O'Farrell, T. J., & Murphy, C. M. (1995). Marital violence before and after alcoholism treatment. *Journal of Consulting and Clinical Psychology, 63*, 256–262.
115. Collins, J. J., Kroutil, L. A., Roland, E. J., et al. (1997). Issues in the linkage of

alcohol and domestic violence services. Longitudinal perspectives on alcohol use and aggression during adolescence. In M. Galanter (Ed.), *Recent developments in alcoholism,* vol. 13 (pp. 387–405). New York: Plenum Press.

116. Center on Addiction and Substance Abuse. (1998). *Behind bars: Substance abuse and American's prison population.* New York: Author.

117. Belenko, S. (1998). Research on drug courts: A critical review. *National Drug Court Institute Review,1,* 1–42.

118. Goldkamp, J. S. (1996). *The role of drug and alcohol abuse in domestic violence and its treatment: Dade County's Domestic Violence Court Experiment.* Final Report. Philadelphia: Crime and Justice Research Institute.

119. Lurigio, A. J. (2000). Drug treatment availability and effectiveness: Studies of the general and criminal justice populations. *Criminal Justice and Behavior, 27,* 495–528.

Permission Acknowledgments

The following articles were previously published. Permission to reprint is grate-fully acknowledged here.

Carroll, K. M., Libby, B., Sheehan, J., & Hyland, N. (2001). Motivational inter-viewing to enhance treatment initiation in substance abusers: An effectiveness study. *The American Journal on Addictions, 10*(4), 335–339. Copyright © 2001 American Academy of Addiction Psychiatry. Reprinted with permission of Brunner-Routledge and Taylor & Francis.

Galanter, M., Dermatis, H., Keller, D., & Trujillo, M. (2002). Network therapy for cocaine abuse: Use of family and peer support. *The American Journal on Ad-dictions, 11*(2), 161–166. Copyright © 2002 American Academy of Addiction Psychiatry. Reprinted with permission of Brunner-Routledge and Taylor & Francis.

Higgins, S. T., Alessi, S. M., & Dantona, R. L. (2002). Voucher-based incentives: A substance abuse treatment innovation. *Addictive Behaviors, 27*, 887–910. Copy-right © 2002 Elsevier Science, Inc. Reprinted with permission.

Kaminer, Y., & Burleson, J. A. (1999). Psychotherapies for adolescent substance abusers: 15-month follow-up of a pilot study. *The American Journal on Addic-tions, 8*(2), 114–119. Copyright © 1999 American Academy of Addiction Psy-chiatry. Reprinted with permission of Brunner-Routledge and Taylor & Francis.

Kasprow, W. J., Rosenheck, R., Frisman, L., & DiLella, D. (1999). Residential treatment for dually diagnosed homeless veterans: A comparison of program types. *The American Journal on Addictions, 8*(1), 34–43. Copyright © 1999 American Academy of Addiction Psychiatry. Reprinted with permission of Brunner-Routledge and Taylor & Francis.

Larimer, M. E., Palmer, R. S., & Marlatt, G. A. (1999). Relapse prevention: An overview of Marlatt's Cognitive-Behavioral Model. *Alcohol, Research, & Health, 23*(2), 151–160.

Martin, S. E. (2001). The links between alcohol, crime and the criminal justice system: Explanations, evidence, and interventions. *The American Journal on Addictions, 10*(2), 136–158. Copyright © 2001 the American Academy of Addiction Psychiatry. Reprinted with permission of Brunner-Routledge and Taylor & Francis.

Miller, W. R., & Meyers, R. J., with Hiller-Sturmhöfel, S. (1999). The community reinforcement approach. *Alcohol, Research, & Health, 23*(2), 151–160.

Noonan, W. C., & Moyers, T. B. (1997). Motivational interviewing. *Journal of Substance Misuse*, 2, 8–16. Reprinted with permission of Brunner-Routledge and Taylor & Francis.

Rawson, R. A., Huber, A., McCann, M., Shoptaw, S., Farabee, D., Reiber, C., & Ling, W. (2002). A comparison of contingency management and cognitive-behavioral approaches during methadone maintenance treatment for cocaine dependence. *Archives of General Psychiatry, 59*(9), 817–824. Copyright © 2002 American Medical Association. Reprinted with permission.

Westermeyer, J., Myott, S., Aarts, R., & Thuras, P. (2001). Self-help strategies among patients with substance use disorders. *The American Journal on Addictions, 10*(3), 249–257. Copyright © 2001 American Academy of Addiction Psychiatry. Reprinted with permission of Brunner-Routledge and Taylor & Francis.

Index

Note: *Italicized* page numbers represent figures or tables.

616.86   Psychosocial
Psy   treatments.

DATE			
6/8/06			
12/11/12			
4/18/18			